D1517444

FINANCE *for* GROWTH

POLICY CHOICES IN A VOLATILE WORLD

A World Bank Policy Research Report

FINANCE *for* GROWTH

POLICY CHOICES IN A VOLATILE WORLD

A copublication of the World Bank and
OXFORD UNIVERSITY PRESS

Oxford University Press

OXFORD   NEW YORK   ATHENS   AUCKLAND   BANGKOK   BOGOTA   BUENOS AIRES   CALCUTTA   CAPE
TOWN   CHENNAI   DAR ES SALAAM   DELHI   FLORENCE   HONG KONG   ISTANBUL   KARACHI   KUALA
LUMPUR   MADRID   MELBOURNE   MEXICO CITY   MUMBAI   NAIROBI   PARIS   SÃO PAULO   SINGAPORE
TAIPEI   TOKYO   TORONTO   WARSAW

and associated companies in

BERLIN   IBADAN

© 2001 The International Bank for Reconstruction
and Development / The World Bank
1818 H Street, N.W., Washington, D.C. 20433, USA

Published by Oxford University Press, Inc.
198 Madison Avenue, New York, N.Y. 10016

Cover photo credits
The five coins: © Copyright the British Museum.
The stock exchange photo: © Danny Lehman/Corbis.

Manufactured in the United States of America
First printing April 2001

1 2 3 4 5 04 03 02 01

Library of Congress Cataloging-in-Publication Data has been applied for.

∞ *Text printed on paper that conforms to the American National Standard
for Permanence of Paper for Printed Library Materials, Z39.48-1984*

Contents

Foreword

T HE WORLD BANK GROUP HAS LONG RECOGNIZED THAT poverty reduction and growth depend on effective national financial systems. Understanding just how finance contributes to development—and how good policy can help guarantee its contribution—has been the focus of a major research effort at the Bank in recent years. This research has included systematic case-study analyses of the experiences of specific countries, as well as more recent econometric analyses of extensive cross-country data sets. *Finance for Growth* draws on this research and uses it to develop an integrated view of how financial sector policy can be used in the new century to foster growth and bring about poverty reduction.

At its best, finance works quietly in the background; but when things go wrong, financial sector failures are painfully visible. Both success and failure have their origins largely in the policy environment. Policy needs to create and sustain the institutional infrastructure—in such areas as information, law, and regulation—that is essential to the smooth functioning of financial contracts. Above all, policymakers need to work with the market to help align private incentives with public interest. As the ever-diminishing cost of communications and information technology leads to greater integration of global financial markets, policymakers face new challenges in ensuring this alignment. Governments must be prepared to recast their policies to take advantage of the opportunities resulting from global integration, and also to guard against the associated risks.

This book draws on the latest research to confirm some long-held views and challenge others. Some commentators have long regarded finance as largely irrelevant to the drive for poverty reduction; but the evidence here shows clearly that financial development has a strong and independent role in increasing general prosperity. Countries that build a secure institutional environment for financial contracts, making it possible for banking and organized securities markets to prosper, will see these efforts bear fruit in the fight against poverty.

Good regulation of financial firms is an essential part of this story. But regulation is also becoming increasingly complex, and this book provides some guidelines for negotiating that complexity. Policymakers must pay special attention to the incentives created by the regulatory system: they should align private incentives with the public interest in such a way that scrutiny of financial institutions by official supervisors is buttressed by supervision by market participants. The book makes it clear that what works best will depend on country circumstances—for example, in some countries introduction of explicit deposit insurance may need to await complementary institutional strengthening.

Although there is much for governments to do, there are other areas where the public sector tends not to have a comparative advantage, most notably in ownership of financial firms. Here again the problem is one of incentives and political considerations. Among other problems, decisions are too often based not on efficiency considerations, but rather on desires to reward particular interest groups. For this reason, well-crafted privatization can yield considerable social benefits. Even when, in a crisis, governments find it expedient to take control of banks, their aim should be to divest again as quickly as practicable—keeping in mind the threats of insolvency and looting by insiders if privatization takes place too rapidly in a weak institutional environment.

Many countries are increasingly relying on foreign firms to provide some financial services. It is inevitable that this trend will continue. For one thing, the financial systems of almost all economies are small in relation to world finance. For another, the Internet and related technology increase the porosity of national financial frontiers. Although governments may need to adopt capital controls on inflows in some circumstances, they would be wise to make sparing use of policies that protect domestic financial firms from foreign competition. The evidence suggests strongly that growth and stability in national economies are best served by ensuring access to the most efficient and reputable financial services providers. Although financial openness does introduce new channels for importing economic disturbances from abroad, those risks are more than offset by the gains.

New developments in communications and information technology will be an important driver for finance, too. Not only will they make finance more international, but they will also help extend its reach, thereby crucially increasing the access of small enterprises and others now excluded in practice from the formal financial system. Informal finance will continue to be important, of course, and that is one of the topics taken up by this year's forthcoming *World Development Report, 2001/2002: Institutions for Markets*, which will complement the current volume.

If implemented, the financial reforms proposed in this book can have pervasive—if often intangible—effects in expanding economic prosperity. At the same time, many of these reforms will be opposed by powerful interest groups. The stakes in this contest are high. The World Bank Group is committed to continuing to work with member countries to develop and implement reforms by helping them to devise national policies that are firmly based on empirical evidence and that draw on good practices from other countries.

Nicholas Stern
Senior Vice President
    and Chief Economist
The World Bank
March 2001

The Report Team

THIS POLICY RESEARCH REPORT WAS WRITTEN BY GERARD Caprio (Development Research Group and Financial Sector Strategy and Policy Department) and Patrick Honohan (Development Research Group), with the editorial assistance of Mark Feige. It takes stock of and synthesizes results to date from a research program on financial sector issues overseen by Paul Collier and Lyn Squire. Original research as background for this report includes work by the authors and by Thorsten Beck, Craig Burnside, Robert Cull, Aslı Demirgüç-Kunt, David Dollar, James Hanson, Philip Keefer, Leora Klapper, Aart Kraay, Ross Levine (now at the University of Minnesota), Millard Long, Giovanni Majnoni, Maria Soledad Martinez-Peria, and Sergio Schmukler.

The authors benefited from conversations with and comments by the Financial Sector Board and by Amar Bhattacharya, Biagio Bossone, Craig Burnside, Constantijn Claessens, Paul Collier, Simeon Djankov, Bill Easterly, Alan Gelb, Thomas Glaessner, James Hanson, Daniel Kaufmann, Hiro Kawai, Michael Klein, Daniela Klingebiel, Luc Laeven, Carl-Johan Lindgren (IMF), Millard Long, Giovanni Majnoni, Donald Mathieson (IMF), Frederic Mishkin (Columbia University), Ashoka Mody, Jo Ann Paulson, Larry Promisel, Jo Ritzen, Luis Serven, and Mary Shirley, many of whom contributed underlying research as well. A good part of the research originated in two large World Bank research projects, Financial Structure (led by Aslı Demirgüç-Kunt and Ross Levine) and Deposit Insurance (also led by Aslı), and data gathered in the more recent Bank Regulation and Supervision project (by James Barth, Ross Levine, and Gerard Caprio) arrived in time to contribute as well. Members of the Financial Stability Forum Working Group on Deposit Insurance made helpful suggestions to chapter 2. The authors would like to acknowledge the excellent research assistance of Anqing Shi, Iffath Sharif, and Ying

Lin, and superb administrative support by Agnes Yaptenco. Polly Means made stellar contributions to the graphics and design. Book design, editing, production, and dissemination were coordinated by the World Bank Publications team.

The judgments in this policy research report do not necessarily reflect the views of the World Bank Board of Directors, or the governments they represent.

Acronyms and Abbreviations

ADR	American depositary receipt
AMC	Asset management company
DIS	Deposit insurance system
DR	Depositary receipt
EU	European Union
FDI	Foreign direct investment
GCB	Ghana Commercial Bank
GDP	Gross domestic product
GDR	Global depositary receipt
GNP	Gross national product
IAS	International Accounting Standard
IPO	Initial public offering
LOLR	Lender-of-last-resort
LTCM	Long Term Capital Management
M2	Broad money
NAFTA	North American Free Trade Agreement
NBC	National Bank of Commerce
NPL	Nonperforming loan
OECD	Organization for Economic Co-operation and Development
PPP	Purchasing power parity
RFC	U.S. Reconstruction Finance Corporation
SEC	Securities and Exchange Commission
SME	Small and medium-size enterprises
SOE	State-owned enterprise
UCB	Uganda Commercial Bank

Overview and Summary

A S THE DUST SETTLES FROM THE GREAT FINANCIAL crises of 1997–98, the potentially disastrous consequences of weak financial markets are apparent. But even when there are no crises, having a financial system that does a good job of delivering essential services can make a huge difference to a country's economic development. Ensuring robust financial sector development with the minimum of crises is essential for growth and poverty reduction, as has been repeatedly shown by recent research findings. Globalization further challenges the whole design of the financial sector, potentially replacing domestic with international providers of some of these services, and limiting the role that government can play—while making their remaining tasks that much more difficult.

The importance of getting the big financial policy decisions right has thus emerged as one of the central development challenges of the new century. The controversy stirred up by the crises, however, has pointed to the weaknesses of doctrinaire policy views on how this is to be achieved. How then should financial policymakers position themselves? This book seeks to provide a coherent approach to financial policy design—one that will help officials make wise policy choices adapted to local circumstances and seize the opportunities offered by the international environment. With informed policy choices, finance can be a powerful force for growth.

This is not a book that relies on the application of some abstract principles; rather, our conclusions are based on an analysis of concrete evidence. Though much remains to be learned, a huge volume of empirical analysis, drawing on a growing body of statistical data, has been conducted on these issues over the past few years. The findings of this research greatly help to clarify the choices that are involved. Many

Financial policymaking is one of the key development issues

This report presents an analysis of the evidence

long-held beliefs have found detailed empirical confirmation for the first time; some new and perhaps surprising discoveries have been made.

In other words, we are asking policymakers to face some facts about finance. It is now possible to define with some confidence the need for a refocusing and deepening of the financial sector policy agenda. In this study, we identify and synthesize what we believe to be the key findings of recent financial sector research, both that conducted at the World Bank and elsewhere, highlighting the policy choices that will maximize growth and restore the financial sector as a key sector for helping to cope with—rather than magnifying—volatility. A few key messages have emerged from this research.

Finance contributes to long-term prosperity

It is obvious that advanced economies have sophisticated financial systems. What is not obvious, but is borne out by the evidence, is that the services delivered by these financial systems have contributed in an important way to the prosperity of those economies. They promote growth and reduce volatility, helping the poor. Getting the financial systems of developing countries to function more effectively in providing the full range of financial services—including monitoring of managers and reducing risk—is a task that will be well rewarded with economic growth.

Governments are not good at providing financial services—

Government ownership of banking continues to be remarkably widespread, despite clear evidence that the goals of such ownership are rarely achieved, and that it weakens the financial system rather than the contrary. The desirability of reducing, even if not necessarily eliminating, state ownership in low- and middle-income countries where it is most widespread, follows from this evidence. However, privatization has to be designed carefully if the benefits are to be gained and the risks of an early collapse minimized.

even when a crisis hits

Even governments averse to an ownership role in banking may find it foisted on them in a crisis. The authorities' focus then must be on getting out as quickly as possible, using the market—rather than government agencies—to identify winners and losers. Drawing on public funds to recapitalize some banks may be unavoidable in truly systemic crises, but they must be used sparingly to leverage private funds and incentives. Procrastination and half-measures—as reflected in lax policies involving regulatory forbearance, repeated recapitalizations, and their ilk—bear a high price tag that will affect the financial system and the economy for years to come.

Achieving an efficient and secure financial market environment requires an infrastructure of legal rules and practice and timely and accurate information, supported by regulatory and supervisory arrangements that help ensure constructive incentives for financial market participants. Success here will promote growth in a way that is tilted towards the poor and will stabilize the economy around the higher growth path; direct access to finance by many now excluded will also be expanded.

Incentives are key to limiting undue risk-taking and fraudulent behavior in the management and supervision of financial intermediaries—especially banks that are prone to costly failure. Instability and crashes are endemic to financial markets, but need not be as costly as they have been in recent years. They reflect the results of risk-taking going well beyond society's risk tolerance. These costs are very real: they represent a potentially persistent tax on growth. This can raise poverty in the near term, and can have longer-term affects on the poor, both through lower growth and through reduced spending on areas such as health and education.

Deposit insurance systems, an important part of the safety net supporting banks, are on the rise in developing countries. It is not hard to see why: not only will a credible system protect against depositor runs, but they are politically popular—not least with the local owners of small banks. However, recent evidence shows that they also lessen market monitoring of banks. Although this may not have weakened banking systems in developed markets, to the extent that these had already acquired reasonably effective regulation and supervision, it is found to heighten the risk of crisis and reduce financial market development where institutions are weak. Thus, authorities considering deposit insurance should make an audit of their institutional framework the first step in the decisionmaking process. Good safety net design needs to go beyond replication of mature systems, and the empirical evidence strongly argues for utilizing known market forces in order to limit the risks that may be associated with introducing deposit insurance.

Banks, securities markets, and a range of other types of intermediary and ancillary financial firms all contribute to balanced financial development. A radical preference in favor either of markets or of banks cannot be justified by the extensive evidence now available. Instead, development of different segments of the financial system challenges the other segments to innovate, to improve quality and efficiency, and to lower prices. They also evolve symbiotically, with expansion of one segment frequently calling for an upgrade in others. The future of some nonbank sectors, notably private pension provision, are heavily dependent on related government policies, whose design needs careful attention.

But well functioning markets need legal and regulatory underpinning—

and a strategy based on harnessing incentives

Good safety nets require good institutions

Diversity is good for stability and development

Open markets can spur development—

Most developing countries are too small to be able to afford to do without the benefits of access to global finance, including accessing financial services from foreign or foreign-owned financial firms. Facilitating the entry of reputable foreign financial firms to the local market should be welcomed too: they bring competition, improve efficiency, and lift the quality of the financial infrastructure. As such, they are an important catalyst for the sort of financial development that promotes growth. Opening up is accompanied by some drawbacks, including a heightening of risk in some dimensions, and will need careful monitoring. It also results in a loss of business for local financial firms, but access to financial services is what matters for development, not who provides them.

as can technology—

The financial sector has long been an early adopter of innovations in information and communications technology. Internationalization of finance (despite efforts to block it) has been one consequence. This has helped lower the cost of equity and loan capital on average even if it has also heightened vulnerability to capital flows. The precise future role of e-finance in accelerating the process of internationalization is not easy to predict, but it will surely be substantial. If volatility may have increased, so too have risk management technologies and their associated financial instruments.

notably for access

Some related credit information techniques, including scoring mechanisms, promise to make an important contribution by expanding what is at present very limited access of small-scale borrowers to credit from the formal financial sector. This will be achieved by lowering the barrier of high information costs. At the same time, a degree of subsidization of overhead costs will still likely be appropriate to contribute to the viability of microcredit institutions targeted at the poor and very poor.

In this overview, after summarizing the main arguments of the book's four main chapters, we analyze the main policy implications, presenting an illustrative stylized application to contrasting country conditions. The overview concludes with a prospect of future research.

Summary

THIS SECTION OF THE OVERVIEW SUMMARIZES THE REASONING of the remaining chapters of the report. We focus on the main findings drawn from the empirical research, and the primary implications of these findings. The detailed arguments and caveats are to be found in the succeeding chapters, along with references to the extensive body of research underlying the study.

Chapter 1: Making Finance Effective

There is now a solid body of research strongly suggesting that improvements in financial arrangements precede and contribute to economic performance. In other words, the widespread desire to see an effectively functioning financial system is warranted by its clear causal link to growth, macroeconomic stability, and poverty reduction. Almost regardless of how we measure financial development, we can see a cross-country association between it and the level of income per capita (figure 1). Association does not prove causality, and many other factors are also involved, not least the stability of macroeconomic policy. Nevertheless, over the past few years, the hypothesis that the relation is a causal one (figure 2) has consistently survived a testing series of econometric probes.

The reason finance is important for growth lies in what are, despite being less obvious, the key underlying functions that financial institutions perform. At one level, finance obviously involves the transfer of funds in exchange for goods, services, or promises of future return, but at a deeper level the bundle of institutions that make up an economy's financial arrangements should be seen as performing several key economic functions:

Financial depth generates growth

The vertical bar shows the interquartile range —the financial depth of 50 percent of the countries at each stage of development lie within this range. The median is shown as a horizontal bar.

Figure 1   Financial depth and per capita income

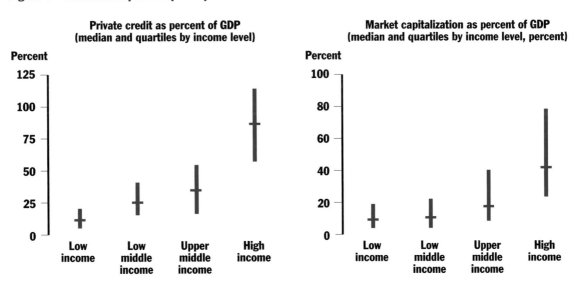

Note: This figure represents the average of available dates in the 1990s for each of 87 countries.
Source: Beck, Demirgüç-Kunt, and Levine (BDL) database.

Figure 2   Financial depth and growth

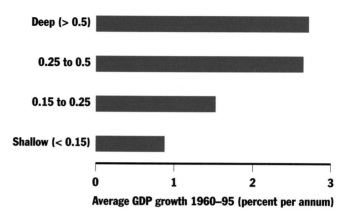

Ratio of liquid liabilities to GDP in 1960

Source: World Bank data.

- Mobilizing savings (for which the outlets would otherwise be much more limited).
- Allocating capital funds (notably to finance productive investment).
- Monitoring managers (so that the funds allocated will be spent as envisaged).
- Transforming risk (reducing it through aggregation and enabling it to be carried by those more willing to bear it).

Rigorous and diverse econometric evidence shows that the contribution of finance to long-term growth is achieved chiefly by improving the economy's total factor productivity, rather than on the rate of capital accumulation.

It is through its support of growth that financial development has its strongest impact on improving the living standards of the poor. Though some argue that the services of the formal financial system only benefit the rich, the data say otherwise. Furthermore, countries with a strong, deep financial system find that, on balance, it insulates them from macrofluctuations.

Bank and equity financing are complements, not substitutes

The evidence on the importance of each of the two major institutional components of finance—banks and organized securities markets—is also clear. There is no empirical support for policies that artificially constrain one in favor of the other. Indeed, the development of each sector seems to strengthen the performance of the other by maintaining the competitive edge of individual financial firms. While banking is more deeply entrenched in developing economies than securities markets and other nonbank sectors (figure 3), distinct challenges face policymakers in trying to ensure that both banks and markets reach their full functional potential. Macroeconomic stability is, of course, one key, but other aspects relate more closely to the microeconomic underpinnings of finance.

With so much of the borrowings by firms coming from banks, the borrowing cost depends on the operational efficiency and competitiveness of the banking market. In this respect, too, the performance of developing economies falls behind. Liberalization has been associated not only with higher wholesale interest rates, but also with a widening of intermediation spreads—at least partly reflecting increased exercise of market power by banks.

One path to lower financing costs through increased competition in financial markets is through the development of equity financing. Here the challenge is to alleviate the problems of information asymmetry. The complexity of much of modern economic and business activity has greatly increased the variety of ways in which insiders can try to conceal firm performance. Although progress in technology, accounting, and legal practice has also helped improve the tools of detection, on balance the asymmetry of information between users and providers of funds has not been reduced as much in developing countries as it has in advanced economies—and indeed may have deteriorated.

Figure 3   Bank-to-market ratio and per capita GDP

Ratio of banks' domestic assets to stock market capitalization

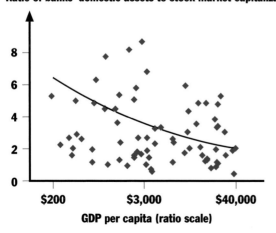

GDP per capita (ratio scale)

At lower levels of per capita income, the value of bank assets tends to be a much larger multiple of stock market capitalization than in higher income countries.

Source: World Bank data.

Finance needs an infrastructure: law and information

The current wave of policy research thus points to the desirability of policy measures that could promote the production and communication of information; limit the exercise of market power, whether in banking or by insiders against shareholders; and ensure an efficient functioning of the organized securities markets. These policies are likely to be more effective if directed to infrastructure rather than directly to the financial structures themselves. It is in the legal area that recent research on effective infrastructure has made most progress—and in areas going beyond the obvious and crucial need to ensure that the creditor's rights can, in the event of default, be expeditiously and inexpensively exercised. Naturally, the government has a comparative advantage in the design and implementation of law, and it needs to address itself to updating and refining laws and legal practice as they relate to financial contracts. Yet, to supplement—or make up for the absence of—government action, there is a clear and practical scope for market participants to amplify regulatory structures where this is needed. Practice in some of the more successful organized stock markets provides good examples of such private initiatives. This presents a promising way forward, especially where the development of public law is difficult.

There has been a major scholarly debate on whether the precise design of laws matter, with recent research focusing on the contrasting performance of financial systems with legal structures of differing origins. The evidence indicates that the main families of legal origin do differ in important respects relevant to financial development—notably in the differential protection they tend to provide to different stakeholders. These differences have been shown to have had an influence on the relative development of debt and equity markets, on the degree to which firms are widely held, or more generally the degree to which they are financed externally, and thus on overall financial sector development. And the policy message from the econometric results systematically points in one direction: far from impeding growth, better protection of the property rights of outside financiers favors financial market development and investment.

Collective savings media help strengthen and upgrade the system

The growth of collective savings—including through investment companies and mutual funds, as well as pension funds and life insurance companies—can greatly strengthen the demand side of the equity market, as well as widen the range of savings media available to persons of moderate wealth, and provide competition for bank deposits. The impact is not limited to the stock market: in mature and emerging markets, contractual savings institutions have been central in supporting numerous market-based financial innovations such as asset-backed securities, the use of structured finance and derivative products, including index-tracking funds and synthetic products that protect investors from market declines. The associated learning and human capital formation, as fund managers tool up to employ such techniques, helps to enhance the quality of risk management throughout the economy. Growth in these funds can also ensure enhanced and stable funding for key niche segments of the financial market, such as factoring, leasing, and venture capital companies. They can also generate a demand for long-term investments, thereby providing a market-based solution to a perceived gap that many governments have tried to fill over the years with costly and distorting administered solutions. Regulation of this sector is something that needs attention in many countries.

Measures that succeed in deepening financial markets and limiting the distorting exercise of market power result in more firms and individuals securing access to credit at acceptable cost. However, what of the poor and of the small or microenterprise borrower? What aspects need special attention to ensure that these do not get passed by despite overall improvement in the performance of financial systems? There is no point in pretending that the problem of access is easily solved. Experience shows that formal financial institutions are slow to incur the set-up costs involved in reaching a dispersed, poor clientele (even with minimal deposit-type services). In looking to improvements, however, two aspects appear crucial, namely information and the relatively high fixed costs of small-scale lending. Recent research focusing on technological and policy advances points to how these barriers can be lowered.

A range of innovative, specialized microfinance institutions, mostly subsidized, has become established with remarkable success. Loan delinquency has been low—far lower than in the previous generation of subsidized lending programs operated in many developing countries—and the reach of the institutions in terms of sheer numbers, as well as to previously grossly neglected groups, such as women and the very poor, has been remarkable. This success has been attributed to reliance on innovation in, for example, the use of group lending contracts exploiting the potentialities of social capital and peer pressure to reduce willful delinquency, dynamic incentives using regular repayment schedules and follow-up loans or "progressive lending," and lighter distributed management structures that reduce costs and enable lenders to keep loan rates down to reasonable levels.

Even without subsidy, some of these techniques can be applied to microlending to the nonpoor. Furthermore, efficient use of credit

Policy choices and new technology may expand access to finance—

9

—notably in the area of microfinance

information can reduce the threshold size for cost-effective lending by the formal, unsubsidized financial sector. Computer technology has greatly reduced the unit costs of collecting information on borrowing history and other relevant characteristics, and has improved the sophistication with which these data can be employed to give an assessment of creditworthiness. While the impact of having this information available alters incentives and market power in subtle—and not always favorable—ways, growth in access to credit information improves loan availability and lowers intermediation costs.

Chapter 2: Preventing and Minimizing Crises

Finance always involves risk

Finance is inherently fragile, largely because of the intertemporal leap in the dark that many financial transactions involve. Not only is money handed over now for the promise or expectation of money in the future, but this is done despite the problems of limited and unequal information both as to the characteristics of one's counterparty (adverse selection) and as to their subsequent behavior (moral hazard). Finance cannot be effective without credit, but credit means leverage, and leverage means the risk of failure, sometimes triggering a chain reaction. In these conditions, expectations can change quickly, leading to swings in asset prices, which in turn may be exacerbated by the possibility of crowd behavior.

Financial markets are in the business of making efficient use of information, but substantial and even growing deviations from equilibrium prices are possible, manifesting themselves as bubbles, or speculative booms and busts. If the countless historical examples of asset price crashes are not sufficient evidence of this, theory, too, explains why, when acquiring information and contracting are both costly, financial markets will never be fully efficient and fully arbitraged. Carefully controlled experiments confirm that individuals are not fully rational in assessing risk: they attach too much weight to recent experience (display myopia), they trade on noise rather than on fundamentals, and they exhibit positive feedback (or momentum) by buying because prices are rising. As well as exacerbating asset-price fluctuations and contributing to euphoric surges of bank lending—followed by revulsion and damaging credit crunches—such behavioral characteristics also provide fertile ground for fraudulent Ponzi schemes.

If finance is fragile, banking is its most fragile part. Bankers have to place a reliable value on the assets they acquire (including the credit-worthiness of borrowers), but banking also adds the complications not only of maturity transformation, but of demandable debt, that is, offering debt finance backed by par value liabilities in the form of bank deposits. The particular fragility of finance, and within it of banking, is true for all countries regardless of their income level, as attested to by the occurrence of banking crises in many industrial economies in the 1980s and 1990s. But banking outside the industrial world is more dangerous still, where crises have been enormously costly—in terms of direct fiscal costs, slower growth, and a derailing of stabilization programs and increasing poverty (figure 4).

Developing countries face several additional sources of fragility. Not only are information problems in general more pronounced, but developing economies are also smaller and more concentrated in certain economic sectors or reliant on particular export products, and accordingly are less able to absorb shocks or pool isolated risks. In addition, emerging markets have seen a succession of regime shifts altering the risk profile of the operating environment in hard-to-evaluate ways, including most prominently

Figure 4 East Asia poverty before and after the financial crises

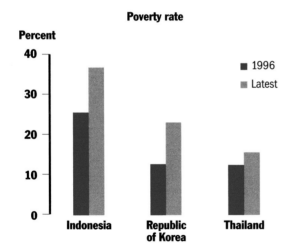

Poverty rises and remains elevated for some time following crises.

Note: The "Latest" column refers to 1999 for Indonesia and Thailand, and 1998 for the Republic of Korea, based on household surveys. Poverty lines are set at $1.50 per day (at 1993 PPP), except for the Republic of Korea, where the national definition of poverty is about $8 per day.
Source: World Bank.

financial deregulation. Moreover, as banking tends to be the dominant force in emerging financial markets, there is more demandable debt, less access to outside equity for firms, and therefore greater fragility. Collapses in equity prices are not innocuous, but are clearly less disruptive than bank failures, which explains the need to focus on the latter.

Financial sector regulation and supervision—the rules of the game in the financial sector, and the way they are enforced—are essential to limiting moral hazard, as well as to ensuring that intermediaries have the incentive to allocate resources and perform their other functions prudently. Although there has been a remarkable convergence on paper in recent years, stark differences remain in regulatory environments around the world, and weaknesses in this area serve as a potential source of added vulnerability in some emerging markets.

Use market-based incentives to supplement regulations

Necessary though headline regulations may be, a clear lesson from recent and historical research is that they need to be supplemented by the use of incentives and information to maximize the number of well-informed, well-motivated monitors of financial intermediaries. Diversity in the set of monitors for banks is desirable not only because of possible differences in information that they may possess, but also because of the varying and possible opaque incentives that they face. But who can monitor banks? There are three main categories:

- Owners, including the board and senior management of a bank, whose net worth should depend on the prudent performance of the institution.
- Markets, meaning all nonofficial outside creditors and counterparties, who should not be under the presumption that they will be "bailed out."
- Official supervisors, who should operate within a well-constructed incentive structure.

The aforementioned factors accounting for enhanced fragility in emerging markets means that they need to ensure that all three monitors are performing this function vigorously. Greater information and incentive problems certainly suggest that it is unwise to concentrate on any one of these groups. And the higher volatility of these markets implies that even adopting "best practice" from industrial economies may fall far short of the mark.

This report urges that authorities go well beyond the existing Basel guidelines. Ensuring that banks are well diversified, which in many small economies means regional or foreign banking, is important. Motivating creditors, such as mandating that banks issue uninsured subordinated debt, is a promising part of the solution, but requires that authorities should focus on improving the information available to these monitors and on the difficult task of ensuring that they are at arm's length from the issuing banks. Also, attention to supervisors' incentives is warranted. Higher present and especially future compensation (through bonuses or loss of generous pensions) need to be coupled with protection from legal prosecution today for effective performance of their job.

In the face of financial fragility, governments provide a safety net of sorts, virtually always through lender-of-last-resort facilities and increasingly through explicit deposit insurance. Deposit insurance is increasingly popular in emerging markets because it appears to be an effective way to stem bank runs, at least in high-income countries, and helps foster indigenous banks. The existence of these schemes, however, may actually worsen the information and incentive environment, increasing the scale and frequency of crises. To some extent, establishment of a formal deposit insurance scheme can be expected to result in greater risk-taking—the age-old moral hazard that tends to be associated with most forms of insurance. That would be an argument against establishing a formal scheme, but it has to be recognized that absence of a formal scheme can be equivalent to implicit deposit insurance—perhaps unlimited in its coverage and potentially also entailing moral hazard. Thus, whether to adopt an explicit system, and what kind of system to adopt, are empirical issues.

The weight of evidence from recent research suggests that, in practice, rather than lowering the likelihood of a crisis, the adoption of explicit deposit insurance *on average* is associated with less banking sector stability, and this result does not appear to be driven by reverse causation. Here the qualification "on average" is key: deposit insurance has no significant effect in countries with strong institutions, but in weak institutional environments has the potential to destabilize. This result is reinforced by the finding that banks, exploiting the availability of insured deposits, take greater risks.

Insurance reduces depositor monitoring, which is not sufficiently compensated by official monitoring where institutions are weak. Moreover, in institutionally weak environments, having explicit deposit insurance is associated with lower financial sector development, in addition to a greater likelihood of crises. Although it may be paradoxical that

There is a need to go beyond the Basel guidelines

the provision of insurance could lead to less of an activity, it may be that when taxpayers in institutionally weak countries see their authorities providing explicit guarantees, they understand that the environment is not conducive to restraining the cost of these guarantees. The result, then, might be that the real insurers, the taxpayers themselves, choose to hide their assets outside the banking system, and perhaps outside the country to avoid being taxed for coverage. This finding runs sharply counter to the popular doctrine that deposit insurance would promote financial deepening—and hence growth—in poor countries.

The role of good institutions—as measured in this research by indicators of the rule of law, good governance (a proxy for effective regulation and supervision), and low corruption—thus seems crucial in reducing the opportunities for risk-taking. Good design of deposit insurance may help lead to better outcomes, but given the delays in improving regulation, supervision, the rule of law, and other basic institutions, authorities considering the introduction of deposit insurance should first focus on addressing these related institutions to reduce the likelihood of excessive risk-taking. And for those who already have explicit deposit insurance, it is by no means suggested that they should suddenly end these schemes—doing so would likely induce a crisis—but instead should reconsider the design of their systems in light of the evidence presented herein. In deciding on design features, this report argues that authorities should draw on empirical evidence and in particular utilize market forces to ensure prudence, rather than simply attempting to copy existing practice—itself quite diverse—of high-income countries. It is overwhelmingly important that governments do not provide banks with an excessively generous safety net, as this will hamper the development of other parts of the sector, as well as potentially underwrite excessive risk-taking.

Chapter 3: Government Failure in Finance

Government ownership of banks is greater in poor countries

More than 40 percent of the world's population still live in countries in which the majority of bank assets are in majority-owned state banks. Government ownership tends to be greater in poorer countries (figure 5). State ownership in banking continues to be popular in many countries for several reasons. First, proponents of state control argue that the government can do a better job in allocating capital to highly productive investments.

Figure 5 Government ownership of bank assets and per capita income

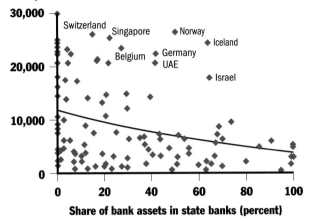

Per capita GDP 1997 in international dollars

Source: World Bank Survey of Prudential Regulation and Supervision; La Porta, López-de-Silanes, and Schleifer (2000).

State banks are more common in low income countries.

Second, there is the concern that, with private ownership, excessive concentration in banking may lead to limited access to credit by many parts of society. Third, a related popular sentiment—reinforced by abuses at, and governance problems of, private banks in many countries—is that private banking is more crisis prone.

Despite the worthy goals often espoused by advocates of state ownership—and though there are isolated pockets of success—achievement of these goals has generally been elusive, to say the least.

Political incentives make governments poor bankers

Government failure as owner is attributed to the incentives imposed on it by the political process, and the few cases of more successful state banks appear to be linked to a stronger institutional environment and dispersed political powers. And important new statistical evidence summarized in chapter 3 confirms that state ownership generally is bad for financial sector development and growth. Greater state ownership of banks tends to be associated with higher interest rate spreads, less private credit, less activity on the stock exchange, and less nonbank credit, even after controlling for many other factors. It is not just financial development that is affected: one study reveals that countries that had greater state ownership of banks in 1970 tended to grow more slowly since then with lower productivity, especially in poor countries and

15

where the protection of property rights was weak. Credit allocation is also more concentrated, with the largest 20 firms—often including inefficient state enterprises—getting more credit where the state ownership is greater. In addition, there is some evidence that greater state ownership is associated with financial instability.

To be sure, there are exceptions: Germany, for example, has had little state ownership of the enterprise sector (outside transport and finance), which has reduced the temptation of allocating credit to government industries. Moreover, the tough penalties there for default and bankruptcy would make life easy for most banks, even those that are state run. However, although it remains possible for developing countries to find ways to reduce the damage done by state ownership, limiting state ownership likely will be easier to implement than the many institutional and political reforms needed to avoid the abuses and inefficiencies of state banking.

Privatization can lead to a more efficient banking sector—

The potential scale of gains from bank privatization are borne out from detailed investigation in World Bank research of one country with comprehensive data and a major privatization experience, namely Argentina. This research suggests that in an incentive-compatible environment, the conduct of privatized banks—as reflected in their balance sheets and income statements—over time begins to resemble that of the other private banks. This is especially true in terms of the ratio of their administrative costs to revenues, and most importantly in terms of credit extended to public enterprises, consistent with the evidence above on improved allocation of resources. As part of the privatization process, the shedding or more efficient employment of staff, though less significant for the overall economy, works in the same direction.

As compelling as the case is for private sector ownership in banking, shifting to private ownership in a weak regulatory environment can lead to crisis—witness the examples of Mexico in the early 1990s, Chile in the late 1970s, and numerous transition economies. While abrupt and premature privatization can be dangerous, so too can be a strategy of hanging on to state ownership. Not only is there the evidence that this lowers growth, but also as the Czech experience points out, continued public sector control of the banking system appears to have facilitated looting—the practice of firms continuing to borrow without the intention of repayment.

but the process should be handled with care

For most countries, abrupt and total privatization is not called for. For one thing, many countries reached an advanced stage of development with modest state ownership. Also, though, a sudden move to private ownership from a lengthy period of state ownership seems particularly dangerous. The authorities would have to be either quite confident in their level of institutional development, or be selling to foreign banks of impeccable repute—and must be willing to gamble on this bet. Accordingly, moving deliberately but carefully with bank privatization—while preparing state banks for sale and addressing weaknesses in the overall incentive environment—would appear to be a preferred strategy. Preparation, in addition to improvements in infrastructure, could include some linkage of compensation for senior managers of state banks to the future postprivatization value of the bank—such as through stock options, an approach that appears to have helped in Poland. To be sure, this approach can only succeed if the process is credible, otherwise the deferred compensation will be too heavily discounted to have any value. As also noted below, sale of state banks to strong foreign banks can be a way of bringing good skills, products, and the capacity to train local bankers, and may even facilitate a strengthening of the regulatory environment. As long as the foreign banks are motivated to protect their reputation to behave in line with the highest fiduciary standards, this approach will increase the speed with which allocation decisions are made on market principles while minimizing the odds of a crisis.

When a banking crisis occurs, authorities need to decide when and how to intervene. When the problem is not systemic, bank creditors and supervisors should be left to proceed as usual on a case-by-case basis through standing channels. However, widespread bank insolvency may force even a government not disposed to take a significant ownership position in the banking sector to become involved in restructuring banks and even their assets (for example, nonfinancial firms) in the process. In many cases, systemic crisis has led to a substantial increase in government ownership or "care-taking." Yet the evidence on governments' limited efficacy as owners of banks suggests that they will not excel at restructuring failed or failing banks either.

Governments should intervene only when the crisis is systemic—

How then can one decide when the crisis has reached systemic proportions and when the government should intervene with other assistance? It is not really feasible to speak in terms of mechanical triggers for this kind of judgment. For one thing, the relevant data either come with a lag, or are very imperfect measures of crisis. Besides, as the economy approaches known thresholds, moral hazard increases and bankers and other market participants may take excessive risks. The authorities would then have little option but to bring forward their intervention even though the trigger has not been reached. Because of such problems, most financial authorities have decided on constructive ambiguity as the main solution.

—and prepare a clear exit strategy

Once the decision to intervene has been taken, the government has several goals. The first is to maintain or restore a functioning financial system. This goal is difficult to debate, though the best means of doing so are not always clear. Second, the government must contain the fiscal costs of its intervention. Care must be taken in designing restructuring plans, such that a preoccupation with minimizing short-term cash costs does not translate into larger long-term fiscal liabilities. On a related third point, governments must also ensure that their restructuring helps minimize the prospects for subsequent crises—notably in terms of the implicit incentive structures.

Unfortunately, as implemented in many countries, government-funded bank recapitalization programs—injecting capital usually in the form of bonds into banks—all too often miss the opportunity to create strong incentives for future prudent behavior. This then suppresses the message that poor performance is costly. Recapitalization without establishing some corresponding financial claim on the bank—and then exercising that claim—is no more or less than a transfer from taxpayers to shareholders, which is the group that keeps the residual value of the bank.

So if government funds are to be injected, there has to be some government involvement. Governments that inject equity will want to make sure that it is used only where needed to fill an insolvency gap, and certainly that it is not looted. Yet they must recognize that they are not likely to function well as bank owners; accordingly their equity stakes in banks should be for a limited period only. One way of achieving both of these goals is for the authorities to make some amount of funding available for recapitalization of banks, but only to those that

Use the market to identify banks to be "rescued"

- Secure matching of private sector funds in some ratio.
- Agree to restrict dividends and other withdrawals by insiders for some time (likewise, contracts for senior managers should be structured to emphasize deferred performance-linked compensation).
- Adhere to stringent transparency requirements.

The virtue of such an approach is that it removes from government or government-sponsored agencies the selection of winners, a process that is ripe for abuse. By openly stating the terms on which it will assist banks and their new shareholders, and ensuring that those terms provide good incentives for the restructured bank going forward, the government is making the best use of market forces while minimizing its direct ownership involvement.

Chapter 4: Finance without Frontiers?

Along with the rapid—albeit uneven—expansion of international debt and equity flows, including foreign direct investment (FDI), there has also been a sharp recent increase in the provision of financial services in many developing countries by foreign-owned financial firms. Financial globalization increases the potential for obtaining growth and other benefits from finance, but it also increases the risks.

In a world where even the largest developing countries have financial systems whose size is dwarfed by the scale and mobility of global finance, policy thinking needs to be refocused on the limited but important scope for domestic policy actions to maximize each country's capacity to secure the best provision of financial services, from whatever source, and to contain the risks of importing volatility.

Apart from China, Brazil is the only developing country with as much as 1 percent of the world's financial system. The financial systems of developing countries are small, and should be managed with that in mind (figure 6). Small financial systems underperform. They suffer from a concentration of risks: the smaller the financial system, the more vulnerable it is to external shocks and the less able its financial system is to insulate or hedge those shocks—unless the financial system is itself securely integrated in the world financial system through

Consequences of being small

Total assets of the banking system in about one third of all countries is smaller than $1 billion; another third have banking systems smaller than $10 billion.

Figure 6   National financial systems ranked by size

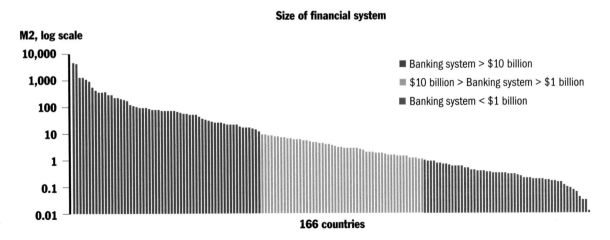

Source: International Financial Statistics.

ownership and portfolio links. Small financial systems also provide fewer services at higher unit costs, partly because they cannot exploit economies of scale and partly because of a lack of competition. Regulation and supervision of small systems is disproportionately costly, and even a well-funded effort would be hard pressed to ensure stability if finance is restricted to domestic institutions operating locally. Many financial systems fall short of minimum efficient scale and thus have much to gain from outsourcing financial services from abroad.

It sometimes seems that a boom-and-bust roller coaster has been imported when the capital account has been liberalized. Undoubtedly, with the wrong incentives, this has been a threat. There have also been tangible gains from external liberalization, and above all there is an inevitability about further opening-up to foreign capital markets and financial institutions. However, despite a huge research literature, there is nothing near a professional consensus on whether the net impact of full capital account liberalization on growth, poverty, or volatility should be regarded as favorable or not.

Governments can no longer hope to maintain a permanent and wide gap between actual and market-clearing exchange rates and real wholesale interest rates without a panoply of administrative controls on international trade, as well as on payments, to an extent that is demonstrably damaging to growth and living standards. That premise does not in itself rule out milder forms of control, including taxes and restrictions on the admission of foreign-owned financial service companies (such as banks), on the purchase by foreigners of local equities, and on international capital movements. The evidence, however, suggests that such restrictions should be used very sparingly.

The internationalization of the provision of financial services, including the entry of reputable foreign banks and other financial firms, can be a powerful generator of operational efficiency and competition, and should also prove ultimately to be a stabilizing force (figure 7).

Foreign bank entry can strengthen the system

Some countries have remained slow to admit foreign-owned financial firms to the local market, fearing that they will destabilize the local financial system and put local financial firms out of business, with the ultimate result that particular sectors and particular national needs will be poorly served. There is no hard evidence, however, that the local presence of foreign banks has destabilized the flow of credit or restricted access to small firms. Instead, the entry of these banks has been associated with significant improvements in the quality of regulation and disclosure. The very threat of entry has often been enough to galvanize the domestic banks into

Figure 7 Comparing the share of foreign and state ownership in crisis and noncrisis countries

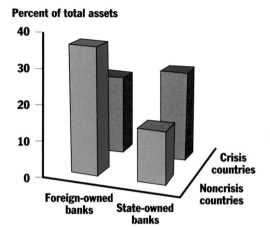

Source: Barth, Caprio, and Levine (2001c).

Ownership structures matter for crisis avoidance.

overhauling their cost structure and the range and quality of their services, with the result that foreign entry has often proved not to be as profitable for the entrants as they may have anticipated.

There may be some downside: pressure on domestic banks from foreign competition could present prudential risks if it erodes franchise value of high-cost operators to the point where they begin to gamble for resurrection. Also, there is the risk that some less reputable foreign bank entrants might prove to be unsound. Evidently these considerations reinforce the urgency of strengthening prudential regulation. Actually, the arrival of reputable foreign banks is usually associated with a systemwide upgrading of transparency (especially if the banks bring improved accounting practices with them).

The most dramatic structural developments in international finance for developing countries over the past decade or so have been the growth in cross-border equity investment, whether in the form of direct foreign investment (where the investor takes a controlling stake) or in the form of portfolio investment in listed or unlisted equities. The dramatic stock market collapses in East Asia during 1997 and 1998 took much of the shine off what had seemed an almost trouble-free liberalization of several dozen equity markets in the previous two decades, highlighting questions about the consequences, benefits, and costs of equity market liberalization.

Despite some setbacks—

For a country that has an active equity market, opening that market to foreign investors is a decisive step that can be expected to influence the level and dynamics of asset pricing. More than thirty sizable stock exchanges in emerging market economies undertook significant liberalization mostly concentrated in a ten-year period from the mid-1980s to the mid-1990s. So it is natural to ask: did the expected effects occur in practice? Were stock prices higher on average than they would otherwise have been? Was there an increase or a fall in the volatility of stock prices?

—equity market liberalization has lowered the cost of capital without much increase in volatility

In practice, these questions are tougher to answer than might appear at first sight. Overall, though, it appears from research findings that equity prices have increased, thereby lowering the cost of capital, without an undue increase in volatility. Opening up has also accelerated improvements in disclosure and the efficiency of the local stock markets, even though these have lost some of their share of the increased business in the listing and trading of local equities.

Before the explosion in international equity investment, the classic form of international finance involved debt flows: international borrowing and lending. Though carefully designed tax-like measures can be somewhat effective in damping short-term debt flows, openness to international flows inevitably impacts domestic interest rates and the exchange rate. Here is where the risks arise, and where macroeconomic, fiscal, and monetary policy has long been directed to containing those risks. Exposure of financial intermediaries and others to exchange rate risks, both direct and indirect, can be a particularly severe source of problems.

Domestic financial liberalization would be possible even without opening up the economy to international capital movements; with the opening-up, it becomes unavoidable. Capital account liberalization weakens and distorts a repressed domestic financial sector, eventually forcing domestic liberalization. If the process is long drawn out, partial liberalization of external and domestic finance can result in a very risky and unsound situation emerging.

Liberalization both of domestic and international finance has resulted in a convergence of interest rate movements, though developing countries are now experiencing some increased interest rate volatility and a structural risk premium, partly reflecting exchange rate and other policy risks.

Continuing developments in computing and communications technology seem sure to reshape the way in which financial services are delivered worldwide. To some extent the impact on developing economies will be an acceleration of the trends of recent years, but there will be qualitative changes too. Economies of scale for some financial services are declining, but increasing for others, while the synergies between financial and other economic services are also changing and often increasing. This will alter the organization of the industry, with consolidation in some areas and fragmentation in others.

This process may present some opportunities for financial service providers in small developing countries, especially where the unbundling of financial products leaves subproducts that can be efficiently produced with low sunk costs, and exploits advantages of location rather than scale. However, the greater potential benefit in prospect for developing countries will be for users of financial services, including services that have often not yet been well developed—such as pensions and other forms of collective savings—and international payments. Technology should allow those countries to access these services on terms comparable to consumers in advanced countries, especially insofar as physical distance from the provider begins to lose much of its importance. Undoubtedly, the accelerating presence of the Internet will begin to make direct international financial transactions available even to small firms and individuals.

The likely speed of these developments, and the extent to which they will displace the need for a local presence of financial service companies, remain unclear. The question that will be increasingly asked is whether smaller developing countries need to have local securities and debt markets in the traditional sense, and even how much of banking needs to be domestic. For policymakers in developing countries the questions will shift to considering the stability of domestic financial institutions in the face of the increased competition. Increased access to foreign financial services will entail more use of foreign currency, and this will accentuate the risks of exchange rate and interest rate volatility for countries that choose to retain their own currency. Once again, heightened prudential alertness will be needed.

Increasingly, countries can choose which financial services to buy and which to build

Policy Implications and Stylized Applications

THE GENERAL APPROACH EMERGING FROM THIS STUDY should be clear. Evidence on the importance of sound financial infrastructure is more important than anyone thought. Unregulated financial systems will fail, often catastrophically, but the wrong type of regulation is counterproductive. The *right* type of regulation is "incentive compatible"—that is to say, it is designed with a view to ensuring that the incentives it creates for market participants help achieve its goals rather than hinder them. More specifically, the right type of regulation

Financial policies should be market-aware

- Works with the market, but does not leave it to the market.
- Keeps authorities at arm's length from transactions, lessening the opportunities for conflicts of interest and corruption.
- Promotes prudent risk-taking, meaning risks borne by those most capable of bearing it, for example, removing distortions that lead to too little direct investment, too little equity finance, too little long-term finance, and too little lending to small firms and the poor.

In short, this is financial policy that is *market-aware*.

The *wrong* type of regulation includes financial repression—the maintenance of below-market and often negative real interest rates, and forced credit allocation. Repressive policies, in many cases the wrong response to an earlier round of crises, created some of the problems we see today, including the underinvestment in skills and in the infrastructure that are needed to support a market-based financial system. The design of the financial safety net also requires careful attention if it is not to become another type of misplaced regulation.

Another wrong solution is excessive reliance on one type of monitor to oversee intermediation. Prudential supervision is by now a universal feature of financial policy, but supervisors are hard-pressed to keep up with financial technology and the speed with which the risk profile of banks can change. Enlisting the help of private sector participants by arranging for well-funded investors to have something at stake in the continued viability of banks, and hence the incentive to monitor them, will be an increasingly important support to direct official supervision. Establishing appropriate incentives for supervisors themselves—recognized in some cases during the 19th century—will help as well and is an idea whose return is long overdue. Political structures that increase the risk that reforms such as these will be delayed need to be addressed, too; in the opinion of some scholars, it is here that the deepest causes of the wave of crisis of the past two decades should be sought.

The recommendations of this report are mutually supportive in some obvious ways. For example, financial systems that are not supported by effective infrastructure and incentives systems will not be entrusted with much of society's savings. A less obvious link is that countries that provide heavily subsidized deposit insurance or a lax regulatory framework will miss out on the benefits of a diversified financial system, because nonbank and capital market development will suffer. Similarly, excessive state ownership is demonstrably bad for competition and usually features active or passive discouragement of foreign banks.

The present condition of the financial system in many countries is far from ideal, and achieving the goals set out here may seem impossibly distant. Yet there are practical implications for all types of countries and all types of initial conditions. Without attempting to provide a detailed tactical design for reform in each case, and without pretending to do justice to the true diversity of country conditions, it is worth briefly sketching the policy implications that can be drawn for policymakers in four contrasting stylized scenarios. Although the initial conditions facing policymakers differ widely, the principles of good policy that emerge from these research findings have an equally wide application.

(a)   *A small low-income country dominated by state-owned financial institutions.*

Here we picture a low-income country, such as many in Africa—but also elsewhere—where the legacy of financial repression and state ownership has hampered the development of a vigorous private financial system. The lessons of chapter 3 are the most immediately relevant for this country. Government ownership has resulted in credit being directed to underperforming state entities; incentives and professional capacity are weak in the banking system, and there may still be a hidden inheritance of doubtful loans. The priority for the state must be to divest itself of its bank holdings and to create a credible policy stance sufficient to attract reputable international bank owners.

Legal infrastructure may need upgrading here, too, as discussed in chapter 1, although it is likely that judicial enforcement is the more relevant weak spot. In financial regulation, the political independence of the supervisors is an issue (chapter 2). Clear legal protection for them is crucial. The temptation to bolster the emerging private banks with a formal deposit insurance system should be resisted in view of the demonstrated moral hazard effects.

Although this country needs nonbanking financial services, such as those of securities markets, it is likely too poor and too small to sustain a liquid securities market on its own (chapter 4). The authorities need to be aiming to remove barriers that prevent borrowers and lenders from accessing international capital markets. Evidently this will need to be supported by stable and sustainable macroeconomic policies, as policy-induced macroinstability may be amplified by this opening-up of capital markets. Achieving minimum efficient scale—both in market infrastructure and in such aspects as payments systems—is going to be a challenge. Exploring the possibilities of regional cooperation on these fronts should bear fruit. If democracy is weak and ethnic conflict high, a significant level of uncertainty will likely prevail, which will deter physical entry by good foreign banks, as will low population density. E-finance or joining a regional financial system may be the best hope of getting access to higher-quality financial services.

(b)   A transition economy with weak rule of law.

Where the rule of law is weak, the financial sector cannot be expected to function well. Tackling this situation will be the primary challenge. The message from chapter 1 is that market participants may have to supplement formal law with private contracts that establish bright-line rules that can easily be verified and enforced, possibly using enforcement through external jurisdictions.

Because the credibility of domestic institutions is so weak, it is hard to align private incentives with social goals. Certainly it will be undesirable to institute deposit insurance, as observed in chapter 2, although it may be hard to withdraw insurance from existing state-controlled banks, which retain an important quantity of household savings in several transition economies. Leveraging credibility by allowing foreign institutions to enter and to compete in the retail market is a preferable solution, which is all the more reason to privatize many such banks as expeditiously as possible (as proposed in chapter 3), although with care to ensure that the new owners have significant capital at stake.

This economy is likely to have a de facto open capital account, with market participants already obtaining financial services from foreign systems (chapter 4). It would be better to recognize this through a formal liberalization so that such access is not an underground or illegal activity.

(c)   A lower middle-income bank-dominated country emerging from a crisis.

Most bank-dominated, middle-income countries have recently experienced banking crises associated with an undue burden of debt. As they seek to recover from these crises, the policy messages are clear. Getting the state out of a direct role in restructuring as fast as possible is important, including using the private sector to identify the banks and nonfinancial firms that are fit to survive. In the medium term, authorities need to find ways to lessen reliance on short-term debt finance. Improved protection of minority shareholders, as noted in chapter 1, is needed to help boost the possibility of issuing outside equity. And no doubt, improvements to the availability and reliability of information will spur nonbank finance.

Also important is better monitoring of the banking system. Even to the extent that the crisis was brought on by external factors, virtually every crisis uncovers banks that have ventured far out on the risk frontier, and that may account for a large fraction of the fiscal cost. In addition to ensuring that excessive risk takers are not "bailed out," better monitoring is crucial here to convince financial sector participants that incentives have changed. Often, even if a formal deposit insurance system was not in place before the crisis, blanket coverage may be now, and it is important that this coverage begins to be limited as soon as possible. If the banks still are fragile or suspect, however, great care is needed, and introducing a subordinated debt requirement—addressing the enforcement problems noted in chapter 2—can both improve monitoring and increase the share of unguaranteed liabilities. Then over time the authorities can announce a schedule of reduction of the ceiling amount of deposits covered by an explicit system. For countries with relatively limited numbers of banks, the German system of private deposit insurance and mutual liability among the private banks in the scheme has much to recommend itself as a way to maximize market monitoring.

Official monitoring of banks also will need improvement, and correcting the "balance of terror" noted in chapter 2 will complement greater central bank independence and allow for vigorous oversight.

Admitting foreign banks also can help stabilize and improve the sector, and middle-income countries are more likely to have good and eager entrants, while chapter 4 shows how beneficial openness to international equity markets can be.

(d)   An upper middle-income country with a still-shallow financial system.

The financial development of some upper middle-income countries remains below average. They seem to have all the basics, but depth, term finance, and a full range of services are lacking. Here, too, the research findings of each chapter are relevant. Often term credit is absent because of uncertainty, both macroeconomic and structural. If high inflation has been a culprit in the past, convincing demonstrations of a longstanding commitment to low inflation is important. Although dollarization (or adoption of some other currency) is one way out of this dilemma, it can create additional problems to the extent that the country is not an optimal currency area with its partner. Another solution, which also can help ensure the quality of regulatory oversight, is fixed and long terms for the central bank governor, ending the ability of finance or prime ministers to remove them without a solid majority of parliament.

The development of long-term suppliers of finance—insurance and contractual savings institutions—also will contribute to a deepening of that end of the market, as it has in Chile, without costly distortions. Markets with poor services can benefit from competition. If there is still a significant (20 percent or more) share of the banking sector in state hands, further privatization will help in this regard. Limiting the state banks' role is also shown to increase nonbank financial sector development, which will improve competition at short and long ends of the financial market. These more sophisticated financial systems will retain many financial services on-shore, but will also rely on the international market for risk-spreading and for more exotic services.

Technology of credit-scoring and credit information can be adopted to help improve the reach of the financial system and the access of small entrepreneurs to it (chapter 1). The incentive conditions and the ability of the authorities to supervise intermediaries effectively can be greatly enhanced in this rather sophisticated environment by relying on carefully designed requirements that have the effect of bringing additional private sector monitors into the picture.

The Next Generation of Research

THIS REPORT REPRESENTS THE CULMINATION OF ONE generation of research on the financial sector, not the first generation, but perhaps the first that has been systematically based on statistical data from across the world. The research findings provide "first-order" solutions to policymakers: overall guiding principles and a sense of strategy. It also highlights key policy issues for the next generation of research. In many cases, the first-order solution needs further amplification and specification beyond overall principles.

For example, given the principles of incentive-based regulation from chapter 2, which particular aspects of bank regulation and supervision deserve greater priority at different stages of development? Or, the case for reducing state ownership in many countries is clear, but how far should authorities go and how quickly? And given the dangers associated with bank privatization, what are the lessons on how to do this process? Although research has begun in this area, it comes too soon after the privatizations to provide definitive answers on the long-run effects. Also, although a basic approach to bank restructuring is proposed in this volume, a more systematic exploration of the links between bank and enterprise restructuring, informed by case studies of systemic crisis countries, would help to guide authorities' decisions in a crisis.

Another area of relative ignorance is how corporate governance and ownership in the financial sector affects reform strategies. When insiders or "oligarchs" control banks and other important intermediaries, they may be able to so influence, or even seize control of, the regulatory apparatus that effective oversight is nonexistent. Although many accept that "one size does not fit all" in the reform process, coming up with practical rules and guidelines for authorities to know when it is safe to proceed along different reform paths is an important priority. Case studies of bank restructuring episodes will likely yield useful lessons in general, but especially in this area, such as by highlighting the fate of different approaches to preventing excessive concentrations in ownership and control.

Our discussion of foreign entry also reveals a range of wider questions about the shifting patterns of financial firm ownership and ownership concentration that need more in-depth research. And, though financial repression is almost a thing of the past in most countries, taxation of finance is still a pressing issue awaiting a synthesis, whether in regard to novel transactions taxes, to international tax competition, or to other aspects.

Ongoing developments in e-finance promise to change the financial landscape in emerging and mature markets. The likely decline in the cost of entering foreign markets may greatly increase the extent to which residents of almost all economies "import" their financial services. This rapidly evolving area needs to be monitored to identify policy problems, options, and solutions. Policymakers will certainly want to know how it will affect credit to small and medium-scale enterprises, though there will be many other effects that also need to be studied. And while e-finance may improve long-run stability, in the near term the increase in competition could have destabilizing consequences. There is already a

Moving beyond general principles—

and monitoring the effects of e-finance

demand to know how countries are handling these pressures and how they are regulating "e-banks" and electronic exchanges.

The trends noted or urged here—better infrastructure, improved incentives, less state ownership, and a more receptive view to importing financial services—will all surely contribute directly or indirectly to a considerable expansion in the role of nonbank intermediaries and capital markets. How to regulate efficiently these markets to contain systemic risk could be *the* key research question of the next few years.

The last several years have seen impressive leaps in our understanding of the importance of the financial sector in development and in the knowledge base for many key issues, but there is still much to be learned.

CHAPTER ONE

Making Finance Effective

"Money is the greatest factor in life and the most ill-used. People don't know how to tend it, how to manure it, how to water it, how to make it grow."

Spoken by Margayya, the "financial expert," in the eponymous
novel by R.K. Narayan (1952)

Much of the renewed focus in recent years on the financial systems of developing countries reflects the rapid and often spectacular deepening in the scale and complexity of the the financial systems of advanced economies. This deepening suggests that the nature of contemporary economic progress may be more finance-intensive than previously thought, and that policymakers in developing countries may need to pay more attention to ensuring that their countries' financial systems can and do function effectively.

For the good reasons reviewed below, policymakers around the world have now made financial strengthening a priority: everybody seems to want to build deeper, more sophisticated financial systems in the expectation that this will contribute significantly to economic performance. This perspective is not uncontroversial, but against the contrary view that finance merely follows and adapts to real economic progress, there is a solid body of empirical research strongly suggesting that improvements in financial arrangements precede and contribute to economic performance.

This then raises the question of how a country can develop a more effective financial system. Is bigger always better? Is there a clear-cut preference for the shape of finance in terms of the relative importance

**Economies are becoming
more finance intensive**

31

of different types of intermediary or market? And what of the infrastructural elements needed to support finance? These matters have become the subject of an active research debate, especially over the past decade when financial systems in transition economies had to be built essentially from scratch, requiring policymakers and scholars to go back to first principles. Contrasts between the shape and approach to structure and infrastructure in different advanced economies have become the focus of examination—paradoxically just at a time when these contrasts have begun to erode.

While there is still much more to be learned from comparative analysis of the causes and consequences of contrasting financial sector performance, recent research allows several important conclusions to be drawn now. *The widespread desire to see an effectively functioning financial system is warranted by its clear causal link to growth, macroeconomic stability, and poverty reduction.* Attempts to discriminate between different structural types of external finance through a preference for banking over market finance, or vice versa, are unwarranted, though, and could be counterproductive.

Efficient functioning of all these markets in intertemporal commitments requires a supporting infrastructure for information disclosure, contract enforcement, and competitive behavior. This contractual and information infrastructure should, if anything, be biased in the direction of directly protecting the interests of the external funds *provider*: the long-term interests of the would-be *user* will be poorly served by an infrastructure that gives potential providers so little protection that they withhold their funds. In addition, the infrastructure should be fashioned in such a way as to limit the exercise of market power not only in banking, but also by insiders—whether in a firm or in the securities markets—against outside shareholders.

To what extent all of these financial services will—or need to be—provided at home by domestic financial firms and markets, instead of being imported or supplied by foreign-owned firms, is a key question to which we return in chapter 4.

Here it is worth pausing to clarify what we mean by financial development, which subsumes both institutions and functions. Starting with money itself, specialized institutions, including intermediaries, markets, and agents, tend to become increasingly pervasive in an economy's financial activities, displacing bilateral arrangements. However, it is worth bearing in mind that, especially in developing economies, much

There is a clear causal link between finance and development

A well-functioning financial system requires a supporting infrastructure

of finance is provided within the family, through partnerships or unincorporated business. Still, while finance can and does exist without specialized financial firms, our discussion is confined to *organized* finance, that is, with funds processed, intermediated, or managed by specialized financial firms or traded in organized markets.[1]

More important than the institutional form taken by these firms and markets are the underlying functions of finance that they perform. While the most evident financial activity relates to the transfer of funds in exchange for goods, services, or promises of future return, it is essential to dig deeper. In fact, the bundle of institutions that make up an economy's financial arrangements can be seen as providing the bulk of the economy's need for several functions deeper than that of simply trading and transfer (Levine 1997; cf. Merton and Bodie 2000):

- Mobilizing savings (for which the outlets would otherwise be much more limited).
- Allocating capital funds (notably to finance productive investment).
- Monitoring managers (so that the funds allocated will be spent as envisaged),
- Transforming risk (reducing it through aggregation and enabling it to be carried by those more willing to bear it).

The main functions of finance

Most textbooks, in addition to the focus on payments systems, dwell on the mobilization and allocation functions, but the monitoring and risk transformation functions are crucial as well. Though the financial sector has no monopoly on the economy's stock of intellectual capital, it is these deeper functions that justify characterizing the sector as functioning like the brain of the economy.

Monitoring means that intermediaries do not merely collect information on firms and allocate loans or investments to them, but also continue to keep track of the recipients' activity and to exert corporate control, whether by enforcing covenants on existing contracts or ultimately by withdrawing or not renewing their financing. These activities are valuable precisely because information is difficult to acquire and costly to verify. In this way, intermediaries serve as "delegated monitors" (Diamond 1984), without which it would be difficult to separate firm ownership and management.

Risk transfer and mitigation likewise can be underrated; the variety of the associated financial instruments and the fact that they occasionally backfire often results in this function receiving less weight than it deserves. Some risks can be alleviated simply by access to liquidity. Thus, entrepreneurs with access to liquid savings—their own and others—may be more willing to undertake riskier but high-yielding projects that raise growth, or investors may be willing to finance a project (or country) if they know that they can get out of it by selling, without their action so driving down the price that the option ceases to have value. Specific risks that all face—from typhoons or *El Niño* events for farmers, to technological shifts for e-entrepreneurs—also can be eased by sharing the risks with investors. Specialized instruments are invented regularly to unbundle and repackage various risks.

How Finance Helps

W E SHOULD THUS SEEK THE MAJOR CONTRIBUTIONS OF finance to economic performance in three dimensions. The first, and likely the most important, is whether there is an overall contribution to long-term average economic *growth*; second, whether it contributes additionally to *poverty* reduction; and third, whether finance succeeds in *stabilizing* economic activity and incomes. In all three dimensions, recent research findings suggest an unambiguously positive role for the formal institutions of finance.

Financial development causes growth

Almost regardless of how we measure financial development, we can see a cross-country association between it and the level of per capita income (figure 1.1). Association, however, does not prove causality and, as the charts show, there is even a very wide variation between the level of financial development between countries at comparable income levels, and this variation persists over time (figure 1.2). Nevertheless, over the past several years, the hypothesis that the relation is a causal one has consistently survived a testing series of econometric probes.

Formal empirical exploration of this issue dates back over 30 years, and there has been a steady accumulation of evidence.[2] Possibly the most striking basic indication that the relationship is one of causality is the fact—evident in figure 2 of the overview—that the level of financial development back in 1960 can help to predict subsequent economic growth even after account is taken of other known determinants of growth (including the catch-up effect of a low initial level of per capita income and the 1960 level of school enrollment). First displayed by King and Levine (1993a), for economic growth up to 1989, this predictive power has continued to be present as growth data for subsequent years is added.

Figure 1.1 Financial development and per capita income

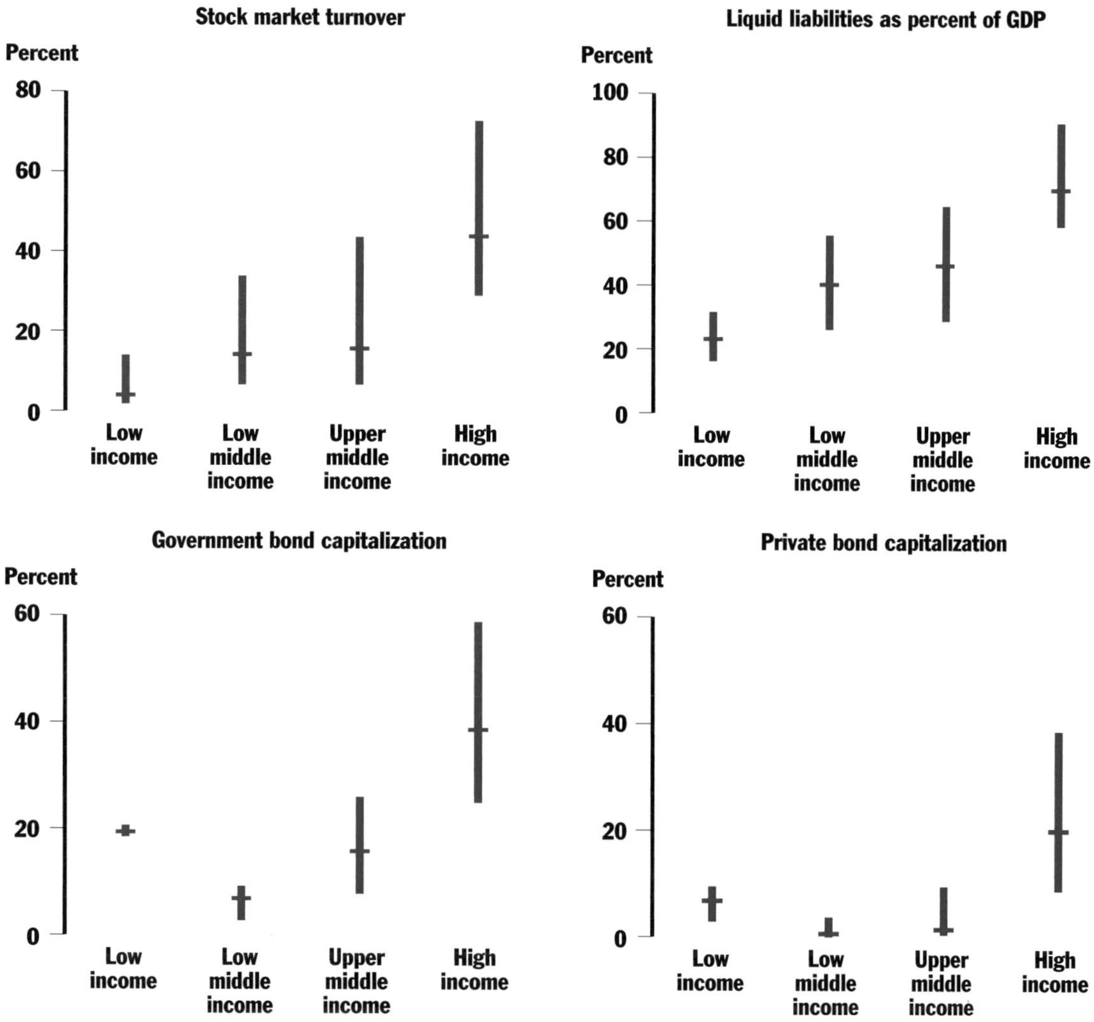

Stock market turnover

Liquid liabilities as percent of GDP

Government bond capitalization

Private bond capitalization

Note: This figure represents the average of available dates in the 1990s for each of 87 countries. The vertical bar shows the interquartile range; the financial depth of 50 percent of the countries at each stage of development lie within this range. The median is shown as a horizontal bar. Data for the bond market in low-income countries is available only for China and India.

Source: BDL database.

Increasing income is generally associated with greater financial depth. Stock market turnover, liquid liabilities of banks and near-banks, and bond capitalization are also generally associated with greater financial depth.

Perhaps the most persuasive of the more recent studies (Levine, Loayza, and Beck 2000) uses a richer data set for the period 1960–95 to make a more comprehensive assessment in particular of the key issue: could it be that the process of economic growth itself feeds back on financial develop-ment, rather than the other way around? Some aspects of the financial

Figure 1.2 Financial development over time

Bank credit to private sector as percent of GDP

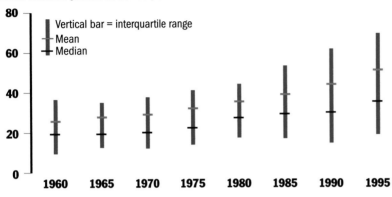

The ratio of bank credit to the private sector is up relative to GDP, but the variance has widened.

Note: The vertical bar shows the interquartile range; the financial depth of 50 percent of the countries at each date lie within this range. The median and mean are shown as upper and lower horizontal bars.

Source: BDL database.

sector clearly are determined prior to recent growth, and what Levine, Loayza, and Beck show, in essence, is that each country's level of financial development can be partly predicted by one such prior factor, namely the origin of its legal system (that is, which of the British, French, German, or Scandinavian traditions it is based on).[3] As we will see, this is not the only role for legal factors in our discussion, but in the present context they provide the essential econometric *instrument*. Levine, Loayza, and Beck go on to show that the *predicted* level of financial development is also correlated with long-term growth (even after also controlling for other standard determinants of growth), thereby seeming to rule out the idea that the finance-development link is all or mostly reverse causality.

Levine, Loayza, and Beck's favored measure of financial development is the ratio of bank (and near-bank) credit to the private sector, expressed as a share of GDP. The emphasis on the private sector reflects the fact that credit to government does not much involve the functions of allocation, monitoring, and risk management. Thus it is not just a measure of financial depth, such as the ratio of money to GDP. Nor is it exactly a measure of the private sector's role in the allocation of credit; a better measure of that is the ratio of the central bank's to other banks' assets. It is worth noting that both of these alternative measures also correlate with GDP growth, and both survive the test for reverse causality. And similar results are available for measures of stock market capitalization and liquidity, as discussed below.

Even higher than would be predicted by a naïve simple regression of growth rates on financial development, the size of the estimated effect is substantial (figure 1.3): a doubling of the ratio of private credit (say, from 19 percent of GDP to the sample average of 38) is associated with an average long-term growth rate almost 2 percentage points higher (box 1.1). To be sure, neither this nor other financial sector ratios are policy variables, and the healthy development of the sector depends on the quality of the infrastructure and incentive environment in which it functions.[4]

It is through its support of growth that financial development has its strongest effect on improving the living standards of the poor. Some argue, however, that the services of the formal financial system only benefit the rich, and even suggest that there may be a price to pay for finance-supported growth in the form of a worsening of the income-distribution in financially developed economies. Nevertheless, available empirical evidence is against any such tradeoff: on the contrary, measures of financial development are, if anything, positively (albeit weakly) correlated with the share of the bottom quintile of the income distribution. Note that poverty in a country is determined by the numbers of the poor and their income. Faster growth affects both. The recent literature on the interrelation between inequality and growth points to the importance of wealth inequality in dampening growth and to

Finance-led growth is pro-poor—

Figure 1.3 Naïve and modeled impact of financial development on growth

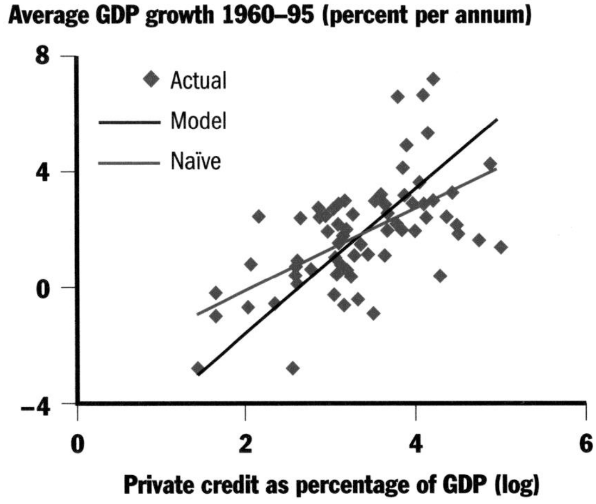

Average GDP growth 1960–95 (percent per annum)

Source: Levine, Loayza, and Beck (2000).

Box 1.1 Using regression coefficients to infer policy effects

IT IS TEMPTING TO USE ESTIMATED REGRESSION coefficients to project what might happen in a country if one of the explanatory variables were to be changed by policy. To begin with, one needs to recognize the limitations of regression analysis; the hazards of noisy and incomplete data and the probability that alternative modeling specifications can alter the quantitative results. Even when we have satisfied ourselves that the selected regression is as good as we can hope for in the current state of knowledge, three further tests must be satisfied before we use the estimated relationship to predict the impact of policy.

First, the relationship must be free of endogeneity bias. Second, there must not be relevant omitted variables that are correlated with the variable being manipulated. Third, the variable really must be controllable.[1]

Take the relationship discussed in the text: private credit ➔ growth. At least the first two problems are clearly relevant and have to be navigated.

The first issue of endogeneity (loosely referred to in the text as "reverse causality") is what has been handled in the cited literature by means of instruments;

this can considerably alter the measured impact, often—though not always—reducing it.

The second issue is also very important. Indeed, it is clear that the private credit variable is only a proxy for a multidimensional but unmeasured impact of financial intermediation on productivity. It works in the regressions, because it tends to be correlated with the other dimensions, but if it becomes a focus of government policy, the traditional correlation with the unobserved, omitted variables will certainly break down, and the hoped-for impact on growth will not occur. (An analogous problem is well known in the theory of monetary stabilization, where it is known as "Goodhart's Law.") In a nutshell, simply boosting credit growth is no guarantee of healthy long-term output growth.

Controllability may be more of an issue when it comes to the institutional factors discussed later in the chapter and elsewhere. Do we really have reliable ways of *measurably* improving legality, say, or the quality of administration? Here the direction of appropriate policy change may be easier to identify than its likely quantitative impact.

---

1. Controllability does not imply an endogeneity bias unless the variable has been manipulated by policy in response to disturbances in the estimated relationship.

a feedback from growth in the direction of reducing inequality. Analysis by Li, Squire, and Zou (1998) of data on inequality in 49 countries suggests that financial development is a positive catalyst in both of these relationships. It is statistically associated across countries not only with higher growth whatever the level of wealth inequality, but also with lower income inequality (as measured either by the Gini coefficient, or by the share of the top quintile) whatever the rate of growth. Further research is needed to see if these results are valid over time, as well as across countries.

The results are not implausible, however. For example, even having access to secure forms of savings can protect poor farmers from the various idiosyncratic shocks that they face, reducing the likelihood that a bad year will put them into the poverty statistics, and access to other financial services can allow them to adopt more advanced technologies.

What of the risk-reduction function? At the microeconomic level, a wider range of financial instruments, including insurance contracts, can pool risk, as well as shifting it to those more willing to bear it.[5] And it seems from recent research that financial development also tends to reduce aggregate economic volatility. For example, Easterly, Islam, and Stiglitz (2001) find the level of financial development (here measured again by the private credit indicator discussed above) to be a strong and significant explanatory factor in a regression explaining the output growth volatility of some 60 countries. A doubling of private credit from 20 percent of GDP to 40 percent is predicted in this regression to reduce the standard deviation of growth from 4 to 3 percent per annum (figure 1.4). Interestingly this improvement is not sustained with further financial deepening: indeed, the authors' estimates suggest that very high values of the private credit measure of financial development could be associated with *higher* volatility of output growth, though the data in this range are sparse. Another warning sign from this study is that volatility in monetary aggregates is also associated with output volatility.

—and generally a stabilizing force—

Figure 1.4   Financial depth and macroeconomic volatility

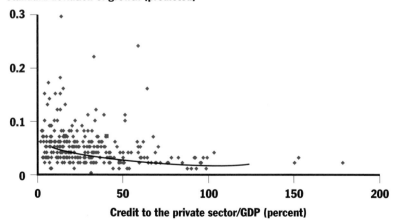

Standard deviation of growth (predicted)

Credit to the private sector/GDP (percent)

The deeper the financial system, the smaller is economic volatility (except perhaps where the share of credit in GDP is very high).

Note: The figure shows the data and fitted value in a regression of the standard deviation of annual GDP growth on financial depth (conditional on other control variables).

Source: Based on Easterly, Islam, and Stiglitz (2001).

—but can amplify inflationary shocks in low- and middle-income countries

Finance is better at protecting against some sorts of shock than others. As shown by Beck, Lundberg, and Majnoni (2001), financial development (measured with the private credit indicator) insulates output growth from terms of trade shocks, but it actually seems to magnify the impact of inflationary shocks on output volatility in low- and middle-income countries. Perhaps it is not surprising that inflationary shocks can matter more in a more deeply monetized economy, but this, too, is a warning sign that expansion of finance is not risk-free. Indeed, deeper finance without the institutional and incentive features recommended in this report can lead to a poor handling or even magnification of risk, rather than its mitigation.[6]

The aggregate empirical evidence thus points to financial development having an unambiguous long-term growth effect, and also to be stabilizing and pro-poor. The finance-growth link is especially well supported by a range of different methodologies, but what mechanisms are involved, and can they be strengthened by judicious policy design? Furthermore, are there risks in seeing financial deepening as a quick fix or short-term engine of growth?

Further empirical exploration by Beck, Levine, and Loayza (2000) has helped to pinpoint the most likely channels through which finance contributes to long-term growth. They show that financial development is not reliably correlated with either national savings ratios or with capital deepening (figure 1.5: where the arrow is almost vertical rather than almost horizontal).

Figure 1.5 Relative contribution of financial development to productivity and capital intensity

Productivity y/k

It's through productivity—not volume—of investment that finance helps growth.

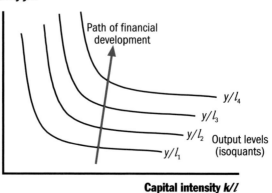

Path of financial development

y/l_4

y/l_3

y/l_2 Output levels (isoquants)

y/l_1

Capital intensity k/l

Source: Based on the econometric findings of Levine, Loayza, and Beck (2000).

Therefore, the contribution of finance to long-term growth is to improve the economy's total factor productivity rather than the quantity of capital.

This meshes well with the finding of Bandiera and others (2000— based on a detailed examination of the multidimensional process of financial liberalization in eight countries over a quarter century) that liberalizing reforms aimed at financial development do not reliably increase aggregate saving. On the contrary, the indications are that liberalization overall, and in particular those elements that relax liquidity constraints, may be associated with a fall in saving. Even a lower overall rate of saving is quite compatible with more rapid growth if it comes with an improved efficiency in the allocation of investable funds.

Although the role of finance in contributing to growth comes through its contribution to productivity rather than the quantity of capital, more developed financial systems do make external finance available to more firms, and specifically tend to favor economic sectors where, for one reason or another, firms need to call on outside finance. Thus, when Demirgüç-Kunt and Maksimovic (1998) compared the actual growth rate of several thousand firms from 30 countries with each firm's estimated capacity to finance long-term growth from internal resources, they found that a greater proportion of the firms in financially developed economies were growing faster than this benchmark. This suggests that financial development is in this sense associated with wider access to external finance. Likewise, looking at the aggregate financing of firms in 36 manufacturing sectors in more than 40 countries, Rajan and Zingales (1998) found that it was the economic sectors that, based on U.S. experience, need to rely most on external finance that grow more rapidly in more financially developed economies.

If specialized financial firms are good at monitoring the users of funds, more reliance on external finance could represent an improvement. In themselves, however, these firm-level and sectoral findings do not necessarily point to a greater efficiency in the allocation of investable resources. After all, efficiency improvements may require diverting finance away from certain firms or sectors. A recent study by Wurgler (2000), also using sectoral data, goes some way to closing the circle by showing that sectoral investment is more responsive to sectoral output growth in financially developed economies. Put another way, in financially less-developed economies, an output slump in a certain sector is less likely to result in investment being cut back in that sector, and vice versa. Evidently this, too, is an imperfect measure of allocative efficiency, but it does cast additional light on the processes at work, which apparently

More finance means external funding for more firms and in particular sectors

include the mobilization of—though not necessarily an increase in—savings, reallocation of investable funds, and increased reliance on external providers of finance to firms, and as such to more external monitoring of firms' managers.

Finance works in the short run too—

Finance also impacts growth positively over shorter periods. Levine, Loayza, and Beck slice their 35 years of data into 7 equal subperiods and find that the correlation of growth rates with the level of financial development is still as high as it is over the longer term. Indeed, if we shorten the period even further, we can find even stronger correlations between private credit expansion and economic growth—but these can be misleading. It is, after all, necessary to distinguish between (a) sustainable growth based on steady productivity gains helped by shrewd allocation of capital resources and monitoring of managers, and (b) transitory growth based on unsustainable rates of borrowing.

but beware: bigger is not necessarily better

This alerts us to a need for caution in pushing for credit expansion as a way of achieving finance-driven growth. Bigger is not *necessarily* better. To be sure, it is a distinguishing mark of the high-income, advanced economies that their financial systems are large in terms of

- The amount of funds intermediated and processed.
- The number and range of firms they embody and the services that they provide.
- The economic resources they employ.

The econometric results we have described suggest that the association is to some extent causal, but it is almost obvious that a headlong rush by developing economies to emulate the scale of advanced financial systems is unwise and potentially costly. For example, attempts to make a dash for financial depth (to improve economic growth through inverting the finance-growth equation) can and have misfired badly:

- Engineering too rapid a rapid growth in domestic credit leads to inflation and depreciation or to institutional insolvency (getting this right is partly a matter of macroeconomic stabilization policy—some of the biggest failures here have been associated with inflow surges of foreign capital, as discussed in chapter 4).
- Creation of publicly owned banks to force the pace of intermediation may instead stifle the creation of financial capacity (see chapter 3).

Box 1.2   Finance as an export sector

THERE IS A VALID ALTERNATIVE PERSPECTIVE HERE that has been seen as relevant, especially for some smaller economies. This is to see finance as a potentially important export sector. To some extent a successful export finance business can be expected as a spin-off from effective domestic finance. The United Kingdom's huge net export earnings from financial services reflect the legacy of a quarter-millennium of technological leadership in finance, built on the Dutch experience in the late 17th century and placed initially at the service of government war finance. Technological and human capital sophistication has also helped Hong Kong and Singapore achieve comparable roles in their region. There is some natural tendency for international

finance to concentrate in a small number of centers, each reflecting a pool of liquidity and expertise, and several regional financial centers have benefited from the existence of repressed financial systems in their geographical neighborhood. (Furthermore, routine back-office financial services can be exported without requiring such a high systemic investment in human resources.) Unfortunately, few have been successful. Many countries attempting to develop finance as an export business have not developed the requisite legal, regulatory, and supervisory structures and have, instead, sought to employ aggressive tax or regulatory competition. What were envisaged as centers of financial expertise have sometimes become little more than centers for money laundering.

- Protection of the financial services sector as an "infant industry" can lead to excess costs and poor services (box 1.2).

Instead, the policy lessons must be derived from closer observation of the processes by which the financial systems of advanced economies have evolved to provide solutions to the financial requirements of firms—and households—in increasingly complex economic environments, thereby providing the platform for further productivity advances. To a large extent, these processes have been market-driven, and many of them occurred in periods when there was little direct government activism in financial markets. Governments in developing countries that want to build on this success can best do so by responding to market needs—not indeed to the particular needs of individual market participants, but to the needs of market functioning overall. In other words, the aim should be not to try to engineer directly an expansion of the financial sector, but to adopt policies that enable financial system participants to deliver the services in which they specialize with the maximum effectiveness, and to ensure in particular that the deep functions most needed by each economy that can be provided by finance are adequately catered to.

Policymakers should focus on the effectiveness of financial systems

Since developing these services involves considerable externalities and network effects, a passive stance is not enough (cf. Stiglitz, 1994). Policymakers must work with the market to ensure optimal financial development, both helping to coordinate the development of interlinked market structures, and also creating the necessary infrastructure for finance.

We look in turn at structures and infrastructure.

Structure

Debt and equity—the basic structural elements

THIS QUESTION OF HOW TO CHOOSE THE OVERALL DESIGN of a financial system emerged suddenly and acutely with the collapse of the planned economy, and the urgent requirement to create a new structure for finance in more than a score of transition economies. Almost immediately, a latent debate between the merits of intermediated and nonintermediated "market" finance came to the fore. This debate has taught us much about the way in which financial systems work, in particular how apparently different institutional structures can perform in apparently quite different ways, but with similar efficiency, the same deep economic functions.

Though the premises of the debate—that bank-based financial systems and market-based systems can be unequivocally ranked in their ability to deliver financial services needed for growth and prosperity—seems, as we will see, to be a false one, it is certainly true that the institutional structures surrounding banks and securities markets have often and for long periods evolved quite differently in different countries.

How are the funding needs of a venture to be externally financed when they are too large to be provided by the promoter themselves? External providers of finance need to satisfy themselves in advance that the returns are commensurate with the risks involved and to continue keeping an eye on things thereafter.

One financing strategy is for providers and users of funds to rely on a bank: a more or less large specialist intermediary that takes the risk of financing the venture on its own books, pools the risk from many ventures, and achieves economies of scale by avoiding duplication in appraisal and monitoring. The bank in turn is kept on a tight leash through its reliance on short-term financing from a large number of depositors, which also has the advantage of giving the depositors liquidity. Bank financing clearly makes sense when information about creditworthiness is easy to interpret but costly to acquire—as for example in a mature industry; the depositors have no reason to disagree with the bank management's information-based judgments.

An alternative financing strategy is for financial claims on the venture to be sold directly to fund providers. If there is a lot of disagreement on the prospects of the venture, this might be a better way of enabling financiers to be matched to the ventures they believe in. Selling financial claims on the open market, where there are both optimists and pessimists among the suppliers of funds, might be a better bet for those seeking finance for innovation than trying to rely on the judgment of a monolithic intermediary (Allen and Gale 2000).

The liquidity of these claims is enhanced by having them listed on an organized securities exchange; without such liquidity, the pool of open market investors will be limited.

Formal financial systems in most countries are dominated by banks, but in some of the most advanced countries the ratio of stock market capitalization to banking assets is very high, and there is a general tendency for the market-to-bank ratio to increase with the level of development both over time and cross-sectionally (figure 1.6, box 1.3). Does this imply that an increased role for market-based finance should be a goal of policy?

This question has been extensively analyzed in recent econometric research, with a striking conclusion: the trend for a general increase in

As countries get wealthier, the relative scale, activity, and efficiency of the stock market to the banking sector all increase.

Figure 1.6   Three measures of the relative development of banks and organized securities markets

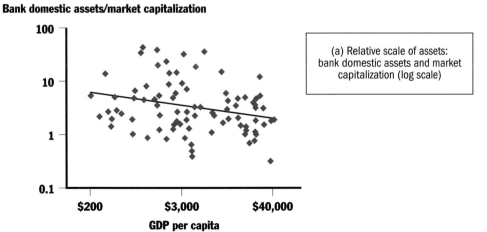

Bank domestic assets/market capitalization

(a) Relative scale of assets: bank domestic assets and market capitalization (log scale)

GDP per capita

(figure continues on following page)

Figure 1.6 *(continued)*

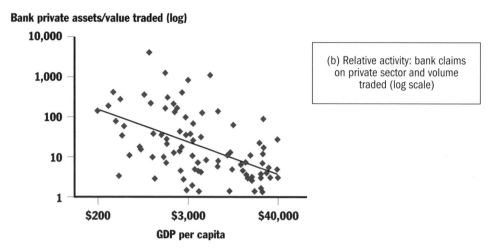

Bank private assets/value traded (log)

(b) Relative activity: bank claims on private sector and volume traded (log scale)

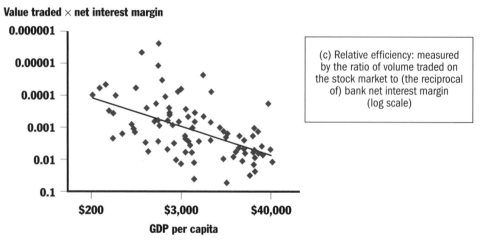

Value traded × net interest margin

(c) Relative efficiency: measured by the ratio of volume traded on the stock market to (the reciprocal of) bank net interest margin (log scale)

Source: BDL database.

Banking and market finance both support economic growth

the share of market finance with economic development *does not* appear to be causal. If one takes the regression models of growth, discussed above, and adapts them by adding various measures of the market-to-bank ratio, the results consistently fail to show any statistically significant impact of these measures of structure on growth. There appears to be no effect, whether on the sectoral composition of growth or on the proportion of firms growing more rapidly than could be financed from internal resources; even bank profitability does not appear to be affected. This is the case regardless of whether the ratio one employs relates to the

Box 1.3 Time, income, and inflation: stylized facts about financial depth

EVEN BEFORE EXAMINING INSTITUTIONAL determinants of financial development and the causal relationship between finance and growth, certain empirical regularities can be detected in the macroeconomic data, linking financial depth, inflation, and per capita GDP with a significant variation along the time dimension.

For monetary depth (M2/GDP ratio), regression analysis of a pooled cross-section and time-series with some 2,700 observations covering more than 120 countries for up to 35 years from the BDL database (Beck, Demirgüç-Kunt, and Levine 2000a) allows us to quantify these macroeconomic relationships and suggests a number of stylized facts:

Monetary depth
- increases by about three percentage points for every $1,000 increase in GDP per capita,
- and by about a quarter of a percentage point every year,

- but falls by about half a percentage point for every percentage point rise in the medium-term inflation rate.

The importance of inflation, especially high inflation, in hindering financial development is stressed by Boyd, Levine, and Smith (forthcoming). Their regressions, which include a wider list of controls and examine nonlinear effects of inflation, confirm the average size of the inflationary impact on financial depth noted above. They also show that high-inflation countries have much lower financial development, but that, beyond a certain point, additional increases in inflation have little further impact.

The trend increase in financial depth has not prevented a secular slowdown in the world rate of growth. This could appear paradoxical in light of the proposition that deeper financial systems help generate growth. One interpretation is that technological changes over time have increased the finance-intensity of growth, implying that deeper financial systems are now required to achieve the same rate of growth as before.

Note: These results are the estimated long-term (cointegrating) relationship from an error-correction mechanism imposing common coefficients across countries except for a country fixed effect. Estimation method: GLS with cross-section weights.

volume of assets (bank deposits, stock market capitalization) or efficiency (net interest margin, stock turnover).[7]

We need not conclude that the type of financing does not matter. One aspect of what seems to have happened is that firms in successful economies have found a mixture of equity market and bank development that suits their own particular financing needs and institutional structures; the higher the level of income, the more likely that mixture will be weighted toward equity. The production technology and product market conditions facing different firms certainly play a role in prompting different approaches to financing decisions. So this evidence by no means runs counter to the need for an appropriate degree of diversity in channels for financing in each country. Instead, the message must be that both development of banking and of market finance help economic growth: each can complement the other.

To be sure, policy has also influenced the relative importance of banks and stock markets in some countries. Often policies favoring one segment have had the effect of stifling another, with the result that the financial system has not developed the optimal range of structures for its needs. For example, in many countries, policies of restricting information or subjecting dividends to multiple taxation stifles the development of equities and fosters relationship debt finance, particularly when interest paid is deductible. Similarly, the relative repression of the Indian and Korean banking systems compared with less interventionism in the nonbank sector clearly contributed to the development of the latter in the 1980s and 1990s. The restriction, from the mid-1930s, preventing U.S. commercial banks from taking significant ownership stakes in nonfinancial firms helped make at least larger firms more reliant on the stock market, as had restrictions from the country's inception on geographical diversification of banks. The striking thing is that these restrictions did not prevent the U.S. financial system from adequately supporting subsequent U.S. growth. A contrasting case is that of the U.K. banks: even though public policy did not impose any comparable restrictions on their activities, they too left room for a substantial contribution from the stock market to the development of the U.K. financial system and economy.

The reasons for contrasting behavior of different financial institutions in different countries will continue to be debated. What recent research findings have established is that they matter much less than was previously thought, and that it is the financial services themselves that matter more than the form of their delivery. Indeed, the variety of the needed services goes well beyond what can be measured in the aggregate data for the scale and activity of banks and markets.

Information asymmetry limits access to equity in developing countries— One reason that the dichotomy between banks and markets may not help much to predict growth is that it does not closely correspond to the dichotomy between debt and equity.[8] A range of different financial instruments is necessary to enable firms in different circumstances to obtain an adequate structure of their financing. Debt is the classic instrument that can be used to deter insiders in a successful firm from pretending that they are unable to remunerate external financiers.[9] With simple debt contracts, the payment is not supposed to be conditional on the firm's performance, and default will trigger a transfer of control (whether of a collateral, or of the firm itself) to the external financiers. *Provided this transfer of control can indeed be relied upon to take place* (and as discussed below, this is by no means guaranteed for developing countries), this gives lenders the confidence that, even if they cannot monitor the firm's performance very reliably, they will be able to move in, take control, and realize the firm's value in the event of a default.

An interesting historical reflection helps confirm that verifiability of outcomes is the central issue. Some of the earliest debt-type contracts, specifically the ship-voyage (bottomry) loans of antiquity, *did* actually make payment partly conditional on one of the readily verifiable aspects of success inasmuch as the debtor did not have to service the loan unless and until the financed ship returned, in which case, as with the junk bonds of more recent times, they paid off handsomely.

And it is important that there should be something left over to take control of: debt is much more available to firms with tangible assets (estimates by Demirgüç-Kunt and Maksimovic (1999) based on the financial accounts of a large sample of listed companies in developed and developing countries indicate that replacing $100 of intangible assets with tangible will increase reliance on debt finance on average by between $36 and $51).

The complexity of much of modern economic and business activity has greatly increased the variety of ways in which insiders can try to conceal firm performance. Although progress in technology, accounting, and legal practice has also helped improve the tools of detection, on balance the asymmetry of information between user and provider of funds has not been reduced as much in developing countries as it has in advanced economies, and may have deteriorated. The problem of monitoring limits the potential for firms to have access to outside equity, and this problem is more acute in developing countries.

Indeed, access to long-term debt financing is limited in developing countries, even for the leading firms. Likely contributory causes are not only information asymmetries and general opaqueness, but also poor collateral law and weak judicial efficiency, making it hard either to write strong contracts or to enforce them in a court of law. Examination of the financial statements even of listed companies clearly shows that the proportion of total assets financed by debt is smaller—and much smaller if we confine attention to long-term debt—in those developing countries for which data are available than in the major industrial countries (figure 1.7). The low average maturity of the debt issued by firms in developing countries is not wholly explained by higher inflation—though there's nothing like inflation for stifling a long-term debt market. That is not to say that these firms have substituted outside equity. While the data do not allow us to identify outside equity

—and along with legal problems, limits the availability of long-term debt

Figure 1.7 Average leverage of listed firms in industrial and developing economies

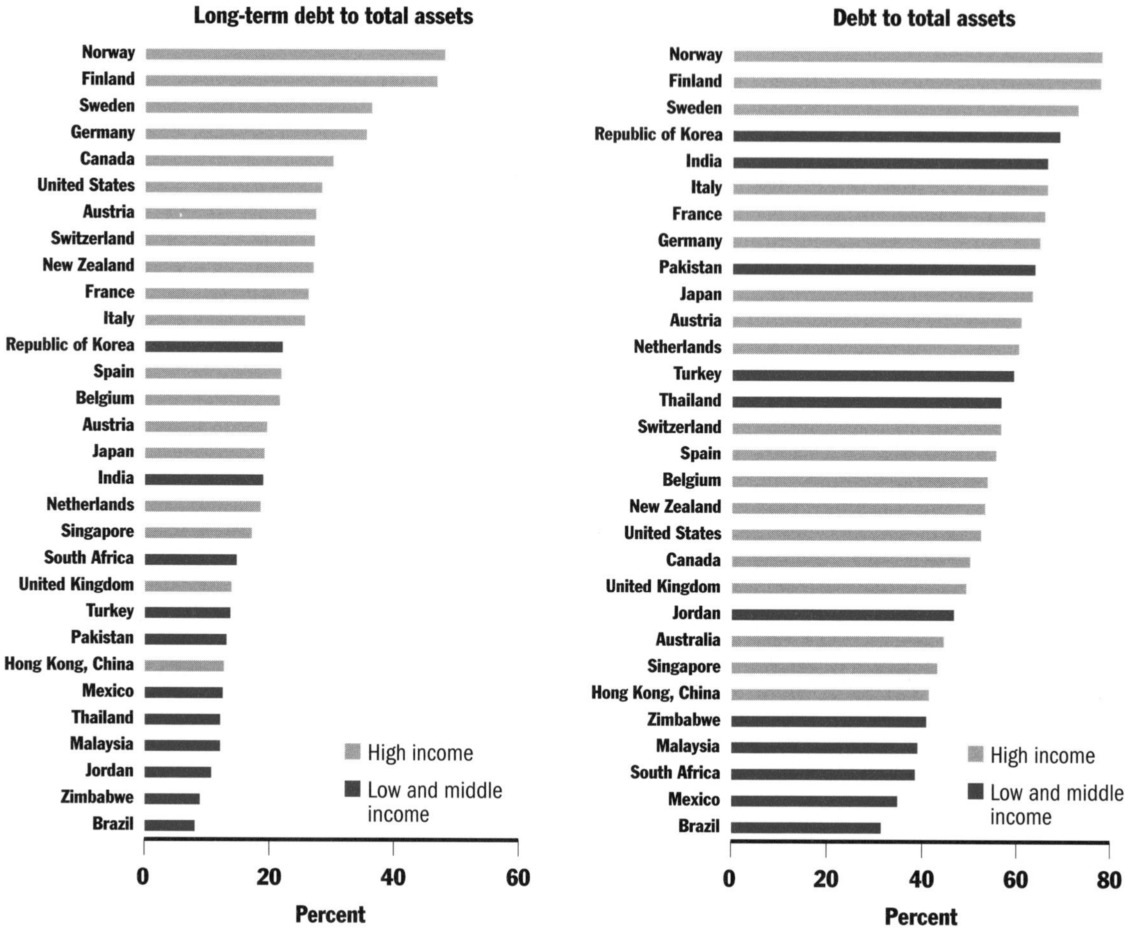

Long-term debt to total assets

Norway
Finland
Sweden
Germany
Canada
United States
Austria
Switzerland
New Zealand
France
Italy
Republic of Korea
Spain
Belgium
Austria
Japan
India
Netherlands
Singapore
South Africa
United Kingdom
Turkey
Pakistan
Hong Kong, China
Mexico
Thailand
Malaysia
Jordan
Zimbabwe
Brazil

High income
Low and middle income

0   20   40   60
Percent

Debt to total assets

Norway
Finland
Sweden
Republic of Korea
India
Italy
France
Germany
Pakistan
Japan
Austria
Netherlands
Turkey
Thailand
Switzerland
Spain
Belgium
New Zealand
United States
Canada
United Kingdom
Jordan
Australia
Singapore
Hong Kong, China
Zimbabwe
Malaysia
South Africa
Mexico
Brazil

High income
Low and middle income

0   20   40   60   80
Percent

Note: Data is for the average of information collected 1981–90.
Source: Based on Demirgüç-Kunt and Maksimovic (1999).

separately, the presumption must be that these firms have been sub-stantially financed by retained earnings and by equity funding from firm insiders; those who are not hampered by the problem of asymmetric information. This is one reason for the growing importance of private equity investment.

Much of the borrowings of firms in developing economies come from banks, and the cost of this finance accordingly also depends on the operational efficiency and competitiveness of the banking market. In this respect, too, the performance of developing economies falls behind. One approximation to this performance is the intermediation spread. The indications are that liberalization of bank interest rates has widened this spread (figure 1.8); indeed, while the median of average quoted spreads in advanced economies shrank during the second half of the 1990s to just over 300 basis points, the corresponding figure for developing economies continued to widen beyond 800 basis points. Some of this increase will have reflected more refined loan pricing in the liberalized environment, better reflecting the higher default risk in the typical developing country bank portfolio.[10] Some, however, will reflect an increased exercise of market power by banks and bankers in internally liberalized banking markets; especially where capital has been eroded by banking crises, banks will be keen to use their new freedoms to build up capital through the exercise of market power. The potential need for policy measures to guard against concentration of market power following banking liberalization is evident, but the authorities may be slow to do so if banks' capital is low because of previous problems: this will be like a hidden quasi-tax on bank customers to restore adequate capitalization (see chapter 2).

Concentration of banking is also demonstrably bad for industrial growth, but, as shown by Cetorelli and Gambera (2001), the effects are

Borrowing from banks is costly in developing countries—

Figure 1.8 Intermediation spreads

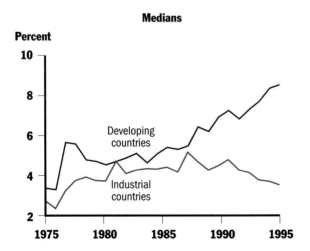

Medians

Percent

Note: The graph shows trends in the median intermediation spread for banks in industrial and developing countries, 1975–99.
Source: Honohan (2001a).

Competition and efficiency gains reduce spreads in the industrial countries; liberalization has allowed for a greater reflection of risks in developing country spreads.

—but equity market development may provide a counteracting competitive force

complicated by the fact that noncompetitive banking systems are particularly adapted for profiting from lending relationships with young firms with heavy financing requirements. (In an uncompetitive market, the banks can expect their initial investment in establishing a lending relationship with such firms to be rewarded with a lengthy stream of profits.) Indeed, the damaging effect of concentration is found to be lower in sectors likely to have a predominance of such firms.

Development of the securities markets—equity as well as debt—may provide a countervailing force to excess profits in banking. Indeed, banking depth appears to be correlated across countries with stock market liquidity (figure 1.9). In attempting to understand stock market development, it is easy to be distracted by the large anonymous equity markets that have become so important in the advanced economies, to the extent that one neglects the fact that, in developing countries, even firms with stock market listings often have the bulk of their equity held by investors who are closely related. Indeed, in historical terms, the first extensive use of formal equity finance was not really to tap an anonymous market, but served as a way of transferring ownership between limited circles of business associates, and so it is for much of equity today, especially (of course), but not only, for unlisted firms.[11]

Still, if the problems of asymmetric information can be overcome or alleviated, outside equity is clearly a financial instrument that can offer considerable advantages to both user and supplier of funds. Equity finance

Figure 1.9 Measures of stock market and banking development

Stock market capitalization as percent of GDP

Bank and stock market development go together.

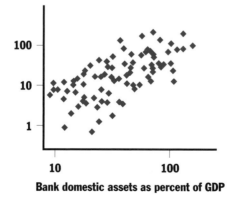

Bank domestic assets as percent of GDP

Source: BDL database.

allows the insider promoters and managers of firms time to complete longer-term strategic projects and to recover from unexpected difficulties without having to incur the costs of reorganization. Although the equity holders may have ultimate ownership rights and stand to gain much if the firm becomes very successful, these advantages depend on the effective functioning of the board of directors giving all shareholders fair treatment.

When this cannot be assured, equity can be sold to outsiders only at a discount. This has been dramatically shown for East Asia in studies by Claessens and others (1999a, b), who have carefully documented the ultimate ownership structure of 3,000 listed firms in 9 countries, tracking group and family control, and thus the degree of de facto control by management or dominant shareholders, often through the pyramid structures that are commonly found—and not only in that region (figures 1.10, 1.11).[12] To some extent, such structures reflect the greater concentration of economic power in developing countries (a point that has consequences for the conduct of prudential regulation also, as discussed in chapter 2). Increasing ownership concentration hurts stock market performance of these shares, which trade at a discount to compensate outside financiers for the likelihood that their interests will be relatively neglected. Here, too, we see that the functioning of the market cannot always be relied upon to reach the optimum, and in this case the corporate governance of the firm and the allocation of resources are what suffer.

Some protection can be provided here by accurate and comprehensive financial reporting, and by laws that require directors to work in the best interests of all the shareholders. Of course, if laws and their enforcement depend in practice on endorsement by the same elite that controls most of the economy's major firms, they may not be in a hurry to provide that endorsement. Still, insiders do not always benefit in net terms from an environment in which they cannot credibly commit to fair treatment of outside shareholders.

These kinds of requirement seem more important than simply establishing a formal organization for facilitating the trading of shares. Nevertheless, once the essentials for the issuance of equities by firms have been established, it becomes important to ensure that trading procedures and practice in the organized stock market are also such that adequate liquidity is available at fair prices. Rapidly evolving practice and technology from mature markets make it much easier than in the past to adopt and implement trading and price discovery mechanisms that are effective and, in short, ensure market integrity both for bond and equity trading (cf. IFC 1998).

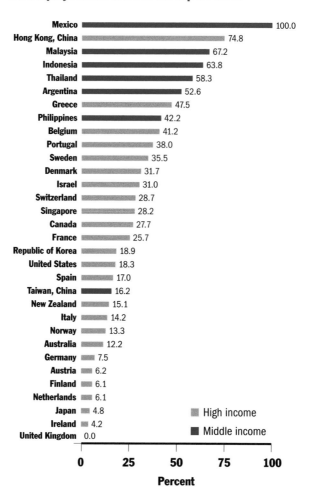

Figure 1.10   Market value of family-owned firms as a percentage of the total equity market value of the top 20 firms

Family-controlled firms holding 20 percent or more equity dominate in some countries

Country	Percent
Mexico	100.0
Hong Kong, China	74.8
Malaysia	67.2
Indonesia	63.8
Thailand	58.3
Argentina	52.6
Greece	47.5
Philippines	42.2
Belgium	41.2
Portugal	38.0
Sweden	35.5
Denmark	31.7
Israel	31.0
Switzerland	28.7
Singapore	28.2
Canada	27.7
France	25.7
Republic of Korea	18.9
United States	18.3
Spain	17.0
Taiwan, China	16.2
New Zealand	15.1
Italy	14.2
Norway	13.3
Australia	12.2
Germany	7.5
Austria	6.2
Finland	6.1
Netherlands	6.1
Japan	4.8
Ireland	4.2
United Kingdom	0.0

■ High income
■ Middle income

Source: La Porta, López-de-Silanes, and Shleifer (1999a); Claessens, Djankov, and Lang (2000).

Forced feeding of a local stock market, however, as has been attempted in many small countries, may be putting the cart before the horse. Many new stock exchanges have been established in recent years despite unpromising conditions. Many have extremely low liquidity and a very small number of stocks traded. Especially with increasing opportunities for international alliances and cross-border listing and trading, it is uncertain how many of these exchanges can and should survive. We will return to the role of small financial systems in chapter 4.

Figure 1.11 "And the owner is...the Suharto family group"

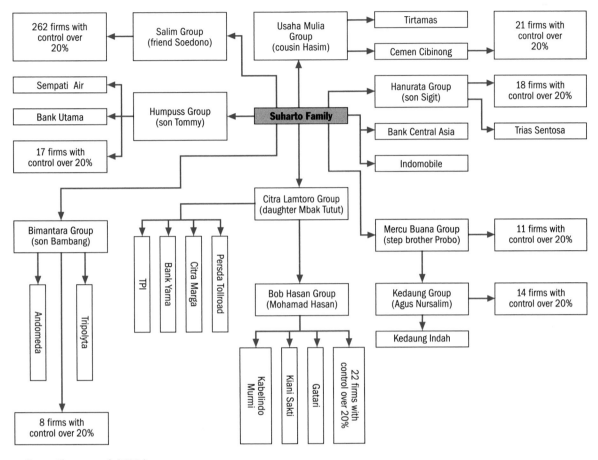

Source: Claessens et al. (1999a).

Financial Infrastructure

IF WHAT IS NEEDED IS TO FACILITATE THE EFFECTIVE FUNCtioning of both debt and equity markets—allowing them to respond to the demands placed on them by the needs of providers and users of funds—this still leaves the question of what policy measures are appropriate? The answer that most naturally emerges from the research results that we have been reviewing and from the disappointing experience from government ownership of financial intermediaries (discussed in chapter 3) is that these policies are likely to be more effective if directed to infrastructure[13] rather than directly to the financial structures themselves.

It is better to focus policies on the development of a solid infrastructure, rather than specific structures

The lessons from examinations of financial structure point to the desirability of infrastructural policy measures that could promote the production and communication of information; limit the exercise of market power, whether in banking[14] or by insiders against shareholders; and ensure an efficient functioning of the organized securities markets.

But what policy measures should these be? For example, what rules and procedures would limit the tendency for participants to misrepresent relevant information, to evade commitments they have undertaken, and to exploit market power? (Here our first principle of policy formation, from the overview, comes to the fore: "Work with the market, but do not leave it to the market.")

It is in the legal area that recent research on effective financial systems has made the most progress—and in areas going beyond the obvious and crucial need to ensure that the creditor's rights can, in the event of a default, be expeditiously and inexpensively exercised. Naturally government has a comparative advantage in the design and implementation of law. One possible approach to policy design in the legal field is to seek to update and refine laws and legal practice in areas affecting finance: to bring the legal structure up to best practice as defined by what is in place in one of the more advanced economies.

Different legal systems provide different protection

Some few years ago a startling assertion, backed up by detailed quantitative research, cast doubt on this bland prescription. In a series of papers, La Porta, López-de-Silanes, Shleifer, and Vishny (1997, 1998) suggested that the choice of legal tradition is not innocuous. Specifically, they asserted that legal systems derived from English common law outperform those derived from the Napoleonic code, both in terms of favoring financial development and in supporting economic growth overall. (According to their research, performance of the other two legal families recognized by legal scholars, the German and the Scandinavian, lay between that of the others.)

These initial findings by La Porta, López-de-Silanes, Shleifer, and Vishny can be interpreted, for example, in terms of the relative protection that is formally granted by the different legal traditions to a firm's managers, controlling shareholders, and other insiders as against outsider financiers, including both creditors and minority shareholders. Indeed, the authors identified a set of key markers indicative of this relative protection in law. For example, if a firm declares bankruptcy, can a secured creditor seize collateral, or does an automatic stay on such seizure kick in (an automatic stay evidently protects the insiders from secured creditors)?

Is management entitled to stay in control of a firm that has filed for reorganization under protection of a court? Are there compulsory provisions for proxy voting by mail? Do all shareholders have equal voting rights and a preemptive right to participate in any new share issues (protecting the minority shareholder)? Can a small minority of shareholders insist on calling an extraordinary general shareholders' meeting? Can directors be sued for oppressive treatment of shareholders?[15]

While the various legal markers cannot readily be assigned a quantitative value in terms of the degree of protection that they do provide, the pattern is fairly clear: using data from 49 countries around the world, the relative protection is closely correlated across countries with the four-way classification of legal origin, and with characteristics of legal rules that are in turn associated with legal origin. Significantly, stronger shareholder rights (measured rather crudely by an average of the markers) are associated with a greater number of listed firms and with higher stock market capitalization; stronger creditor rights are associated with a higher level of bank credit and bond finance. This finding, that legal protections do help support financial market development, is confirmed and reinforced by the Levine, Loayza, and Beck paper (to which reference has already been made, and which again uses the legal origin variable as an instrument to help control for the possibility of reverse causation).

Thus legal origin is correlated with financial development, and finance helps economic growth, but it may be a mistake to make the leap to saying that legal origin itself was a major causal determinant of economic growth. More recent econometric work suggests that the causal paths are more complex. Two recent studies propose alternative mechanisms, either of which seems to describe the data more accurately. Both emphasize historical conditions in the countries adopting legal systems from the core European countries.

- The first (Acemoglu, Johnson, and Robinson 2000) distinguishes between colonies that were exploited by the colonial power and those that were settled by colonists: only in the latter (econometrically identified by the lower mortality rates experienced by colonists) could the benefits of well-designed legal and other institutions have an effect.
- The second paper (Berkowitz, Pistor, and Richard 2000) emphasizes what they call legality, that is, the degree to which legal institutions are actually working effectively. In practice, legal origin

does also correlate with legality, and with the same ranking. But Berkowitz, Pistor, and Richard take a different tack, arguing that countries where alien legal systems were directly transplanted from the source country to unreceptive environments (or even to receptive environments if the transplant was indirect and hence somehow imperfect) failed to develop effective legality.

Each of these views leads to a different explanatory variable, and the econometric results indicate that each of these variables outperforms the legal origin as an explanation for economic growth. Perhaps the key message from these studies is not that successful development required benevolent colonial leadership, but rather that the nature of the historical interaction with European centers was often destructive of or inimical to the effectiveness of local institutions.

The protection of property rights favors financial market development and investment

The last word has not been written on this matter, but even if it is not itself a strong independent causal influence on economic growth, the debate and the analysis of the role of legal origin has deepened our understanding of legal structures in the functioning of financial systems. The research has shown that the differential protection of different stakeholders has had an influence on the relative development of debt and equity markets, on the degree to which firms are widely held, or more generally the degree to which they are financed externally, and thus on overall financial sector development.

Specifically, the proposition that legal origin influences financial development is not statistically overturned by the colonial and transplant theories discussed above. Indeed, Beck, Demirgüç-Kunt, and Levine (2000b) show that legal origin continues to be an important explanatory factor for various measures of *financial* development in cross-country regressions. (It is the persistence of this link that allows us to the use legal origin as an instrument to help identify the causal impact of finance on growth as discussed above.) The colonial variable also appears to be significantly correlated with financial development—the transplant variable less so.[16]

And the policy message from the econometric results systematically point in one direction: far from impeding growth, better protection of the property rights of outside financiers favors financial market development and investment.[17]

Lest it be thought that this observation is too obvious, let it be recalled that this perspective—attractive and conventional to providers of finance—is not uncontested. Indeed, there is something to be said on theoretical grounds for the alternative view that providers of finance should not be protected too much. After all, growth depends on entrepreneurship, which is provided by the insider promoters of the firm; giving them insufficient legal protection might dampen their enthusiasm for new ventures. From another perspective, we can see that providing too much legal protection to claims over collateral could encourage lazy banks, which fail to exploit their skills in the social function of project appraisal and monitoring, relying instead on taking collateral and on its legal protection (this scenario is worked out theoretically by Manove, Padilla, and Pagano 2000).

Although theory shows that too many protections to creditors may stifle entrepreneurship—

And one must clearly avoid elevating contract fulfillment and enforcement beyond its true value. As Keynes (1923) memorably remarked, "the absolutists of contract…are the real parents of revolution." These and similar arguments have a degree of validity, but the net judgment must be an empirical one, and here all the recent evidence points to the problems being of insufficient protection of claim holders rather than the contrary. The absence of a "credit culture," that is, the incentive and practice of borrowers to repay, does elicit the predictable response from would-be lenders. Furthermore, the absence of restraints on the abuse of insider power to tunnel out the resources of a firm out of sight of the minority shareholders makes them reluctant to provide equity finance in the future. Failure to establish these norms holds back the development of financial markets, thereby limiting entrepreneurial access to an adequate range of financial instruments at reasonable cost.

the evidence suggests that the greater risk is of insufficient protection

Despite the retreat of government from many spheres of economic activity, and although over-regulation and counterproductive rules for financial markets have often been a problem, it would be hard to deny that government needs to have a role in this field of ensuring adequate financial infrastructure.[18] Where government has wholly absented itself from the ultimate responsibility for licensing and prudential supervision of banks, for regulation of the public issuance and trading of securities, or for creating and supporting the legal system needed for conflict resolution in matters of contract, the results have been bad.

The government should work with the markets to develop a financial infrastructure

Hence, the first key principle which by now is almost self-evident: in designing and implementing policy for the financial sector, the government must work with the market to develop the effectiveness of market functioning, but it cannot leave these matters to individual market participants or to the market as a whole.

There is clear scope for market participants to enhance regulatory structures—

Yet, to supplement—or make up for the absence of—government action, there is a clear and practical scope for market participants to amplify regulatory structures where this is needed. Practice in some of the more successful organized stock markets provide good examples of such private initiatives. Indeed, most markets impose some disclosure and corporate governance requirements over and above those provided for in general company law, the better to give confidence to market participants. They also create special rules for trading procedures in the market, including the prohibition of insider trading, front-running, and various forms of collusive practice among market specialists.

An instructive recent example, with evident potential application in developing countries, is the way in which the German stock market—the privately owned Deutsche Börse—reacted to a perception that disclosure requirements for listed companies were too weak to generate a high level of shareholder confidence. Accordingly, there were few new listings. The problem could be traced to the traditional approach of German accounting, which imposes a requirement of reporting prudence that, while protecting the interests of creditors (whose main requirement is to have early warning of solvency problems), has the effect of concealing the actual financial strength of a firm, exactly the information needed by a would-be shareholder. A general reform of accounting standards to approximate the International Accounting Standard (IAS) is envisaged for Germany, as for many other countries, and should help solve this problem. Meanwhile, the stock market, though obliged to admit any company that satisfies statutory listing requirements, decided to create a new high-profile segment of the market with greater disclosure requirements. Admission to this new segment, the Neuer Markt, requires quarterly reporting to IAS standards. Since its establishment in 1996, it has been associated with an explosion of new issues attributable to increased shareholder confidence.[19]

Like all self-regulatory organizations, the Deutsche Börse cannot dispense altogether with the courts: although a company listed in the new segment has voluntarily accepted the tougher rules and could be removed from the Neuer Markt list in case of violation, there could be future disagreements over compliance that might have to be resolved in the courts. If they are to be effective, attempts to augment the law with the private contracts of a self-regulatory organization need to be designed in such a way that recourse to the courts is unlikely, for example by making the rules themselves as transparent as possible. The term *self-regulatory organization*

(SRO) is, of course, problematic, because most such organizations in financial markets will need some degree of outside regulation if only to limit abuses of the market power that such organizations can wield.[20]

In attending to the design of laws and market regulations, however, we must not lose sight of the evident importance, already alluded to, of legality, and in particular that existing rules should be enforced. Several of the cross-country econometric studies to which reference has been made also show that survey-based assessments of the rule of law and quality of government also matter for financial development.

At the simplest level, taking a real estate collateral for a loan is of limited use if attaching or repossessing the collateral is known to be difficult in practice (even though, for example, the borrower's willingness and ability to provide such collateral may suggest that they are likely to be committed to the neighborhood, and that protecting their local reputation may be of some importance to them). Likewise if bankruptcy law and procedures are ineffective, unsecured lending by outsiders to a firm becomes highly risky. Indeed there is good evidence that firms borrow less where bankruptcy proceedings are less widely observed (Klapper 2000).

Correcting deficiencies at the level of the courts is a task that goes beyond the scope of this review. Pending wholesale legal reforms, however, progress can sometimes be made by market participants exercising such sanctions as are available to them. For example, in the case of abuses by corporate insiders, delisting by the exchange may be an effective sanction even if the efficient and fair courts are not available. Securing a secondary listing on a foreign market, or of a depositary receipt, can also export the problem, a point to which we return in chapter 4.

Another example of how market regulations—in this case deficient ones—can matter as much as substantive corporate law is the notorious case of the investment companies that acquired ownership over large swaths of the Czech corporate sector following the mass privatizations there by offering their shares for the mass privatization vouchers. Although there were rules governing the conduct and transparency of licensed investment companies, they did not protect the outside shareholders—those who had exchanged their vouchers for investment company shares—from seeing investment company licenses surrendered and the entity converted into a largely unregulated holding company (Coffee 1999). Many of the largest funds were so converted, facilitating the effective looting or "tunneling" of much of the fund's assets to insiders to the detriment of the outsiders who

—but they must be enforced

Experience illustrates the hazards of an inadequate infrastructure

61

had sold their vouchers for fund shares. Another type of problem in the Czech case related to the deficiency of rules for trading, as distinct from corporate governance and transparency. It was permissible to trade in listed shares without reporting the amounts and prices to the exchange: in practice, deals on the exchange became the exception and were often concluded at false prices; the true market-clearing prices became opaque.

Investment companies and mutual funds illustrate in a dramatic form the need for careful protection of outside shareholders. The design of regulation for this sector, which can greatly strengthen the demand side of the equity market, as well as widening the range of savings media available to persons of moderate wealth and providing competition for bank deposits, is something that needs attention in many countries.

Contractual savings and the stock market: a symbiotic development

Actually, the development and strengthening of the stock market and of managed funds often go hand in hand.[21] Managed funds, particularly private pension funds and other contractual savings funds—with their appetite for longer-term investments, often (though not always) including market-traded equities—can be a significant driver of stock market development.[22] It is as a block of significant investors—with the muscle to require rules and legislation to improve market integrity, efficiency of trading mechanisms, and corporate governance (including better disclosure to, and protection of, minority shareholders)—that pension funds and other institutional fund managers can make their largest contribution to improving the stock market. This will not happen until their equity holdings have reached a critical mass of, say, 20 percent of the market, a figure that may take some time to be achieved: in particular, the accumulation of pension funds is a gradual process. It will also not happen where the strategy of the funds is to take majority shares in affiliated nonfinancial firms, as is the case for the main pension funds in some countries.

And it is not just the stock market that benefits from the emergence of pension funds, life insurance companies, and other contractual savings institutions. In mature and emerging markets, they have been central in supporting numerous market-based financial innovations, such as asset-backed securities, the use of structured finance and derivative products, including index-tracking funds and synthetic products that protect investors from market declines. Catastrophic risk bonds placed by insurance companies are yet another example of the financial innovations emerging from this segment, and the process is likely to continue, with an apparent market gap in longevity-based derivatives. The associated learning and human capital formation, as fund managers tool up to employ such techniques, helps to enhance the quality of risk management throughout the economy.

Building up these funds can also ensure enhanced and stable funding for key niche segments of the financial market, such as factoring, leasing, and venture capital companies. These in turn are a key to ensuring that smaller-scale firms can get access to financing at reasonable cost, a point to which we return below. They also generate a demand for long-term investments (required by life insurance providers and firms selling annuities if they are to match their obligations with assets of comparable maturity), thereby providing a market-based solution to a perceived gap that many governments have tried to fill over the years with costly and distorting administered solutions. Thus, contractual savings institutions expand the range and depth of financial services provided not only to their own policyholders and plan participants, but to a much wider range of financial sector actors.

While the emergence of private pension funds is neither necessary nor sufficient for a well-functioning stock market, it is thus well worth ensuring that the preconditions for contractual savings development are in place. This is true, not only for the longer-term benefits that will accrue to pensioners, policyholders, and other customers, but also for the spillover effects that can result for financial sector development if the pension fund industry is competitive and innovative.

Indeed, public policy design in relation to pension funds needs to go a lot further than is the case for most other parts of the financial sector. The reason is that the development of private pension funds is everywhere strongly influenced, if not wholly driven, by tax concessions designed to encourage saving for old age, or by government mandates that make such saving compulsory. The so-called second pillar of pension provision relates to privately managed funds established in response to official mandate (the first pillar is tax-financed; the third is voluntary saving, but may be tax-advantaged). In making pension saving compulsory, the government is inevitably drawn in to defining what is to qualify as pension saving and approving the financial firms that will manage pension schemes. The same applies, though to a lesser extent, for tax-advantaged saving media. This implies that the government must also take some responsibility not only for prudential issues, but also to ensure that its interventions do not distort market incentives, resulting in, for example, a cartelized pension industry mis-selling at exorbitant prices to a largely underinformed customer base.[23]

Special issues for pension fund policy

Many pension fund system policy design issues remain unresolved in the literature, and there is a wide dispersion of practice internationally on matters such as the following:

- If pension saving is to be mandatory, should the mandate apply to the individual or to the employer? (There are cost savings to having the employer arrange for the funds to be set aside, but there is also a loss of transparency and perhaps of the incentive to ensure that the funds are well invested.)
- What is the allowable fee structure to be charged by funds? (Should fees be paid up-front or made proportional to investment return? Should funds be constrained, in the interest of transparency and fairness, to charging all participants the same price, or does such price-fixing lead to worse distortions in terms, say, of marketing expenses?)
- Should pensioners be allowed to divide their savings into more than one fund? (The preferred mix of asset types may vary, especially with age, but where switching between accounts is allowed, costly and probably wasteful marketing expenses tend to mushroom.)
- Should fund managers be obliged to offer a minimum return guarantee? (Guarantees may encourage herding of investment strategies, though there is evidence to suggest that this happens even in the absence of guarantees.)
- What types of annuity contract or other drawdown arrangement should be allowed? (Compulsory annuitization eliminates longevity risk, but introduces counterparty risk; variable annuities allow the pensioner to participate in market returns—and risks—during the drawdown period.)

Resolving these matters shades into complementary public policy issues that go well beyond the scope of this report, such as the nature of government-provided pension schemes and the portability of accumulated benefits in employer-provided plans and other aspects of income redistribution policy.

If a consensus has emerged, it is around the principle that the rigid investment rules that often channeled much of pension savings to poorly remunerated government-sponsored assets should become a thing of the past. To be sure, conditions in many countries, especially where the pension industry is embryonic, where customer sophistication or access to information is limited, or regulatory capacity is weak, dictate that conduct

There are many unresolved issues in policy design for pension funds

in the pension industry should still need to be constrained by explicit quantitative rules, especially against concentrations of risk, going beyond a general requirement of prudence. The trend, however, should be toward relaxation of arbitrary quantitative investment rules as soon as conditions permit, so that pension funds can play their full and potentially substantial part in the provision of essential financial services.[24]

Access

MEASURES THAT SUCCEED IN DEEPENING FINANCIAL markets and limiting the distorting exercise of market power result in more firms and individuals securing access to credit at acceptable cost. But what of the poor and of the small or microenterprise borrower?

Greater access to finance can help households escape poverty and tap the talents of the less privileged

Access issues are important for at least two distinct reasons. First, they directly address the empowerment aspect of poverty. Limited access to finance is a contributor to persistent poverty in that it severely limits the potential for poor households to exercise their own entrepreneurial abilities to escape poverty. Second, there are externalities in finance for small and medium-size enterprises (SMEs). One way of thinking of this is to recognize that each would-be small entrepreneur begins with an idea: small firm creation is often the only way to embody these ideas, and they will not be brought to realization without the necessary access to finance. Many of the ideas will be bad ones, but some will prove to be of enormous social benefit as contributors to the growth process. Which is which will not easily be determinable unless they are exposed to the marketplace. Without detracting from the growth-contribution of larger firms, a financial system so structured as to give access only to those who are already established and prosperous fails to deliver in this dimension.

Much-discussed as the two key obstacles to access are (a) the fact that the poor and start-up companies alike have a lack of collateral and (b) fixed costs, including those of information acquisition, monitoring, collection, and enforcement that can be prohibitive for small financial contracts and transactions. With limited access to the conventional formal financial sector, small-scale, poor, or isolated firms or individuals have had recourse to a huge variety of informal or quasi-formal financial arrangements. They also employ a range of nonfinancial approaches to securing needed services that the formal financial system fails to offer them.

Extensive informal financial networks exist in most countries—

Informal finance is very important in many regions and for certain groups in almost all regions of the developing world.[25] It comes in different forms, ranging from *susu* men—providing a haven for the savings of market women, secure as much from thriftless and importunate family members as from theft—to rotating savings and credit associations (*roscas*) which, by pooling regular savings and lending the pooled sum out in turn to the members, can reduce the average time taken for a member to access a target investable sum. Everywhere there is the traditional moneylender, the pawnbroker, and trade-related and tied credit, but probably the largest part consists of nonintermediated bilateral financial arrangements between friends or relatives, whether of loan or equity type, or a mixture.[26]

In the absence of collateral or of functioning or practical legal enforcement mechanisms, informal finance substitutes a range of alternative incentive and information devices, including social enforcement of penalties for willful default, social collateral, and pledging, where possession and use of the asset offered as collateral is transferred to the lender.[27]

but these are poor substitutes for more formal means of intermediation

The indications are that the scale of informal finance is inversely related to formal financial depth, but, extensive and rich though it is, informal finance hardly provides a perfect substitute for well-functioning formal finance with its ability to mobilize funds on a large scale and pool risks over extensive areas. The comparative advantage perceived for informal finance in solving enforcement and information problems is relevant mainly to small-scale and isolated customers. For example, an extensive empirical literature on the effectiveness of informal financial systems in pooling risk in villages concludes that, though many such institutions exist, and often operate at a relatively substantial scale, the volatility of individual household consumption is still far from being fully insulated from idiosyncratic household risk.

Informal finance aside, households with inadequate access to formal finance fall back ex ante on self-insurance through such means as choice of low-risk (and potentially low average yield) production processes, and on choice of nonfinancial assets with good risk-reduction characteristics (such as the purchase of cattle), or on marriage and migration strategies (marrying into a family in a remote village can help spread consumption risk); and ex post on a variety of coping strategies, including mobilizing additional household labor resources.

If there is to be improved access to formal finance, this must be achieved by addressing the two fundamental problems of information and the relatively high, fixed costs of small-scale lending. Recent research focusing on technological and policy advances points to how these barriers can be lowered. Much attention has focused in recent years on a range of innovative, specialized microfinance institutions, mostly subsidized and often targeted at lending to the poor, which have become established with remarkable success. The features that have been emphasized in studies of these microfinance institutions include (a) the rather low rates of loan delinquency—far lower than in the previous generation of subsidized lending programs that had operated in many developing countries, and (b) the reach of the institutions in terms of sheer numbers, as well as to previously grossly neglected groups, such as women. These elements of success have certainly been remarkable. This success has been attributed in part to reliance on innovation inspired by informal finance, for example:[28,29]

Microfinance can reduce the problems of information and costs for small-scale lending—

- The use of group lending contracts exploiting the potentialities of social capital and peer pressure to reduce willful delinquency.
- Dynamic incentives using regular repayment schedules and follow-up loans or "progressive lending."
- Lighter distributed management structures that reduce costs and enable lenders to keep loan rates down to reasonable levels.

These innovations, developed from the "bottom up" in poor countries such as Bangladesh, Bolivia, and Indonesia, now begin to be imported into advanced countries whose poor continue to be relatively badly served by the formal financial system.[30]

Though small in terms of dollars lent, these programs are important in terms of the number of beneficiary households, and further rapid growth is envisaged. Hence, it will be of some importance to target the resources where they have the greatest social impact, and to avoid swamping fragile social structures by imposing too many demands on them. However, even these programs have not been very successful in directly reaching the poorest of the poor.

but they often cannot help the poorest of the poor

Their interaction with the remainder of the financial system is likely not decisive for the continued success and evolution of microfinance programs. One illustration of the lack of interaction is the fact that loan performance of BRI in Indonesia was almost unaffected by the 1997–98 crisis that almost swept away the main banking system. To be sure, as some unsubsidized banks learn the value of the techniques, they might become competitors able to cherry-pick some of the subsidized sector's

borrowers, but this need not be much of a threat to the continuing social effectiveness of the specialized microfinance entities directed to the
poor. It may, however, be necessary for them to become part of the formal credit information system, discussed below, to protect themselves
from exposure to borrowers who have, unknown to them, accessed other
sources of finance.

While the revolution in microfinance has thus been associated with
lending techniques that can and have resulted in profitable banking, it
would be a mistake to think that this does away with any scope for
subsidized lending programs targeted at the poor. Four facts highlight
the distinctions that need to be made:

- Many of the largest and most prominent of the microfinance intermediaries require ongoing subsidies.
- Microenterprises are not necessarily operated by poor people.
- Most microfinance programs typically do not directly provide credit
  to the poorest of the poor.
- Operating expenses mean that real interest rates on microloans
  tend to be very high: affordable if applied to some forms of economic activity (for example, very short-term loans for merchan-
  dising), but implying a cost of capital far in excess of wholesale
  money market rates.

These considerations point to a double conclusion. First, unsubsidized
microcredit can be an important element of the financial system, drawing
not only on techniques exploiting the concept of social capital, but also on
improvements in information technology for credit appraisal, as discussed
below. Second, potential economic benefits can also be obtained from
subsidized microfinance targeted at the poor. It may not be realistic to
assume that the need for such subsidies will be eliminated over time.

**The lessons from earlier
subsidized credit programs
remain valid for
microfinance**

Detailed research evaluating the social rate of return of subsidized
microcredit programs has become an active area. Some types of lending
seem more effective than others: lending to women in particular seems to
convey higher social returns on average. It is of some importance to target
available subsidies where they have the greatest social impact. As an aspect
of applied public finance, a full discussion of subsidized microfinance lies
outside the scope of this report, but the sorry history of early generation
of dysfunctional subsidized credit programs has taught many lessons that
remain valid and that must continue to be applied in subsidized microcredit
programs of the new style targeted at the poor (Adams, Graham, and von

Pischke 1984). Among those lessons are the need to enforce hard budget constraints, to avoid loan interest charges so low that they allow round-tripping, to choose carefully and adhere rigorously to the target group, and so on. Furthermore, the high visibility and popularity of these programs among donors itself presents risks: it is crucial to avoid swamping the often-fragile social structures that sustain these institutions by imposing too many demands upon them. (To take just one example: when funding from donors ramps up the supply of credit, how easy is it for each institution to verify that the loan it is now making is not just going to repay another falling due to a different microlender?)

As far as unsubsidized microcredit is concerned, new attention to improving the information infrastructure promises to yield benefits.

The collection, processing, and use of borrowing history and other information relevant to household and small business lending has been a rapidly growing activity in both the public and private sectors (see Miller (forthcoming) for a review of the recent worldwide expansion of credit registries). Computer technology has greatly reduced the unit costs here and improved the sophistication with which the data can be employed to give an assessment of creditworthiness. While the impact of having this information available alters incentives and market power in subtle—and not always favorable—ways, the consensus of recent research is that the growth of access to credit information improves loan availability and lowers intermediation costs. Comparing data from 43 countries, Jappelli and Pagano (1999) found the volume of bank credit to be significantly higher in countries with more information sharing, even after controlling for the effects of different degrees of legal protection for creditors. It is not hard to see why. For one thing, better information allows banks to offer better rates to more creditworthy customers, thereby allowing the market to escape at least partly, from the adverse selection trap that Stiglitz and Weiss (1981) showed can lead to credit rationing. Knowing that your credit performance will be accessed by future lenders also reduces moral hazard by stiffening the costs of delinquency. Furthermore, sharing information they have gathered can also mean that lenders lose some of the market power that goes with that information.

We cannot assume that these technologies can fully overcome the greater underlying information deficiencies encountered in many developing countries, but they can help.

There are drawbacks, of course, and they pose interesting policy challenges. To avail themselves of the benefits, borrowers must tolerate some

Improving the information infrastructure and technology can lower intermediation costs—

—outweighing potential drawbacks in the forms of lost privacy and credit discrimination

invasion of privacy. Since discrimination between the creditworthy and others is the purpose of credit appraisal, statistical credit-scoring models that make use of personal information other than credit history may have the socially undesirable effect of reinforcing pockets of disadvantage, whether geographical, ethnic, or other. Credit discrimination on specified grounds is outlawed in some countries, and even if enforcement is difficult, there is a need to guard against socially damaging effects of this type: this is clearly a potential downside of credit information systems. Also, the information-gathering industry has a natural tendency toward concentration or even monopoly (90 percent of credit information for the small business sector in the United States is provided by the market leader, Dun and Bradstreet).

The issue of privacy is of considerable practical importance. Barron and Staten (2001) show how much of the predictive value of credit information is lost when even modest privacy requirements are imposed. Specifically, the law in several countries precludes the sharing of positive information on credit history (that is, only defaults can be reported). Without this, though, it seems that a lender with a target default rate of no more than 3 percent would have to reject three in every five applicants, more than twice as many as if the full range of credit information were available (cf. table 1.1).[31] Of course the issue of privacy protection is a much wider and rapidly evolving one, but this evidence on how

---

Table 1.1 Effects on credit availability of adopting a negative-only credit scoring model for various default rates

| Target default rate (percent) | Percent of consumers who obtain a loan | | Percent decrease in consumers who obtain a loan with negative-only model |
	Full model	Negative-only model	
3	74.8	39.8	46.8
4	83.2	73.7	11.4
5	88.9	84.6	4.8
6	93.1	90.8	2.5
7	95.5	95.0	0.5

Note: The full model predicts creditworthiness using both positive and negative information about borrowers credit history; cut-off credit quality is adjusted to reach target default rate. The negative-only model does the same, but ignores any positive information.

Source: Calculated by Barron and Staten (2001), based on a large sample of credit histories from the U.S. credit information firm Experian.

valuable—to most borrowers as well as to lenders—is the sharing of objective information on credit history suggests that countries with tight privacy laws should consider whether they can be relaxed to allow for such sharing to a lender from whom the borrower has sought credit.

The establishment of public, or government-controlled, credit registries in some countries has incidentally finessed the issue of monopoly. Long established in certain European countries, partly as a side effect of central bank requirements for preapproved private paper as collateral against money market support, a large number of such registries have recently been established, especially in Latin America. The recent surge is an understandable response to concerns about aggregate loan performance in the countries concerned, and about the quality of information on which bank lending decisions were being made. Countries that already had a private credit registry were much less likely to establish a public one. However, while the public registries represent a step forward, they are unlikely to remain the dominant force in credit information relevant to small-scale lending. Only information on the large exposures is likely to be of much direct value to the prudential regulators, whereas it is at the small end of the scale of loans that the information sharing aspect comes to the fore. Indeed, the establishment of public registries has not precluded the subsequent creation of private registries. Given the increasing volume of cross-border lending, it is likely that communicating networks of private registries will increasingly tend to acquire the comparative advantage here. The appropriate policy stance should be to facilitate this development, for example by ensuring that the threshold loan size for compulsory reporting to the public registry is not unduly low.

Conclusions

RECENT RESEARCH FINDINGS PROVIDE CLEAR GENERAL pointers for the design of government financial sector policy. They confirm that financial development does matter, it is pro-poor and it reduces aggregate volatility as well, contributing to growth. Even if the results do not express a preference as between bank-led or stock market-led structural approaches, they do provide plenty of indications of what needs to be protected through infrastructural measures. Both lenders and would-be borrowers benefit from improved protection of the rights of creditors, minority shareholders benefit from protection from concealment of information and other abuses by firm insiders, and financial development is enhanced when exercise of market power by banks and others is restrained. Improved information infrastructure has been shown to help improve access for small borrowers, as have the innovative management and operational techniques of specialized microcredit institutions.

There are indications, too, of where government subsidy is and is not helpful. Although attempting to subsidize interest rates is likely to be counterproductive, there may be a case for carefully designed subsidization of private information infrastructures to overcome problems of fixed cost and to release the externalities that can be triggered by greater access on the part of small firms to formal finance. Public money may also be fruitful in strengthening judicial and accounting infrastructures, as well, of course, as in prudential supervision and regulation, even though some cost recovery may here be possible.

Thus the landscape of a smoothly performing and progressive financial system is sketched, but how to avoid the pitfalls of crisis, insolvency, and collapse? That is the topic to which we now turn in chapter 2.

Notes

1. Organized finance covers *formal* financial intermediaries and markets, as well as entities such as rotating savings and credit associations (*roscas*) which, though specially organized for finance, are informal in the sense of not having a legal existence or falling within the scope of government regulation. Note that it has been important in many developing countries to distinguish between these and the emergence of unregulated financial intermediaries offering securities to, or taking deposits from, the general public (see chapter 2). Almost all the data employed in this study refer only to the formal financial sector.

2. Goldsmith (1969) may be said to be the pioneer, and among the first to develop this cross-country empirical initiative were Gelb (1989), King and Levine (1993a and b), and Gertler and Rose (1994). Levine (1997) provides an authoritative review of the theoretical and empirical literature.

3. Among the statistical hurdles passed by these legal origin variables is Hansen's test for instrument overidentification. In addition to using the legal origin

instrument, Levine, Loayza, and Beck (2000) also employ a dynamic panel instrumental variable technique with essentially the same conclusions. Contrasting time series methodologies are also employed with similar conclusions by Neusser and Kugler (1998) and by Rousseau and Wachtel (1998), though their data are limited to Organisation for Economic Co-operation and Development (OECD) countries.

4. Replacing the average ratio of private credit to GDP of Congo (Kinshasa) with that of Malaysia or Thailand predicts an increase in Congo's average growth rate of more than 6 percent per annum, not far off the actual difference of about 7 percent between the growth rates of Congo and either of the other two. Of course, such calculations need to be made with care, as indicated in box 1.1.

5. There is an interesting discussion of the demand for risk reduction in de Ferranti and others (2000).

6. The multiple problems of the highly monetized centrally planned economies following liberalization

may be cited as an example here; likewise the inappropriate use of derivatives in Mexico, 1994, described in chapter 4.

7. Levine and Zervos (1998a and b), Demirgüç-Kunt and Levine (1999), Beck, Demirgüç-Kunt, and Levine (2000a), Demirgüç-Kunt and Huizinga (2000a), Demirgüç-Kunt and Maksimovic (2000).

8. For example, the mean debt-to-equity ratio for listed firms plotted for 30 countries in figure 1.7 is only loosely correlated (R = –0.40) with the markets vs. banks structure index devised by Demirgüç-Kunt and Levine (2001).

9. We use the term to include managers, directors, and dominant shareholders of a firm.

10. A further explanation could lie in a link between higher funding interest rates and the higher riskiness of lending (cf. Agénor, Aizenman, and Hoffmaister 1999).

11. Baskin and Miranti (1997) document the use of common stocks in the 19th and early 20th centuries.

12. Cf. La Porta, López-de-Silanes, and Shleifer (1999a) for the advanced countries. A study by Khanna and Palepu (1999) of the monitoring of Indian industrial groups also emphasizes the chilling effect on opaqueness on outsider investment. Note, however, that some countries heavily reliant on family ownership, according to figure 1.10, have experienced strong and resilient economic performance.

13. The term "financial infrastructure" is intended to capture the framework of rules and systems within which firms and households plan, negotiate, and perform financial transactions. As such, it would include legal and regulatory structures (including rule and contract enforcement mechanisms); supervisory resources and practices; information provision (for example, accounting and auditing rules and practices, credit bureaus, rating agencies, public registries); liquidity facilities; payments and securities settlement systems; and exchange systems (for example, trading and listing services, trading rules, communication and information platforms).

14. Openness as an approach limiting market power in banking is discussed in chapter 4.

15. Indeed, English common law sees directors as fiduciaries of the shareholders with a duty of loyalty to them (Johnson, McMillan, and Woodruff 1999).

16. Surprisingly, a variety of political structure variables fail to perform well in predicting financial development in this study; we return to political factors in chapter 3.

17. In extreme cases, even a liquid financial sector willing to lend may find no takers if property rights are insufficiently protected. Johnson, McMillan, and Woodruff (1999) provide some interesting survey-based evidence from Eastern Europe and the former Soviet Union (countries that, incidentally, are not included in the legal sample of La Porta and others) showing that, in 1997, it was differences in firms' perceptions of the security of their property rights that determined their willingness to invest, and not any question of access to outside finance.

18. Though, for the case against government regulation of finance, see Easterbrook and Fischel (1991).

19. A good account of this process in Johnson (2000), which also shows that the listing boom is not an "Internet effect."

20. For a discussion of the actual and potential role of SROs in finance, see Bossone and Promisel (2000).

21. The following paragraphs draw freely on Vittas (2000).

22. Indeed, statistical causality analysis favors the hypothesis that short-term fluctuations in stock market capitalization follow changes in the asset size of the contractual savings industry (Catalan, Impavido, and Musalem 2000).

23. Measures, parallel to those employed for banks and discussed in chapter 2, need to be designed to ensure that approved pension funds are prudently managed by experienced professionals, that they are secure against looting (for example through adequate auditing, and segregation of assets to be held by an external custodian), that they retain an adequate solvency reserve and that there is adequate transparency of their operations (cf. Rocha, Hinz, and Gutierrez 1999).

24. For further discussion of current issues in pension fund regulation, see James, Smalhout, and Vittas

(1999); James and Vittas (2000); Srinivas, Whitehouse, and Yermo (2000); Vittas (1998, 2000).

25. Besley (1995) provides a wide-ranging survey of the literature on informal finance.

26. Cf. the interesting insurance-cum-equity features of local lending uncovered by Udry (1994) in Northern Nigeria.

27. This method has been used, for example, to finance temporary emigration.

28. Success has also required attention to more mundane aspects neglected by an earlier generation of subsidized microfinance institutions, such as a realistic interest rate structure, a well-trained and incentivized staff, and good management information systems.

29. For the performance of these institutions, see Morduch (1999) and Sebsted and Cohen (2000).

30. The recent success stories of microfinance based on group lending has somewhat overshadowed the steady effectiveness of credit cooperatives and credit unions, which have long functioned as quasi-formal but decentralized institutions in many countries, employing some of the techniques discussed above, but usually relying for the bulk of their resources on member savings.

31. The specific comparison is with more restrictive law in Australia compared with what is allowed in the United States (itself closely defined).

CHAPTER TWO

Preventing and Minimizing Crises

"Any sudden event which creates a great demand for actual cash may cause, and will tend to cause, a panic in a country where cash is much economized, and where debts payable on demand are large."

Walter Bagehot (1873)

WHEN MAJOR FINANCIAL CRISES OCCUR, ALL who depend on financial services suffer. Depositors can lose their funds or have their accounts frozen and value eroded by inflation. Good borrowers get cut off from credit. Issuers of debt and equity finance find that markets have dried up. Pensioners may find their living standards diminished. Holders of insurance policies may find their counterparty bankrupt. And taxpayers often foot a bill that otherwise could have permitted much-needed expenditures on other items. Even those so poor that they do not use the financial services of the formal sector may find their incomes slashed in the resulting recession, and informal financial funds may dry up as well (box 2.1).

Recent decades have seen a record wave of crises: by millennium-end, there had been 112 episodes of systemic banking crises in 93 countries since the late 1970s—and 51 borderline crises were recorded in 46 countries. These crises both were more numerous and expensive, compared with those earlier in history, and their costs often devastating in developing countries.

This chapter first examines why finance is so fragile—especially in developing countries, and all the more so in banking—and it discusses the costs of financial and banking crises, and their causes. Banking crises

Recent financial crises have been more numerous and expensive than in the past

Box 2.1   Poverty and crises

WHEN CRISES OCCUR AND LENDERS BECOME MORE risk averse, small firms are the first to be rationed from access to credit, which is an important reason why small business failure rates soar during financial crises. Not surprisingly, then, poverty can rise sharply and remain high for some time following a crisis.

Number of people living in poverty

Year	Indonesia	Republic of Korea	Thailand
1990	80.9	14.7	18.4[a]
1996	50.6	4.7	7.5
1998	—	9.1	7.6
1999	76.3	—	9.7
2000	70.3	6.0	8.7

— Not available.
Note: Figures for 2000 are estimates.
a. 1988 data.
Source: World Bank.

Even with the recovery and projected decline in poverty rates in 2001, the number of poor people is expected to return to precrisis levels only in Thailand, and remain high in Indonesia and the Republic of Korea. As serious as this impact is, the poor get hit again when the bill comes due, as loan losses sooner or later have to be covered (figure 2.1). Fiscal costs of bank insolvency, which represent injections of government funds, must be covered by tax increases, expenditure reductions, or inflation, all of which hit low-income households hard. Even if authorities attempt to put on controls to prevent capital flight, experience shows that wealthy households are best able to avoid them; middle- and low-income families' funds are then left to bear the burden of higher taxes, so income distributions usually deteriorate for at least several years after a crisis. Subsequent growth "…tends not to eliminate the higher level of inequality generated during a severe economic downturn" (Lustig 1999). Consequently, preventing financial crises is an important and potentially effective instrument to sustain growth and avoid poverty.

are the main focus, and although currency misalignment is a common element of a banking crisis, so-called twin (banking cum currency) crises are deferred until chapter 4.

How can society be provided with financial services without incurring the costs of these crashes? The incentive structure, the product of market forces interacting with the regulatory environment, is undoubtedly the key factor in the stability and functioning of the financial sector, so the second section of the chapter, Regulating Banks: Harnessing the Market, turns to reform in this area. Just as liberalization of private initiative in the financial sector and real and financial technological developments have been part of the story in the increased vulnerability of finance in recent decades, so creative initiatives to harness the private sector and technology are key to bringing the social risks of finance back under control.

A key facet of the incentive environment is the safety net provided for banks. The 20th century was marked by the rise of safety nets for the banking sector, the main components of which are the lender of last resort facility and deposit insurance. Although much has been written on the former, research on deposit insurance has been mostly theoretical and limited to the United States until recently. Given the recent expansion of explicit deposit insurance systems around the world, we then focus in the third section, Financial Sector Safety Nets, on when and how they can best be designed. An excessively generous safety net for banks—or state ownership, discussed in chapter 3—can be a key factor behind the bank dominance and the fragility in many emerging markets.

Finance is anything but static: once a set of rules is promulgated, the nature of finance makes it especially easy for participants to move their business into different forms or jurisdictions that can nullify the goals of reforms. This regulatory arbitrage will vary directly with the extent to which regulations neglect the optimizing behavior of participants. Financial systems in which incentives encourage prudent risk-taking will, other things equal, be more resilient, less a source of shocks, and therefore better able to assist in risk mitigation. And as incentive-compatible regulation is combined with an infrastructure that encourages efficient market functioning, economic growth will be stimulated by intermediaries with the incentives and wherewithal to engage in prudent risk-taking. This does not mean relying naïvely on markets to do the job, but rather shaping incentives of private agents and regularly revisiting the effects of various changes on them, what might be termed dynamic regulation. To understand better the consequences of the current regulatory environment, as well as the advantages and disadvantages of any reforms, authorities must focus on the underlying incentives.

It may be necessary to go further than setting out a program of regulatory reform and safety net issues in this area. We have to ask whether there are deeper reasons why such reform has not long since been put in place in most countries. Is it really a failure of regulatory design, or could it also reflect weakness in the political institutions? Is it in the interest of some interest groups and their political sponsors that a lax regulatory environment and a safety net with perverse incentive effects be maintained even though they increase the risk of socially costly bank failure? That issue goes beyond the scope of this chapter, and indeed beyond much research, though we return to related matters in chapter 3.

The incentive structure is key to the stability and functioning of the financial system

Why Finance Has Been So Fragile...and Remains That Way

All people are most credulous when they are most happy; and when much money has just been made, when some people are really making it, when most people think they are making it, there is a happy opportunity for ingenious mendacity. Almost everything will be believed for a little while, and long before discovery the worst and most adroit deceivers are geographically or legally beyond the reach of punishment. But the harm they have done diffuses harm, for it weakens credit still further.

Walter Bagehot (1873, p. 151)

IN PERFORMING ITS ESSENTIAL FUNCTIONS, FINANCE REGULARLY involves the exchange of money today for the promise of money in the future, usually with some form of return. This intertemporal nature, combined with well-known information problems that admit adverse selection and moral hazard behavior, is at the heart of the fragility of finance. Each party to this trade enters into the contract with expectations about a host of variables that will affect the likelihood of repayment. Expectations change, perhaps quickly, and lead to swings in asset prices, which in turn may be exacerbated by the possibility of crowd behavior.

To be sure, there is some truth in the idea that financial markets normally make a reasonably efficient use of information in the sense that it is hard for an investor consistently to earn excess returns—at least on a risk-adjusted basis—using publicly available information. Indeed, even information that is not widely available can quickly become embodied in market prices as long as there are enough well-financed, informed investors.

The efficient market hypothesis can not explain speculative booms and busts

Although the "efficient markets" hypothesis is a useful benchmark for describing the evolution of market prices in normal times, it is hard-pressed to explain the scale of price movements in turbulent conditions. Although itself more than a fad, stock in the efficient markets hypothesis "...crashed along with the rest of the market on October 19, 1987. Its recovery has been less dramatic than that of the rest of the market" (Shleifer and Summers 1990, p. 19). Indeed, there are sound theoretical reasons why financial markets cannot be efficient and fully arbitraged if information is less than perfect and contracting is costly (Grossman and Stiglitz 1980). Substantial and even growing deviations from equilibrium prices are possible, manifesting themselves as bubbles, or speculative booms and busts. And bubbles are more likely when, as is found in experiments, individuals are not fully rational in assessing risk; excessively weight recent experience (display myopia); trade on noise rather than on fundamentals; or exhibit positive feedback (or momentum) by buying because prices are rising.[1]

The "behavioral finance" view that asset markets are prone to bubbles finds confirming evidence in countless episodes of sudden asset price collapses, with greater or less involvement by the banking sector. An augmented and updated version of Kindleberger's (1978) list (table 2.1) shows the regularity of major incidents since the 15th century, as well as the diversity of the objects of speculation. Real estate, a common stumbling block for banks in the latter half of the 20th century, has earlier antecedents in the list, but there are also many other targets from commodities—mineral, such as copper, silver, and gold, or even vegetable; to mines; all sorts of company shares, financial and nonfinancial, notably utilities such as canals and railroads; and latterly paper money and financial derivatives.

Ponzi, or pyramid, schemes, in which investors are gulled into giving funds to nefarious characters who promise impossibly high rates of return (typically rationalized through complex, apparently "fail safe" means) also illustrate the characteristic fragility of finance.[2] These schemes gain credibility by actually paying the promised returns to early investors out of the cash generated from later investors. Although it is doubtful that there is a country that has not seen these schemes, their occurrence in so many transition economies in the 1990s testifies to their link to opaque environments and times of structural change. In some cases, such as the Romanian pyramid of the mid-1990s, railroad traffic even in other countries was said to be affected by the rush to get to the town of Cluj, where investors could get into a scheme promising to repay 8-fold in 100 days—an annual rate of return of 250,000 percent. The scheme collapsed shortly before threatening to overtake Romanian GDP, notwithstanding the fact, relatively unique for these schemes, that there was not even a clear story of how the funds were to be invested.[3] Shortly thereafter, Albania saw a series of schemes the aggregate size of whose liabilities rose to an estimated 50 percent of GDP and whose collapse led to widespread street violence and 2,000 casualties.

If finance is fragile, banking is its most fragile part, for it adds the complications, not only of maturity transformation, but of demandable

Table 2.1   Selected financial crashes (grouped by the object of speculation)

Year	Commodities	Companies	Real Estate	Banks	Financial Assets
1400				Bardi & Peruzzi (Florence), 1348	
1500	Gold (New World), 1550s			Medici (Florence), 1492	Bourse loans (Antwerp), 1557
1600	Coins in Spain, 1618	Dutch East India Co., 1636–40	Canals, elegant houses (Holland) 1636–40	Fugger (Augsburg), 1596	
	Tulips, 1640				
1700		**South Seas (London), Companie d'Occident (Paris), 1720**		**Sword Blade (London), Banques Generale & Royale (Paris), 1720**	
				British country banks, 1750s	British gilts in Amsterdam 1763
		British and Dutch East India Co., 1772 Dutch East India Co., 1783			
	Sugar, coffee, 1799	French canals, 1793		British country banks, 1793	Assignats (France), 1795
1800	Exports, 1810 and 1816		Biens Nationaux (France), 1825		
		British, French canals, 1820s	Chicago, 1830–42	British country banks, 1824	Foreign bonds, foreign mines, new companies, Britain, 1825
	Cotton in Britain, France; exports in Britain 1836	British railroads, 1836	Chicago, 1843–62		
	Sugar, coffee in Hamburg, wheat, 1857	British and French railroads, 1847	Chicago, U.S. public land, 1853–77	Germany, 1850	Foreign mines, Britain, France 1850
	Cotton, 1861	French and U.S. railroads, 1857		Overend Gurney (London), 1866; Credit Mobilier (Paris), 1867	
	Gold (New York), 1869 Petroleum (U.S.), 1871	U.S. railroads, 1873	Chicago, Berlin, Vienna, 1878–98	Germany 1870s	
	Copper (France), 1888; Petroleum (Russia), 1890s	Panama Canal Company, France, 1888 U.S. railroads, 1893	Argentine public lands; Chicago, 1890s	Union Generale (Paris), 1882 Barings (London), 1890	Foreign bonds, France; British discount houses, 1888

(table continues on following page)

80

Table 2.1 *(continued)*

Year	Commodities	Companies	Real Estate	Banks	Financial Assets
1900	Copper, U.S., 1907			Knickerbocker Trust (New York), 1907	
		International Mercantile Marine, 1914			*Bills of Exchange, London, 1914*
		General Motors, 1920	U.S. farmland, 1918–21	Creditanstalt (Austria), 1931	**1920s: German reichsmark, French franc** Mergers, U.K.; foreign bonds, new shares, N.Y.
			Florida, 1920s	500 U.S. banks, 1932–33	
		Penn Central Railroad, 1970			FDI, U.S. conglomerates, sterling, 1960s
	Oil tankers, 1974	Burmah Oil, 1974; Pertamina (Indonesia), 1975	U.S. farmland 1970s		U.S. dollar, 1973
	Gold, 1978–82	*Chrysler Auto, 1979*	U.S. Southwest, California 1970s–80s	Banco Ambrosiano (Italy), 1982	*LDC debt*
	Silver, 1980			*U.S. S&Ls, 1980s* ***Argentina, 1980–89*** ***Chile 1981***	**U.S. dollar (1985) FDI in U.S., 1980s** **Junk bonds (U.S.), 1989–90**
	Coffee, cocoa etc., 1986		U.S. REITs, offices, malls, hotels; Japan, Sweden 1980s	*Japan, U.S. 1980s–92* ***Sweden 1990***	**Japanese shares, 1980s;** ***Vietnamese credit cooperatives*** Korean mergers, 1990s Emerging market shares, 1990s Romanian, Albanian Ponzi Schemes
		PanAmerican Airways, 1991 Guinness Peat Aviation, 1992		BCCI, 1991 ***Mexico 1994*** Barings (Singapore), 1995	Derivatives (Orange County; Metallgesellschaft, Ashanti Gold Mines), forex futures, options
	Copper, Japan 1996				
		Korean Chaebols; Thailand 1997	***Thailand, 1996–97***	***Indonesia, Republic of Korea, Malaysia, Thailand 1997–98***	**Russian bonds, long term capital management, 1998** High tech stocks, U.S. dollar 1997–??

Note: Items in italics indicate government support and items in bold indicate a major crash.
Source: Kindleberger (1998); Caprio and Klingebiel (1999); authors.

Banking is the most fragile part of a financial system—

debt, that is, offering debt finance backed by par value liabilities in the form of bank deposits. This particularly fragile structure of its liabilities may be needed to keep the bankers on their toes and to give large depositors the comfort that they can withdraw as soon as they suspect problems. Banks arose precisely to finance relatively illiquid investments with mostly short-term liabilities (and the fragility of their liability structure has been seen by some scholars as an essential part of their make-up—without which paradoxically they might not be able to function at all. Cf. Diamond and Rajan 2000; Calomiris and Kahn 1991).[4] It also, however, makes banks—and even the whole banking system—susceptible to a sudden withdrawal of deposits. Although all outsiders will have difficulty in monitoring banks, depositors—other than the largest—are likely to be weak at monitoring and also will have an incentive to "free ride" on the monitoring efforts of others. Even if insolvent banks are the first to see a withdrawal of deposits, the contraction of lending by some banks can produce legitimate solvency concerns about others to the extent that aggregate credit shrinks. Indeed, even when banks seem to behave prudently, the bursting of asset bubbles can impair the ability of debtors to repay and induce doubts about banks' health.

and a limited crisis may affect the whole banking network through contagion

Thus, banking may be characterized by the *possibility* of contagious runs, in which a run on one bank leads to runs on other, possibly healthy, banks. In contrast, equity mutual funds, which invest in stocks and pay a return that varies with the return on their portfolio, may suffer from sharp swings in prices, but not from the possibility of contagious runs. However, contagious runs, in the sense that healthy banks are brought down by failures at weak banks, in fact are difficult to find, at least in industrial economies. Even during the U.S. Depression, Calomiris and Mason (2000) find that individual fundamentals explain the runs of 1930 and 1931, but not the 1933 episode, which they link to a generalized run from dollars because of the expectation of a devaluation. The fear of contagious runs may be more marked in emerging markets, because of greater information problems, but emerging markets also may face a greater tendency toward generalized runs, since shocks sufficiently large to change macropolicies or affect the solvency of the banking system are more common (below). And as noted below, the cost of crisis also involves the ensuing credit crunch, all the more so in economies without alternative channels of finance.

The particular fragility of finance, and within it of banking, is true for all countries regardless of their income level, as attested to by the occurrence of banking crises in several industrial economies in the 1980s and 1990s. Banking outside the industrial world, however, is more dangerous still, where crises have been enormously costly (figure 2.1).

The cumulative losses of the failed banks are only one aspect of the cost of a banking crisis. In attempting to arrive at an estimate of the total true economic cost it is necessary to distinguish between three key components:

- The stock component is the accumulated waste of economic resources that is revealed by the insolvency. At least part of the capital deficiency of the failed banks represents depositors' funds that have been wasted in unrecoverable loans that were applied to unproductive purposes, such as empty offices and closed factories.

Figure 2.1   Total fiscal costs (increases in the stock of public debt) relative to GDP in the year of crisis

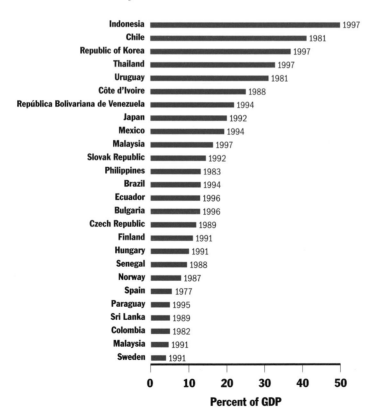

Banking crises have been costly.

Source: Honohan and Klingebiel (2000); Caprio and Klingebiel (1999).

Banking crises have real costs

- The public finance component of the true economic costs arises because of the way in which the fiscal authorities tend to assume a large part of the net capital deficiency of the banks, in order to bail out the depositors and others directly affected by the crash. From an economic cost calculation, this cash "fiscal cost" is merely a transfer to depositors, but it also entails a deadweight economic cost that could represent a sizable fraction of the amount transferred where the marginal cost of social funds is high. The point is that the expenditure cuts, additional tax revenue that will be required to finance them, and/or the inflation tax have distorting effects in themselves, especially in developing countries with weak revenue-raising systems. Thus, for example, "merely" servicing the debt incurred as a result of the Indonesian banking crisis means spending sums that could have doubled health *and* education spending. Moreover, in many emerging markets, the fiscal costs are sufficiently large to derail macroeconomic stabilization programs, with costly consequences.

- The flow component of the economic cost arises from the output slumps with which banking crises are almost always associated. This clearly represents an economic cost inasmuch as resources are underemployed until the economy picks up again. Channels through which this disruption can occur include a collapse of investment and other spending either because of a general loss of confidence, or through a restriction of access to credit (reflecting would-be borrowers being strapped for collateral; lenders' reaction to the crisis by raising creditworthiness standards or attempts to remain liquid; or the loss of information capital, essential for making loans).[5] Payments system failure, though rare, can be another channel for triggering recession. As well as a transitory dip in output below full employment levels, these channels can result in further loss of trend output if the lack of intermediated credit depresses long-term productivity growth.

The larger the initial capital deficiency of the failed banks, the larger the cash fiscal cost and the larger each of the components of the true economic cost is likely to be. Estimates, of varying reliability, of the cash fiscal cost have been made for many crises. Total fiscal costs in developing country crises during the 1980s and 1990s breached the $1 trillion dollar level by 1999. These fiscal costs likely overstate the fiscal component of true economic costs, but may be used as a general indication of the relative and absolute magnitudes of total economic costs.

Alternatively, attempts have also been made to capture a rough estimate of the additional flow economic costs, typically by comparing actual output with some hypothetical "no crisis" output path. It is very hard, though, to guess what part of an output slump is caused by the banking crisis—often a latent banking crash only becomes evident when it is triggered by an exogenous economic shock that also directly contributed to recession. The measured output dip likely overstates the true flow economic costs, but it is correlated with measured fiscal costs, and intriguingly is of the same order of magnitude (figure 2.2).[6] As Boyd and Smith (2000) observe, many crises, though serious at the time, have a small fiscal cost and a relatively low output cost. In figure 2.2, however, about one crisis in three has a cumulative GDP cost of 20 percent or more, and given the uncertainty in times of crises, authorities cannot know whether they will have a small or a large crisis. Given the depth of the recessions, the proverb that an ounce of prevention is worth a pound of cure seems applicable.

Developing countries suffer several additional sources of fragility. First, information problems in general are more pronounced, as noted in the

Figure 2.2 Estimates of fiscal cost of and output dip for 39 banking crises

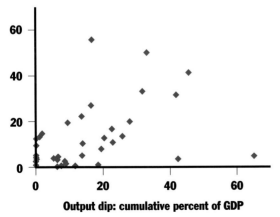

Fiscal and output costs generally go hand in hand.

Note: The chart shows that the fiscal cost of crises is correlated with the subsequent output dip (measured as the total output loss—relative to trend—over the period during which growth remained below precrisis rates).
Source: Honohan and Klingebiel (2000).

Structural issues can make emerging markets more vulnerable to financial crises—

discussion in chapter 1 on the accounting and legal systems. This information problem has to be addressed in any recommendations on lessening vulnerability. Poor information makes it easier for banks not just to take risks unwisely, but also to engage in deliberate related lending, which according to both anecdotal evidence and now empirical research (La Porta, López-de-Silanes, and Zamarripa 2000) is characterized by much higher nonrepayment rates.

Second, developing economies are smaller and more concentrated in certain economic sectors or reliant on particular export products, and accordingly, they are less able to absorb or pool isolated shocks. This in part explains the greater macroeconomic volatility displayed by developing economies in different parts of the world in comparison with the industrial countries (figure 2.3).

Since the portfolios of most financial intermediaries in emerging markets are overwhelmingly concentrated in domestic assets, shocks to the local economy would be more destabilizing even with the best regulation and supervision (chapter 4 will delve into possibilities of importing financial services as a way to lessen this vulnerability). As suggested below, regulation and supervision, with some notable exceptions, are not the strongest there.

Figure 2.3   Volatility by region, 1970–99

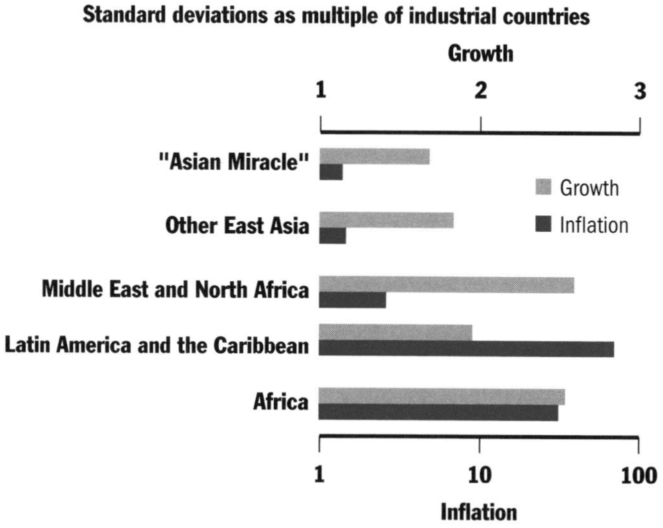

Developing countries display greater nominal and real volatility, compared with industrial economies.

Standard deviations as multiple of industrial countries

Note: The median of the historical standard deviations of GDP growth and inflation for each group of countries is expressed as a multiple of that for industrialized countries.
Source: Caprio and Honohan (1999); *International Financial Statistics.*

Not surprisingly, greater economic volatility translates into financial markets. Although based on just a few cases with a long availability of data, figure 2.4 shows not only that equities enjoy a far higher return than either bills or even bonds in emerging markets relative to that in high-income countries, but the differences in volatility are even more dramatic. Given their greater volatility, then, even if local banks diversified in emerging markets, or were equally well regulated, they would enjoy much less stability than banks in the safer haven of most high-income countries. Exchange rate volatility also has had marked consequences in developing economies

Figure 2.4   Volatility in asset markets

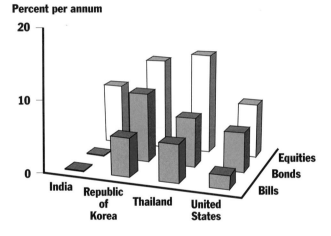

Stocks can pay better in emerging markets...

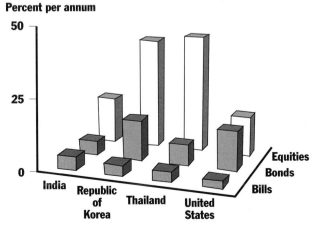

...but are riskier still.

Source: International Financial Statistics; IFC Emerging Markets database; available data, 1975–99.

because they largely have had to borrow in foreign exchange. Thus, increases in dollar interest rates often induce a larger increase in domestic lending rates, to the extent that the currency risk premium rises. This additional volatility affects firms and their financiers. Chapter 4 will return to this theme of volatility and small financial systems.

—including the domination of banks in the financial systems—

Third, emerging financial markets are dominated by banks (figure 3 in the overview), meaning more demandable debt, higher debt-to-equity ratios, possibly inducing greater fragility. If a firm is 100 percent financed by debt, then even a small shock that reduces its projected revenues or raises its interest cost can result in the firm's becoming insolvent. Equity acts like a buffer, providing the firm with greater flexibility in comparison with the need to service fixed debt repayments. High debt-to-equity ratios were found to be a factor in the East Asian crises; although these ratios did not in general increase in the immediate run-up to the crisis, their high level meant that the firms and the economy were highly fragile (Claessens, Djankov, and Xu 2000).

Similarly, if firms can only obtain financing that has to be renewed frequently—every 90 days or more often—they are in a less flexible position to deal with unanticipated shocks, compared to those with a higher mix of long-term debt. Thus, the relative underdevelopment of non-bank finance and capital markets means that when developing country banks get into difficulty, the impact on the entire financial sector and the economy is greater than in industrial countries, where nonbank intermediaries and markets are generally better developed. More financing through equity-type instruments transfers the risk to those more willing and able to accept it. Availability of equity finance thus represents an important potential buffer for the finance of firms, and indirectly for their bankers. The equity market can be seen as a spare tire for finance (Greenspan 1999). Collapses in equity prices are not innocuous, but are clearly less disruptive than bank failures—which is why this chapter focuses on the latter.

Unbalanced financial systems with bank dominance are in part a response to the greater information problems in developing markets—hence the importance of improving this part of the sector's infrastructure (chapter 1)—but also likely reflect excessive "subsidization" of banking through the safety net (described below) or state ownership, which provides an implicit safety net for all bank creditors. State ownership itself appears linked to fragility (chapter 3).

Fourth, in addition to short-term volatility, there have been a succession of regime shifts altering the risk profile of the operating environment in hard-to-evaluate ways, including most prominently financial deregulation. In line with prevailing intellectual trends and following the example of industrial countries, emerging market authorities removed or eased administrative controls on interest rates, bank-by-bank credit ceilings, rules for the allocation of credit to preferred sectors or borrowers, limits on new entry, and even opening the capital account. Dismantling many old controls would ultimately have become inevitable, but academics, advisers, and policy officials alike failed to realize the complexity of the task they had undertaken.

The enthusiasm with which liberalization was adopted in some countries in the absence of necessary institutional underpinnings left financial systems facing largely uncharted territory. New owners and inexperienced bank supervisors tried to feel their way to an assessment of what safe-and-sound banking would mean in practice. At a minimum, this situation suggests a fifth factor behind emerging market crises, namely a regulatory and incentive environment ill prepared for a market-based financial system, and in particular one that encouraged or condoned excessive risk-taking.

Poor sequencing of financial liberalization in a poorly prepared environment has undoubtedly contributed to bank insolvency. Countries abandoned controls on bank liabilities—notably interest rates—but the time to create and implement oversight of assets was greatly underestimated. Only if institutional underpinnings are strong is financial liberalization unlikely to add to the risk of systemic bank failures (Demirgüç-Kunt and Detragiache 1999). It would be misleading, however, to conclude that greater reliance on market forces was always the underlying source of bank failure. In many cases, financial liberalization has revealed a long-standing underlying insolvency of the banking system, which became unavoidably clear as the banks emerged from the sheltered environment that allowed or required them to cross-subsidize loss-making lines of business.

Authorities did not liberalize finance in a vacuum, but rather as part of a general move away from heavier government intervention. The structural economic transformation in many transitional and developing countries created a new economic and political landscape and placed bankers in a brave new world with a shortage of skills and experience for judging

—and the poor sequencing of financial liberalization

the level of risk. With all these changes, in addition to those entailed by the revolution in technology, communications, and financial engineering, plus the seemingly fickle behavior of international investors, it is hard for bankers, governments, and regulators to judge what sources of volatility are likely to be important, and thus what constitutes sound banking.

These factors behind emerging market crises suggest first that, while moving in the direction of the market-based regulatory framework may help, the special factors that characterize these economies necessitate even more robust measures.

Regulating Banks: Harnessing the Market

Prudential regulation promotes systemic stability

FOR AS LONG AS THERE HAVE BEEN BANKS, THERE ALSO HAVE been governments setting a number of rules for them, such as maintaining the purity of coinage and regulating exchange at medieval fairs, holding high, even 100 percent reserves (in 16th century Europe and later in U.S. banks), maintaining interest rates below usurious levels, and providing credit to the ruler, especially in times of war. Modern financial regulation includes an array of instruments designed to improve the informational efficiency of financial markets, protect consumers against fraud and malfeasance, and preserve systemic stability.[7] Prudential regulation promotes systemic stability. Whether or not there is a deposit insurance scheme, the official prudential supervisors in effect act as delegated monitors for depositors, exploiting economies of scale to overcome information problems that would be beyond the resources of small depositors.

Narrow banking could throw the baby (intermediation) out with the bathwater (crisis)

Many proposed rules for reducing banking risk look promising at first sight, but prove to have serious drawbacks and can only be recommended, if at all, where all else has failed. One recurring example is the idea of narrow banking, a proposal with a lengthy history (box 2.2). It amounts to saying that, given the particular fragility of the liability structure of banking, why not make banks safe by forcing them to hold safe assets? As with many recommendations for finance, so-called narrow banking plans may fit some countries, such as those that, following a crisis, have banks with balance sheets dominated by government paper. Although these plans in general have merit, they do not address the need for intermediaries to intermediate risk, the act of which can create a problem when it goes wrong, but which can be an enormous benefit to growth when done well. If narrow banks hold

Box 2.2   Narrow banking

BANKS THAT TAKE DEPOSITS AND DO NOT MAKE loans are not new, (and) with the original goldsmiths—those who guarded depositors' gold—being the earliest example of "100 percent reserve" banks. As bankers learned that not all depositors wanted their funds returned simultaneously, they began to lend out part, embarking on fractional reserve banking, but a number of countries had or still have banks that mainly hold safe instruments. In 1864 the U.S. National Bank Act required note-issuing banks to hold $111.11 in government bonds for every $100 of notes issued, and this system remained in force until the 1930s. Similarly, postal savings banks in many now industrial economies and some ordinary saving institutions (such as in France and the United Kingdom) required that deposits be invested in government paper. In these cases, however, 100 percent reserve banks were only part of the banking sector, and other banks would take deposits and make loans.

The Depression in the United States and in particular the extreme panic in early 1933, culminating in the banking holiday of March 1933, led to proposals by Henry Simons and a number of other prestigious economists for a 100 percent reserve banking plan as the model for the country. Banking problems regularly unearth new interest in this proposal, as seen during the U.S. Savings and Loan crisis and in Argentina in the 1995 crisis.

The basic plan is simple: if all banks hold only deposits backed by high-grade instruments, such as short-term treasury bills, perhaps even quite high-grade commercial paper, the payments mechanism will be protected (except from a run on the currency, which can be averted only if sufficient reserves are denominated in foreign currency). As is the case with U.S. money market mutual funds, failure can only occur because of fraud, which is relatively unlikely in this context. Other financial intermediaries, or the non-bank subsidiary of a financial conglomerate, according to these plans, would be allowed to lend, but they could not call themselves banks, and they would not be eligible for any deposit insurance. Thus, the goal is to attempt to convince depositors that if they want a guaranteed return, it will be a low one, and that funds placed in risky investments can be lost.

The history of finance suggests that plans would be evaded. Thus, the U.S. National Bank Act was made less effective as banks began to issue liabilities that were not reservable, and therefore yielded proceeds that could be lent out profitably. Also, plans to encourage excessively easy financing of government deficits could encourage excessive borrowing, in particular in countries with inadequate fiscal controls and established checks and balances in government. Transition to narrow banking could be tricky and, as noted in the text, the fundamental problem of intermediation would remain.

Still, narrow banking might be suitable for some countries as part of crisis response. For example, in countries where all or most of the banks have had large parts of their assets replaced with government funds, these banks already are virtually narrow banks, and a separate institution could be licensed to make loans. Some regulations would be needed to encourage transparency of the nonbanks, and an education campaign would be required to ensure that depositors were aware of their exposures.

Source: Phillips (1995).

safe assets, but other intermediaries finance risky investment, the latter will pay higher interest rates, and if the history of finance is any guide, almost certainly attract many depositors, eventually make losses, and eventually mount lobbies for government protection.

Thus, for most countries, it seems safe to assume that narrow banking will not solve the fragility problem. Moreover, there may well be a tradeoff between stability and efficiency. If the formation of narrow banks did not lead to a large migration of assets to nonbank intermediaries, the allocation of resources to efficient investments might be seriously impeded. Although banking has declined some in relative importance in advanced countries, it remains significant and in developing countries is the dominant portion of the financial sector.

Although small investors can suffer losses in nonbank finance, too, (and official safety nets are sometimes provided to consumers in segments of the insurance and pension fund industries), failures and losses in financial markets that do not extend to the banking system are much less likely to have catastrophic systemic effects on the payments and credit system.[8] For this reason, nonbank financial intermediaries and markets are also objects of generally lighter government regulation—from the greater oversight in pensions and insurance to less oversight in stocks, futures, and derivatives markets.

The transition to modern prudential regulation is difficult

Financial sector regulation and supervision—the rules of the game in the financial sector and the way they are enforced—are essential to limit moral hazard, as well as to ensure that intermediaries have the incentive to allocate resources and perform their other functions prudently. In the 1980s and 1990s, many developing countries began making the transition away from supervisory systems aimed at ensuring compliance with government directives, such as directed credit guidelines and other portfolio requirements and toward what might be called the basic Basel standard, which is one of supervised capital adequacy. As noted earlier, this transition has not gone smoothly, and evidence suggests that liberalization, at least as conducted, even contributed to the recent spate of banking crises.[9]

Authorities should use incentives to harness market forces

In response to these crises, there has been a boom in the creation of detailed standards that are being promulgated in banking (and other areas of the financial sector). These standards may ultimately induce improvements in the regulatory environment, but the absence of a clear sense of their relative importance or how they function in the disparate institutional contexts found in emerging markets reduces their impact. The outcome of research on financial systems, on the other hand, suggests that, rather than a large number of standards, authorities in emerging markets should focus on using incentives to harness market forces that favor effective and efficient financial markets, and employ individual standards in so far as they contribute to this purpose. To some extent, this means imposing tough rules—not only requiring minimum capital ratios, but perhaps more robust restraints, such as minimum diversification guidelines (or tailoring capital requirements to the concentration in banks' portfolios) or requiring a certain proportion of the bank's liabilities to be in the form of uninsured subordinated bonds. The degree to which the authorities can use such rules to exploit market information and market discipline depends to some extent on the level of overall financial market development.[10] This section examines the extent of regulatory convergence between developed and emerging markets, including the problems of applying regulatory choices in the former to the latter, and then focuses on how the market can best be harnessed to help produce safe and sound finance.

Although there has been a remarkable convergence on paper in recent years, stark differences remain in the regulatory environments around the world. Thus, at the time of the 1988 Basel Accord, which recommended a minimum risk weighted capital adequacy ratio of 8 percent, some developing countries did not even have capital requirements, and many that did had low ratios (2–5 percent not being uncommon) and did not engage in prudential supervision to verify them. By 1998–99, of 103 countries reporting, only 7 had minimum capital ratios under 8 percent, and 29 had minimum capital ratios of 10 percent or more, only one of which was from the OECD region. And more than 93 percent of all countries (88 percent in emerging markets) claim to adjust capital ratios for risk in line with Basel guidelines.

It is easier, however, to adopt "headline" regulations, such as capital adequacy ratios, but more difficult to implement the underlying procedures and to acquire the necessary supervisory skills to give teeth to these rules. Unfortunately, capital by itself is an inadequate indicator of the health of a bank. The true net worth of a bank depends on the quality of its portfolio which, for many banks, is dominated by illiquid loans that cannot easily be valued or "marked to market." This problem is all the more real in developing countries, where volatile prices and thin or nonexistent markets render such estimates hazardous. All too often a bank is truly insolvent long before its accounts tell us so. If capital is actually negative, risk adjustment is irrelevant.

What matters for true net worth is capital net of provisions for loan losses, but accounting rules in many countries permit bankers to be optimistic and underprovision. If the bank has reached a reasonable *measured* capital adequacy ratio only because it made no provisions against loan loss ($P = 0$ in Table 2.2), we can safely say that its true capital is below standard. Even an insolvent bank (with a true P of 10

A convergence of headline regulations—

but wide disparities in their effective enforcement—

notably the accounting for loan loss provisions

93

Table 2.2 Typical balance sheet

Assets		Liabilities	
Cash	10	Demand deposits	100
Liquid investments	20	Other debt	30
Loans at historical value	100		
Less provision for loan losses	$-P$		
Property	10	Capital	$10-P$

or more) can remain in business for months or even years, provided it does not run out of cash. As long as the net inflow of deposits and the interest received on performing loans are sufficient to pay operating expenses and interest on deposits, closure can be deferred. Depositors and supervisors may be lulled into a false sense of security if accounting rules are flouted. Accounting rules in some countries still have some way to catch up.

Rather than rely on historic values, bank supervisors classify loans into forward-looking categories, such as "normal," "specially mentioned," "substandard," "doubtful," and "loss," and regulations implicitly attach loss probabilities to each of the last three categories by requiring a certain percentage (typically 20, 50, and 100, respectively) of the value of loans to be provisioned in the bank's accounts (usually in addition to some general loan-loss provision of 1 or 2 percent of the entire portfolio). Indeed, here too our survey shows that requirements are on average slightly tougher on paper in low-income countries. What is important here, though, is that the provisioning requirements should actually correspond to subsequent loan-loss experience.[11]

Unfortunately, ensuring adequate, forward-looking classification of loans is not straightforward. Especially when economic conditions move out of the normal, or for the large or unusual loans that are often the weak point of a reckless bank, experience may be a poor guide, even to the banker. The high-risk environment and rapidly evolving economic structure of most developing countries obviously exacerbate the severity of this problem. Realistically, in the face of resistant bank management, given the inherent difficulty in understanding the true risks, supervisors often can do little more than rely on a backward-looking measure: insisting on provisions being made when the loan goes into arrears. In this respect, the accounting rules or standards vary widely. In particular, low-income countries typically are more lenient than the upper-middle-income group (figure 2.5). Also telling is that one in three low-income countries allow banks to treat interest that is in arrears as earned income, at least for a time. In Thailand interest accrual on nonperforming loans was allowed for up to 360 days in 1997 and for 180 days in many African countries. In most countries it is still more difficult to prevent a bank from concealing a nonperforming loan simply by "evergreening," that is, by making a new loan to cover the repayment. Most tellingly, Cavallo and Majnoni (2001) show that whereas industrial countries build up provisions in good times and draw them down as the business cycle weakens, there was no such variation in the developing countries in their sample, again suggestive that convergence to industrial country norms is more superficial than real.

In sum, measuring the size of the buffer is a challenge that is far from being under control. Although not published, the Basel Core Principle assessments are understood to be revealing that developing countries are considerably further from full compliance than their industrial country counterparts. Headline regulations are promulgated without having the information needed for verification or without putting in place the incentives that might help reveal it.

Less rigorous loan classification standards apply in lower income countries.

Figure 2.5   Classification of substandard loans, 1997

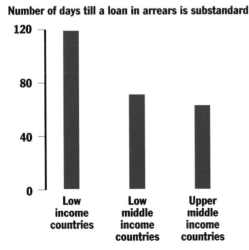

Number of days till a loan in arrears is substandard

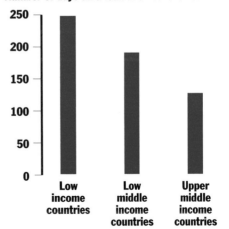

Number of days till a loan in arrears is doubtful

Source: Barth, Caprio, and Levine database.

Good supervision can improve the health of the financial system—

One should not be dismissive of the ability of official supervisors to uncover problems. Empirical evidence exists that they can and do provide independent information. For example, Jordan, Peek, and Rosengren (1999) found for the United States that the release of adverse supervisory information resulted on average in a 5 percent decrease in the bank's stock price, suggesting that the release did contain news. Not surprisingly, there was some variation. Banks that had already disclosed bad news saw little effect, and there was little evidence of contagion, in the sense of other banks' stock prices reacting when another bank disclosed information, except in the case of a common, regional shock for banks in the same region.

This evidence shows not only that good supervision can have an effect in that it does reveal additional information and can lead to the issuance of supervisory actions designed to stop imprudent behavior. It also points to the advantages of greater disclosure in that markets can pressure banks to adjust as soon as possible and before a crisis results.

How does one get good supervision? The Basel Committee guidelines provide supervisors' views on this, and there is little doubt that factors such as the independence of the supervisory agency are key to good supervision.[12] Here we note the issues related to the incentives that supervisors face.

It must be recognized that the environment in which prudential regulation and supervision is being conducted differs markedly between industrial and developing countries. In addition to the greater volatility of emerging markets, income and wealth tend to be much more highly concentrated than in industrial countries, and recent evidence shows that this holds for the ownership of corporations as well (figure 1.10). It is not hard to see that this adds to the challenges faced by supervisors, by increasing the likelihood that the financial firms under their supervision are controlled by extremely powerful individuals.

but incentive structures often make this difficult

The result can be a skewing of the "balance of terror"—the risks and rewards faced by official supervisors in many countries. First, supervisors generally are paid less well relative to salaries in private banks, and in many developing countries turnover is becoming even more of a problem than in industrial countries. Second, deferred income—a potential bonus, in effect—can result from lax supervision, since only a few countries, regardless of income level, have prohibitions on supervisors moving to work for banks. Third, there is no deferred penalty—neither through a loss of bonuses, which generally are not offered—nor by a forfeiting of pensions. And last, in several countries well into the middle-income range, such as Argentina and the Philippines, supervisors can be sued for their actions and be held personally liable, so they face a very real penalty now for vigorous action.

This is precisely the opposite of the optimal compensation structure for those charged with enforcing laws and regulations that has long been recommended for eliminating malfeasance even when it is difficult to detect bad conduct.[13] So, a priority for securing better supervision is to pay bank supervisors well, even by reference to other public servants: the probability of detection of malfeasance is low and, as seen in figure 2.1 above, the cost of laxity on their part is high. Given that it may take some time for supervisory laxity to be evinced, deferred compensation would be the best way to motivate supervisors. Thus, providing them with a generous pension as a deferred bonus, and then removing or reducing that pension for violations of good supervisory practice will help improve incentives. In addition to the common view that supervisory agencies require a high degree of independence to reduce political interference, if supervisors were simultaneously protected against private actions taken against them personally (as in many industrial countries), more countries would be able to benefit from more vigorous enforcement.

Transparency and accountability alone are not sufficient for better supervision. This approach may be sufficient, for example, to ensure that central bank governors behave responsibly in setting monetary policy, because exchange rate and/or bond markets provide a ready assessment of their actions. Also, most central bank governors do not face lawsuits for tightening policy, nor are they rewarded in the future for lax policy. Although the reaction to the U.S. savings and loan problems was to reduce supervisory discretion—through mandatory, prompt, corrective actions—the growing difficulty because of the plethora of financial instruments in observing the risk position of banks is leading to more discretion for supervisors, for example, by having them agree with banks on how they model risk and then penalizing them for violating the model. This is not an easy area to monitor. To the extent that developing country supervisors move in the same direction, it will be particularly important that greater discretion is accompanied by greater oversight *and* a corrected balance of terror.

Although it is necessary in many countries to improve supervisory compensation, it is both unlikely and costly to pay supervisors salaries that are equivalent to senior bank officers. Forcing greater revelation of information is the standard way to limit the required increase in the

Correct the "balance of terror"—

efficiency wage, so something like the above subordinated debt proposal is especially important to force greater disclosure of market information and sentiment.

—and supplement official supervision with market-based monitors

Although the financial conditions of banks are difficult to assess even in industrial countries, the above suggests that it is especially risky in emerging markets to put excessive reliance on official supervision. The recurrence of fraud, defalcations, and crises demonstrates that the information and incentive problems that dominate finance are not easily eliminated. Moreover, differences in institutional development and economic volatility, combined with the ability of financial market participants to adjust to regulation, mean that rather than precise forms or rules, authorities need a strategy for approaching financial sector regulation, and the strategy has to go considerably beyond convergence to industrial country norms.

With greater income and ownership concentration, it is more difficult to maintain adequate independence of supervisory agencies. Also, the information environment, the degree of public oversight of supervisors (not just disclosure, but the degree of sophistication of the press on financial matters), and the basic incentives that supervisors confront all will operate to yield less effective supervision. Political interference in bank supervision has happened even with good checks and balances, such as in the United States as savings and loans had members of Congress lobby for lighter regulation and reduce regulatory capital requirements. These potential problems are likely to be more pronounced where ownership concentration is greater (for example, the República Bolivariana de Venezuela in the early 1990s, in which a senior central bank official owned shares in a bank).

Besides, just as authorities in developing countries were making the transition to supervised capital adequacy, the goal posts were moving. First, the complexity of modern finance has amplified the difficulty of supervising on a transaction-by-transaction basis. In part, with the growth of derivative instruments, banks can now shift their exposure within minutes, so that reviews of their current exposures convey less information as to their health than they would have previously. As already mentioned, this has led middle- and upper-income countries, where such instruments are more prevalent, to shift the focus of supervision to the bank's risk management systems, though experience with this approach is still limited.

Second, as noted above, banks are adept at adjusting to a set of rules. The arbitrary risk weights of the 1988 Basel Accord were easy to evade, and indeed sparked a decade of financial innovation at least in part with this purpose in mind.

The answer from recent and historical research on financial systems is remarkably clear, though as just seen, not always as simple as it appears: use incentives and information to maximize the number of well-informed, well-motivated monitors of financial intermediaries.

Use the private sector to extend the reach of the regulator

Understandably, diversity in the set of monitors for banks is desirable not only because of possible differences in the information they may possess, but also reflecting the varying and possibly opaque incentives they face. Who else, though, apart from official supervisors, can monitor banks? Three classes of monitors should be considered:

- Insiders, including the owners, the board, and senior management of a bank, whose net worth should, in an ideal world, depend on the prudent performance of the institution.
- Rating agencies.
- Markets, meaning all nonofficial outside creditors and counterparties.

Owners earn returns on the capital they have invested. These rewards will be based on current and expected future profits, or the so-called franchise value. Profits in turn will derive from the regulatory framework that constrains banks to various activities and ways of doing business. If the profits from prudent banking are high, and if the threat that banks could lose their bank license (and thus their equity and the related rewards) is real, owners will be motivated to preserve their franchise value. Majority owners and senior managers may be in the best position to surmount information problems, but as numerous bank failures show, such as the famous 1995 Barings episode, owners of large, complicated intermediaries still face these problems. Minority owners do not necessarily have any better information than the general public.

Banks often reward risk-taking

Bank directors have the responsibility of representing all owners, and of disclosing accurate and timely information on their institution. Better and more timely information will improve the ability of all outsiders to monitor them. Most countries in theory make bank directors responsible for accurate disclosure, but only a third (most of which are in high-income economies) have enforced penalties. Enforcement is critical. Stiff penalties for inadequate disclosure, and more generally for excessive risk-taking, is a way of increasing the liability of owners beyond just the capital they have invested for the performance of the bank.

If bank directors and majority owners were highly motivated to engage only in safe and sound banking, they would likely endeavor to effect a compensation system for senior bank management that would reward prudence. However, the fallout from the Long Term Capital Management (LTCM) fiasco revealed that senior executives of a few large international banks were forced out—the good news—for making similar bets as LTCM, but—the bad news—they were able to take multimillion-dollar bonuses with them. In all likelihood, this reflects the predominance of banks that are willing to gamble and hence offer compensation packages that attract risk takers.[14] Authorities could try to correct for this market failure by making capital ratios or deposit insurance premia a function of the compensation structure for senior management. Supervisors in many advanced economies do look at risk management systems that banks have and grade them on this effort. The suggestion here is that the source of the risk management system, executive compensation, rather than its advertised manifestation, be factored in to regulation. The compensation structure also should be disclosed—not just the raw salary, but how bonuses and other forms of compensation are determined (John, Saunders, and Senbet 2000).

One recent proposal for bringing the views of private market participants on bank risk to bear was advanced in 1999 and 2001 Basel Committee discussion papers seeking to reduce the arbitrariness of the risk weights attached to bank capital requirements by proposing that the weights instead be derived from ratings publicized by approved external credit assessors (for example, rating agencies). Although this proposal would appear to be an attempt to "harness the market," it is instructive to consider several problems facing implementation of this proposal, especially in developing countries. Among the better known difficulties are the following:

The problems with rating agencies

- It is unclear how reliable rating agencies would be where information costs are high, the ratings industry is at best nascent, and where banks often pay for their own ratings.
- Ratings are based on expected default rates, but capital is intended for unexpected losses.

In addition, however, are a number of less-recognized points that are highlighted by a focus on incentives (Honohan 2001b). First, the usual moral hazard problem will be exacerbated. If it is announced that banks will have to hold capital in accordance with the riskiness of their portfolio, each borrower will have the incentive to secure a favorable rating, even though it continues to place the bank—and the deposit insurance fund, if one exists—at risk. Bankers, assuming that they have decided to make the loan, will be motivated to collude or go along with a favorable depiction of their borrowers, because it will give them greater freedom in making capital decisions.

Second, raters may release less information about borrowers so as not to lose business. And most serious of all, rating agencies are not paid to anticipate the risk of correlated, systemic shocks, so even if the average rating of a borrower is accurate for normal times, it will not be for a crisis. This problem is especially serious as *developing country authorities may believe that by using ("market based") ratings, they are protected against crises, when in fact they are not*. Even though rating agencies in the United States do a fair job on individual firm ratings, their ratings perform less well on emerging market paper precisely because it is difficult to estimate systemic shocks in small, volatile economies.

Thus, it is important for authorities to use market forces, but this discussion illustrates that it is equally important to understand what the incentives are and how they operate. Also, rather than worry about how to motivate rating agencies to take proper account of correlated factors, authorities should focus on banks, which can and should be looking at their entire portfolio and how it varies or is exposed to different risks. Compelling banks to disclose certain information can be part of this process so that agents external to the bank *who have the right incentives* will put this information to good use. Relying on rating agencies puts excessive burden on entities that may not have as much to lose as bank creditors do.

Given the incentive that equity holders and other insiders may have to increase risk, and the uncertainties of relying on rating agencies, it is all the more important to consider how the incentives of other bank creditors can be aligned with the social goal of limiting bank risk. Although small depositors may choose to "free ride" on other claimants, large creditors, *if they have no expectation that they will be compensated for their losses*, have clear incentives to monitor banks. Recent proposals attempt to capitalize on this incentive by forcing banks to issue subordinated debt, that is, a fixed claim that is only senior to equity. Not enjoying the upside gains of equity holders, but holding almost as much of the downside risk, subordinated debt holders would be highly motivated to police banks for excessive risk-taking. Also, they would not bother with a "loan-by-loan" analysis that is part of the current Basel Committee process, but rather be concerned with the overall risk that banks face. Other large creditors—such as other banks in interbank markets—would also be motivated to monitor banks as well, as long as

Outside creditors can act as monitors—

—and a subordinated debt requirement is a promising, but not fool-proof, way to improve market monitoring

they were not under the presumption that they might be "bailed out" if the bank got into difficulties.

Subordinated debt is not new—as of 2000, 92 of 106 countries responding note that they allow subordinated debt to fulfill some part of their capital requirement. However, those countries in compliance with the Basel Committee guidelines in effect regard it as cheap equity, and to that extent only make eligible long-term debt, and then limit the use of such debt. This, however, ensures that rollovers of the debt will be relatively rare. Also, the fact that it is not required to be issued and is not policed then leads to its issuance to firms that are not at arm's length. Yet regular issuance, tradability, and arm's-length issuance all are needed to ensure better monitoring. To prevent this debt from becoming a kind of "junk bond," it will be necessary to put some cap on the interest rate that can be paid. If these features are present, subordinated debt holders will be even more concerned to avoid a bank that is taking imprudent risks than at present. Far from being cheap equity, this kind of subordinated debt can be a valuable discipline. There is much to be said for requiring its issuance, especially for larger banks in each country. To provide reliable monitoring, subordinated debt holders would become an important lobby group to press for a number of the improvements to infrastructure and information noted earlier, particularly related to the disclosure of information.

To be sure, subordinated debt proposals (box 2.3) can be quite difficult to implement. Capital markets in developing countries are thin, though a requirement that banks issue this debt would deepen them somewhat. Most importantly, a key to its success is to ensure that the issuers are truly at arm's length from the holders of the debt, meaning that they neither should be related parties, nor should the issuer be allowed to provide comfort or guarantees to the holders. Ensuring this is not a trivial concern, and is an excellent reason for not relying exclusively on subordinated debt holders to ensure safety and soundness. Greater reliance on subordinated debt and on other uninsured creditors' monitoring, however, seems to be a worthwhile initiative in middle-income countries.

Notwithstanding the difficulty of ensuring arm's length between banks and the holders of subordinated debt, early results from Argentina are promising. Even though subordinated debt only began to be required there in 1998, and though its implementation was delayed by the East Asian crisis, banks that were largely compliant saw lower deposit rates,

Box 2.3 Subordinated debt proposals

SUBORDINATED DEBT CAN SERVE AS A BUFFER TO absorb losses, but probably its most valuable contribution is by the signal it can provide as to bank riskiness. This signal both will serve as a discipline in the market, as banks find it harder to renew their subordinated debt or find the interest rate thereon rising as risk increases, but also by the indirect signal it provides to others, including bank supervisors. The latter benefit could be great. One problem with so-called prompt, corrective action proposals is that the criteria for intervention still leave significant responsibility to supervisors, which may be particularly difficult in countries in which the institutional independence of the supervisory agency is in doubt. A recent study of the Board of Governors of the Federal Reserve System (1999) noted that one difficulty for official supervisors—the burden to prove that banks may be taking excessive risks—does not hold for subordinated debt holders, who instead get to place the burden of proof on bank managers who need funding. Supervisors could use either the interest rates or ability to issue subordinated debt as a signal to increase monitoring of risky banks or to take mandated actions, or both.

How should it be issued? A requirement that banks issue this debt regularly in 'lumpy' and relatively homogeneous forms would produce a well-informed monitoring system for banks; the regular issuance would continually "refresh" market information, in that banks would presumably find it advantageous, and markets likely require, current information at the time of issuance. If the subordinated debt instrument is relatively homogeneous, then the rate at which it trades could be more easily compared across banks, thereby facilitating monitoring.

In addition to tradability, maturity matters, and the balance of opinion appears to be weighted to the medium term of 2–5 years. While Federal Reserve System interviews with U.S. market participants suggested that market depth would be greater with 3–5 year maturity, Calomiris has proposed for emerging markets as well that banks be required to issue 2 percent of their nonreserve assets (or 2 percent of risk-weighted assets) on a monthly basis with 2-year maturity, so that every month they would have to refinance 1/24th of this debt. Calomiris (1999) also notes that banks in trouble could pay higher interest rates, but he would limit this by imposing an interest rate cap. That would mean that highly risky banks would be forced to shrink the asset side of their balance sheet and eventually close or otherwise restructure their operations when they could not comply with the subordinated debt requirement

Whereas regular issuance would impose discipline on issuers, there is a tradeoff between this gain and the cost to banks—and their customers—from more frequent and smaller issues, because of transaction costs. Indeed, very small banks in emerging markets likely could not pay these costs, so Calomiris has recommended that small banks be allowed to satisfy a subordinated debt requirement by "issuing" large deposits to a qualified institution. Because it is the larger banks whose stability is essential for the health of the overall system, and for which early intervention is important, this limitation is not likely to be severe. Last, to increase the likelihood that subordinate debt holders will be at arm's length from the issuing banks, it may be necessary to put restrictions in place that could limit the attractiveness of this paper.

Source: Board of Governors of the Federal Reserve System (1999); Calomiris (1999); Evanoff and Wall (2000).

faster growth in deposits, a lower capital ratio, and a substantially lower ratio of nonperforming loans compared with noncompliant banks (figure 2.6). More formal econometric analysis confirms that the subordinated debt requirement there has encouraged better monitoring and greater prudence in risk management (Calomiris and Powell 2000). Even if only good banks were able to issue subordinated debt there, this fact of itself conveys important information to supervisors. The above evidence that credibly uninsured creditors are more likely to provide monitoring of banks strengthens the promise of subordinated debt in improving the market monitoring of banks (Evanoff and Wall 2000). Again, however, it is important to stress that subordinated debt should not be thought of as a single cure for unsafe banking, but rather as a potential tool in the regulatory arsenal.

Financial Sector Safety Nets

Deposit insurance schemes are increasingly spreading to emerging markets—

I N THE FACE OF BANKING FRAGILITY, IT IS NATURAL FOR depositors to hope for redress from government when things go wrong, but this expectation in itself can contribute to the fragility. Although governments have a variety of mechanisms, such as the central bank discount window and other lender-of-last-resort (LOLR) facilities, which can be employed as part of a safety net for banks, explicit deposit insurance schemes are increasingly becoming a key

Banks that complied with subordinated debt requirements paid lower deposit rates but enjoyed faster deposit growth, a lower capital ratio, and a lower rate of nonperforming loans.

Figure 2.6 Subordinated debt in Argentina, 1996–99

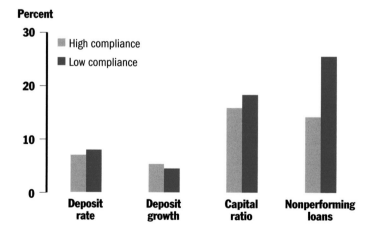

Source: Calomiris and Powell (2000).

component, have an important impact on overall incentives, and therefore are the focus of this section. Governments typically remain more ambiguous about their LOLR function, which has been the subject of an enormous literature.

Not surprisingly, deposit insurance arose where banking was most fragile—U.S. states in which banking was conducted in unit banks (banks that were not permitted to branch) beginning with the N.Y. Safety Fund in 1829. Some 14 states (all with unit banks) adopted deposit insurance; some failed shortly after their establishment, while others lasted until being done in during the agricultural collapse of the 1920s. Only three systems—those that harnessed market forces—were judged successful.

Still, by the late 1920s, the much better survival rate of branching banks appeared to have "won the day" for branching vs. unit banks (with or without deposit insurance) until the political realignment on this issue during the Depression. After the adoption of a national deposit insurance system in the United States in 1934, the number of explicit systems in other countries grew slowly for the first 30 years, with only 6 being established, and then took off (figure 2.7).

Most deposit insurance systems are set up with either or both of the stated objectives of protecting the overall stability of the banking system, and protecting individual, especially small, depositors. In the pioneering U.S. case, although political debate may cloud the true underlying purpose, scholars accept that it was systemic stability rather than small depositor protection that was the key factor (Golembe 1960; see box 2.4).

—with the goals of protecting the stability of the banking system, and the savings of small depositors

Figure 2.7 Explicit deposit insurance systems: the rise of deposit insurance around the world, 1934–99

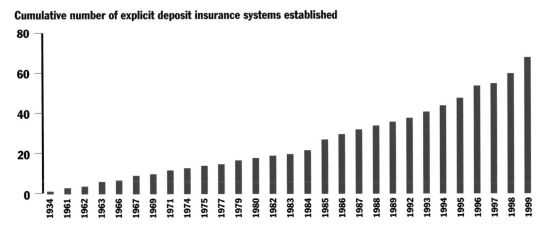

Cumulative number of explicit deposit insurance systems established

Source: Kane (2000).

Box 2.4   The rise of deposit insurance?

Deposit insurance was not a novel idea; it was not untried; protection of the small depositor, while important, was not its primary purpose; and, finally, it was the only important piece of legislation during the New Deal's famous "one hundred days" which was neither requested nor supported by the new administration. (Golembe 1960, pp. 181–82)

FOLLOWING THE ESTABLISHMENT OF THE N.Y. Safety Fund (1829–66), Vermont (1831–58) and Michigan (1836–42) established similar schemes. All experienced severe losses in the panic of 1837, New York then allowed free banking, and its safety fund was done in as better banks switched to become free banks and thereby avoid the losses associated with poor (public sector) supervision and limited premia. Vermont and Michigan also saw failures in the panics of 1857 and 1837, respectively, also because of adverse selection and poor supervision. Indiana (1834–65), Ohio (1845–55) and Iowa (1858–66) established more incentive-compatible systems: restricted membership, unlimited mutual liability, all privately administered, and with powers to restrict dividends and impose other restrictions and penalties on member banks.

These cases could not have differed more from the first three systems, in that there were few failures and, like the states with branching (but without deposit insurance), they weathered common shocks quite well. Interestingly, coverage was broad, but with unlimited mutual liability, the greater the coverage,

the greater the liability and thus the stronger the incentives to police one another. The systems ended with the taxation imposed by the National Banking System, and not because of crisis.

The post-Civil War period saw eight other states adopt deposit insurance, and all perished with the agricultural crisis the 1920s, with the exception of Mississippi and South Dakota, whose schemes made it until 1930 and 1931, respectively. So those schemes with mutual liability and private administration saw few failures, little or no evidence of fraud, did not perish in crisis, and avoided suspension during panics.

Rather than continuing to pay for the failures by themselves, unit banking states regularly sought the protection of the federal government, as 150 bills for a federal deposit insurance system were introduced unsuccessfully between 1886 and 1933. Representatives from branching states continually opposed the attempt to make their voters pay for the fragility of unit banking. The successful legislation was passed in 1933 *after* the bank run was ended by a bank holiday and reopening of far fewer banks, but without including any ex post compensation for depositors and with a low initial ceiling. Political compromise appears to have been key: Carter Glass, chairman of the Senate Banking Committee and a long-time foe of deposit insurance, acceded to it as part of a deal with Representative Henry Steagall to win passage of Glass' plan for the eponymous banking act that separated commercial and investment banks. Glass later said that the compromise was a mistake.

Sources: Calomiris (1992), White (1997), and Golembe (1960).

Other means of protecting small depositors were recognized, such as the savings banks in Europe, which largely invested in safe instruments. The U.S. deposit insurance legislation was passed by Congress in the midst of the banking crisis, though the run on banks—which was linked to fears of devaluation and other measures that might be adopted by the new administration—had stopped before it went into effect.

More recently, some countries have adopted or expanded deposit insurance during crises. For example, after two crises in the 1980s, Argentina abandoned deposit insurance in 1992, only to adopt a system of limited coverage in 1995 in response to the Tequila crisis. Thailand moved to blanket insurance in 1997, including coverage of deposits at finance companies. Mexico is the first developing country recently to have put in place plans to reduce blanket coverage, following its experience with the 1994 crisis, so experience with this transition is necessarily limited among emerging markets. The sharp increase in the 1990s resulted in part from the spread of deposit insurance to transitional countries, and to some African states, perhaps reflecting the prevailing wisdom that deposit insurance would lead to a safer financial system.[15]

The systems that countries adopted differed dramatically. As mentioned, some countries cover all deposits—including interbank and foreign currency deposits—and are even generous in extending the coverage to a broad array of institutions. However, most deny—at least in principle—coverage for interbank funds, so as to induce banks, which are large and supposed to be sophisticated relative to many others, to monitor one another.[16]

Figure 2.8 shows the dramatic dispersion in the stated coverage of deposit insurance relative to per capita GDP, for those countries with limits on coverage.[17] Compared to the relatively modest protection in high-income countries, some of the poorest countries offer the most generous protection, going well beyond the scale of the deposits of the poor—though the extremely low level of average income in countries like Chad needs to be kept in mind to put their coverage in perspective.[18]

Some deposit insurance schemes are funded or administered by the private sector, or both. And whereas many deposit insurance systems are prefunded, some 10 systems—mostly in Europe—as of 1999 were unfunded, with the power to make assessments on individual banks when needed. Most deposit insurance systems feature a flat premium, but about a quarter feature some differential pricing, in effect an attempt to vary the premium with the riskiness of the individual bank, though the differential itself is small and not always collected.[19]

It is not hard to see why explicit deposit insurance systems have become increasingly popular. The political calculus is in their favor. For one thing, they can appear to be a direct and seemingly costless solution

Deposit insurance schemes are politically popular—

107

Figure 2.8   Deposit insurance coverage

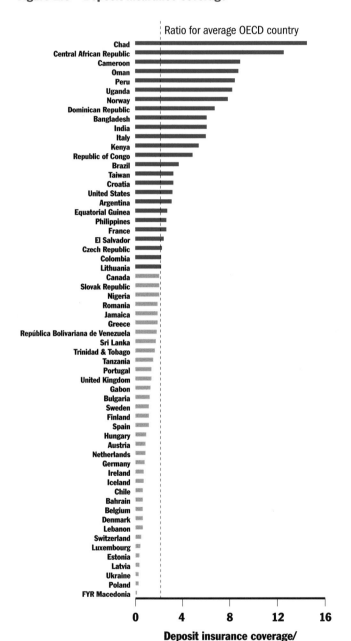

Deposit insurance coverage is relatively generous in low-income countries.

Note: For Germany only compulsory coverage is shown; the private voluntary systems have higher limits, with each depositor protected up to about 30 percent of bank capital.
Source: Demirgüç-Kunt and Detragiache (2000).

to the problem of bank panics and runs. Protection of small depositors is also politically attractive. There are other political forces favoring the introduction of deposit insurance, too. For example, a deposit insurance scheme can help small local banks in emerging markets acquire or retain their market share of deposits that might, in the absence of insurance, migrate to large and especially to foreign-owned banks.

Last, by providing a deposit insurance scheme, the government may feel that, in political terms, it is also buying the right to step in with regulatory intervention, as necessary, including the right to close unsound or insolvent banks. This argument, however—that deposit insurance is a necessary quid pro quo for the authority to close banks—goes too far. Almost everywhere in the past century, banking has not been a right, but a privilege, regulated by the state—and for good reason. Banking law properly requires licenses to be granted only to "fit and proper" individuals, and with the possibility that the license can be revoked for improper actions, which should be defined as any that violate banking regulations.

The logic underlying the more persuasive political considerations is not without merit. Credible deposit guarantees undoubtedly do forestall runs. Prompt repayment of their deposits is clearly a valuable protection for small depositors at failed banks, especially protecting them from inflationary erosion (though, as noted, there are other ways of offering safe savings media to low-income households, including postal savings banks—or even mutual funds restricted to secure money market assets). And explicit deposit insurance does favor small banks, although if it comes at a high cost, governments would need to consider the tradeoffs carefully.

Less evident in the political arena, but long recognized by specialists, is the fact that deposit insurance has the potential to induce greater risk-taking, or so-called moral hazard behavior. Limited liability allows bank owners to walk away from their losses—giving them the option to put the losses to depositors or other parties. However, by reducing the incentive of insured depositors to monitor banks, deposit insurance can greatly accommodate risk-taking if accompanied by lax regulation and supervision.

Perhaps the most persuasive argument in favor of an explicit deposit insurance scheme is the thought that it can represent a limit to the government's commitment to depositors. Absence of an explicit system may really represent unlimited implicit coverage. By placing a modest limit on the amount of deposit coverage, can the government effectively signal that it is not likely to indemnify depositors beyond this limit?

Clearly, the net impact of adopting an explicit system and (if so) of implementing various design features are empirical issues, and turn chiefly on the tradeoff between the gains from protecting depositors and the losses from reduced market monitoring. Until recently, virtually no systematic empirical research used data on emerging markets to address these questions. A recent World Bank research project (led by Demirgüç-Kunt), however, furnished both a database for researchers worldwide and the answers to several key questions on the impact of adopting explicit deposit insurance on financial sector stability, the ability for markets to exert discipline on banks, and the development of the overall financial system. In the process, conclusions on key design issues for authorities are emerging.

—but may cause economic damage—

The weight of evidence from this research is surprisingly clear cut, suggesting that in practice, rather than lowering the likelihood of a crisis, the adoption of explicit deposit insurance has been associated *on average* with less banking sector stability, and this result does not appear to be driven by reverse causation. Here the qualification "on average" is key: deposit insurance shows no significant destabilizing effect in countries with strong institutions; only where the institutional environment is weak do problems arise. The natural interpretation of this result is that banks, exploiting the availability of insured deposits, take greater risks. The presence of explicit insurance reduces depositor monitoring, and this matters if official supervision is insufficient, as where institutions are weak. The role of good institutions—as measured in this research by indicators of the rule of law, good governance (a proxy for effective regulation and supervision), and low corruption—thus seems crucial in reducing the opportunities for risk-taking (Demirgüç-Kunt and Detragiache 2000).

by encouraging risk-taking in institutionally weak settings

That explicit deposit insurance could be positively correlated with banking crises should not be considered too surprising, because *when it is credible*, it facilitates deposit gathering by banks regardless of the risks they undertake.[20]

Even without explicit insurance, depositors could infer an implicit government protection. At lower levels of institutional development, however, confidence in such implicit insurance may be low. There is no certainty at all that the government will, in the event of a failure, be able or willing to pay out even to small depositors, let alone large depositors and shareholders. This uncertainty keeps depositors motivated to monitor banks (to the extent that they can), especially given that they cannot rely on strong official supervision of the banks in an environment of poor skills, a weak information and regulatory base, and often political interference. In contrast, the announcement of an explicit scheme acts like a signal that bailout funds will be easier to get, even from a government operating in a weak institutional setting.[21,22]

Although these remarkable econometric findings have not, of course, gone unchallenged, it has so far proved impossible to dismiss them. True, in a recent working paper Eichengreen and Arteta (2000, pp. 44–45) contend that there is "at least as much evidence that deposit insurance… provides protection from depositor panics…as that it destabilizes banking systems." In arriving at this conclusion, however, they focus on a more limited sample of countries and crises. In particular, omitting countries with better institutions makes it hard for them to detect the importance of institutional quality in determining the overall effectiveness of deposit insurance, as well as of different design features.

Confirmation of the adverse impact of explicit deposit insurance on market discipline can be seen in the price that banks have to pay for their deposits. Examination of individual bank accounts shows that illiquid banks tend to pay more for their funds, partly reflecting depositors' concern to ensure their own liquidity, but the premium on interest expense for illiquid banks is less if a generous deposit protection system is in place. Interestingly, these findings come from a different cross-country database than that used in assessing the link with crises and, as such, provide important additional evidence. Inasmuch as they draw on individual balance sheet and income statement data from some 2,500 banks in up to 43 countries, this may be more telling direct evidence of the way in which deposit insurance can affect incentives (Demirgüç-Kunt and Huizinga 2000b). Although deposit insurance weakens market discipline even in advanced countries, the effects seem to be offset by better official oversight and still more effective market monitoring.

Martinez-Peria and Schmukler (2001) also found similar evidence in Argentina (in the early days after adopting explicit insurance), Chile, and Mexico of the market disciplining risky banks by demanding higher interest rates. Interestingly, though, in this case even insured depositors displayed some disciplining effect, which may represent a lack of credibility toward the insurer's commitment to or speed in paying out.[23] Still, where deposit insurance appeared most credible (in Chile), uninsured depositors appeared to be more effective monitors of bank risk.

The lower interest rates point to the advantages gained by bank shareholders from the existence of deposit insurance, a gain that, in aggregate, is rarely paid for through insurance premia. "Correct" pricing would remove this subsidy, but it appears that it is easier to adopt deposit insurance than to price it correctly—and correct pricing is difficult in many emerging markets. If the value of bank equities as quoted on an efficient stock market truly reflects the risks and returns facing the bank's shareholders, it is possible to infer the ex ante value of the deposit insurance scheme to each bank by examining the leverage of the bank and the variance of its stock price (box 2.5). The calculated values can be substantial, and this tool could be used by supervisors to predict bank failure, as Kaplan (1999) showed for Thailand.

Box 2.5 Implicit value of deposit insurance to the bank's shareholders

A BANK WHOSE DEPOSITS ARE INSURED CAN ACCESS such deposits at close to the market price for risk-free deposits regardless of the risk it is taking on the asset side of its portfolio. Some of the risk, however, is passed through to shareholders, and in an efficient equity market, the price of a risky bank's equity will be lower on average and more volatile. Employing standard arguments from the theory of option pricing, it is possible to infer from the volatility and level of the equity price, the market's beliefs about the probability of the bank failing and of the insurer having to pay out.

Using these probabilities, we can calculate the annual implicit subsidy—or expected insurance payout—for each bank. Although the formula is complex, only three variables are needed for this calculation, the equity volatility, the ratio of equity to deposits, and the dividend yield. The following table presents a ready-reckoner allowing the implicit annual subsidy value to the shareholders of deposit insurance for any bank given only the equity volatility and the ratio of equity to deposits. (The table assumes zero dividend yield.) Risky banks—those with relatively little equity and volatile earnings—enjoy a large subsidy.

Annual implicit safety net subsidies as a percentage of the market value of equity

E/D \ σ_E	50	60	70	80	90	100
1	0.5	1.6	4.1	8.5	16.6	29.1
2	0.5	1.6	4.0	8.4	15.6	27.9
5	0.4	1.4	3.4	7.4	13.3	24.7
10	0.4	1.3	3.0	6.5	12.2	20.6
20	0.3	1.0	2.4	5.0	9.5	15.7
50	0.1	0.5	1.2	2.7	5.0	8.5

Note: σ_E is percentage annual volatility (standard deviation) of equity returns, E/D is the market value of the bank's equity as a percentage of the value of the bank's deposits. The dividend yield is assumed to be zero.
Source: Laeven (2000).

Contrary to a popular view that deposit insurance might be needed in poor countries to give the confidence to allow the financial deepening that is needed (cf. chapter 1) to support growth, the data suggest that, in institutionally weak environments, having explicit deposit insurance leads to *less* financial sector development (Cull, Senbet, and Sorge 2000). Although it may be paradoxical that the provision of insurance could lead to less of an activity, it may be that when taxpayers in institutionally weak countries see their authorities providing explicit guarantees, they understand that the environment is not conducive to restraining the cost of these guarantees. The result, then, might be that the real insurers, the taxpayers themselves, choose to hide their assets outside the banking system, and perhaps outside the country, to avoid being taxed for coverage.

When an explicit insurance system is adopted, the government takes over some of the monitoring function of banks. This requires both transparency—the ability to detect as well as possible the risks that bankers are taking—and deterrence—the ability to convince bankers that rules will be enforced. Deterrence in turn depends on the accountability of government officials, in particular those in the deposit insurance and related regulatory agencies (Kane 2000). Better levels of institutional development—in the legal systems, accounting and auditing standards, and the political environment or quality of government—will make it more difficult for bankers to gamble with insured deposits, or for government officials to refrain from disciplining them.

So if we combine these three features—transparency, accountability, and deterrence—into the overall "institutional environment," the argument can be summarized in figure 2.9. Deposit insurance—whether explicit or implicit—provides the social benefit of protecting insured depositors, but at the expense of socially costly moral hazard behavior. We can picture the level of depositor protection provided by a functioning explicit system (the top panel) as being a given, independent of the remainder of the institutional environment. With an implicit one, some level of social protection usually will be provided, depending on what the government wants and is able to provide ex post. This may, however, as pictured in figure 2.9, be somewhat larger in countries that have achieved a higher overall institutional quality, if only because the better-developed tax systems there will permit greater coverage.

At low levels of institutional development, moral hazard behavior (the middle panel) can run rampant with an explicit system—bankers will

Deposit insurance schemes may inhibit financial sector development where institutions are weak

113

Figure 2.9   Deposit insurance: net benefits

Social protection benefits

Deposit insurance schemes balance the social benefits of security...

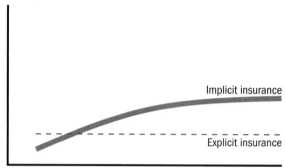

Institutional environment

Moral hazard costs

...against the social costs of moral hazard.

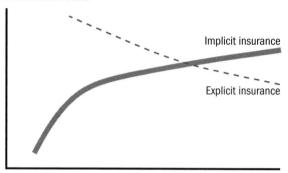

Institutional environment

Balance of advantage: explicit over implicit insurance

When institutions are weak, the costs of explicit deposit insurance outweigh the benefits.

Institutional environment

Source: See text.

have access to deposits, thanks to the insurance, but with weaker oversight. This opportunistic behavior, however, will tend to be reduced with a better institutional environment. In contrast, when the environment is weak, there likely is little moral hazard with an implicit system, as depositors will expect little protection—indeed, they may keep their wealth outside the banking system and even outside the country.

The bottom panel sums up the net benefits, with the key message that adequate infrastructure for enforcing contracts is of paramount importance for ensuring net gains from explicit deposit insurance. Although it is not evident at what cutoff point explicit deposit insurance might yield a net gain to a country, the need to do an "audit" of the state of transparency, deterrence, and accountability prior to its adoption is clear. Governments at the low end of this spectrum that want to institute an explicit system should first focus on improving the related institutions—including the regulatory environment (discussed below) in order to reduce the likelihood of excessive risk-taking. Importantly, no evidence exists that there is any cost to waiting to adopt deposit insurance. In addition to the evidence noted here, that deposit insurance in weak environments tends to lower financial development (and thus growth), *all high-income countries reached that stage without explicit deposit insurance*.

When authorities determine that their system is appropriate for explicit deposit insurance, certain design features should be kept in mind. One way to determine design is to look just at industrial countries and follow what they do, or otherwise try to infer best practice from first principles (Garcia 1999). Moreover, the Financial Stability Forum's Working Group on Deposit Insurance has been asked to develop guidance on deposit insurance to assist countries that are adopting or significantly reforming a deposit insurance system, and a report is expected in the fall of 2001. Wide differences, however, exist in the design of industrial country systems. More important, success may depend on replicating other institutional features of advanced countries as well.

Another method to complement this approach would be to look at lessons derived from cross-country experience. The econometric findings of Demirgüç-Kunt and Detragiache (2000) and Demirgüç-Kunt and Huizinga (2000b), already discussed above, and based on data from a wide range of countries, also point to several features of explicit schemes that can influence the degree to which they weaken market discipline or increase the risk of crisis, in particular, coverage, governance, and funding.

Don't just copy a deposit insurance scheme from another country

Limit coverage—

Coverage: The results suggest keeping coverage as low as is consistent with the perceived need to protect small depositors.

There is room for disagreement on what the ceiling should be, but a rule of thumb suggests a figure of one to two times annual per capita GDP as sufficiently generous to protect small depositors while still maintaining significant market discipline. Interbank deposits should be excluded.

Governance: Involving the private sector in the management and administration of the fund can help limit the reduction in market discipline and the impact on systemic risk, but is no cure-all.

This issue of governance has received less attention recently, but the key role of private involvement in mutual bank guarantees was at the heart of successful deposit protection systems in the early days. Mutual guarantees are to be found, for example, in such successful mid-19th century U.S. state-based systems as in Indiana, Iowa, and Ohio (all of which featured unlimited mutual liability and were relatively successful—White 1997), and in the clearinghouse associations in the 19th and early 20th century. It is also a feature of several current deposit insurance systems, most notably that of Germany. Private sector involvement and even responsibility for deposit insurance illustrates the principle of the government harnessing the private sector to achieve its ends. Purely public schemes are more prone to crisis, and they reduce market discipline, but private sector deposit schemes at times have failed, and they can run out of funds in a systemic crisis.[24]

Importantly, it is easier to achieve private sector involvement in name, but without the exceptional oversight that characterizes some cases, such as the German system. Thus, private systems appear to work best in the presence of mutual liability and are best conceived of as a first round of defense against all but systemic crises, at which point the government can step in—much as the risk against catastrophic loss against earthquakes or hurricanes is handled.

The second potential drawback is that private schemes are based on peer monitoring, which (as observed by Calomiris 1992) is more likely to work when the coalition is relatively limited in numbers. Beyond some point, members may be tempted to "free ride" on the monitoring of others. In the German system this problem is addressed by the existence of several deposit insurance systems for different groups of banks. Smaller numbers of banks may also promote safety by boosting their franchise value and accordingly providing bankers with greater incentives to behave prudently. Still, private coalitions could be used to stifle competition, and

—involve the private sector in sharing the risk—

governments may have to make a decision on where to draw the line between competition and stability. The high costs of banking crises in developing countries suggests giving greater weight to stability. Moreover, many developing countries, in particular the smaller ones, already have a relatively small number of banks, compared with those in their industrial counterparts. Also, as is suggested in chapter 4, firms and households are rapidly gaining access to financial services from abroad, so that finance is becoming more competitive even in small countries.

Finally, deposit protection systems like those in Germany may be successful because of the institutional and regulatory environment in which they reside. The strong antibankruptcy bias of German law and the effective regulatory and supervisory system likely are important as well.[25] Interestingly, applying the methodology of box 2.2 to a sample of 12 countries, Laeven (2000) concludes that German banks take the very low risks, and have the lowest gross subsidy from deposit insurance. Private management, mutual liability, and the antibankruptcy bias likely explain this result.

Funding: The regression results introduce the possibility that keeping the scheme unfunded, though with access to funds, may help protect market discipline. Funding likely increases confidence that payout will be prompt. The case against funding, though, is controversial and not conclusive. The U.S. savings and loan crisis showed that unfunded (or underfunded) schemes could result in greater forbearance and higher-cost resolutions as the insurer struggled to protect depositors of weak banks. In addition, it is sometimes argued that the decision to fund deposit insurance may be accompanied by better oversight. Nevertheless, the cross-country econometrics points to the fact that funds can be abused more easily in weak institutional environments, and it seems far easier to set up a fund than to protect it from looting. These findings should be borne in mind by authorities considering whether or not to fund. Leaving the scheme unfunded, but with the ability to access funds from the government, should allow a quick response while permitting oversight to minimize abuse. Ex ante funding should only be considered when legal and regulatory institutions are developed sufficiently to prevent looting.

In sum, authorities considering the adoption of deposit insurance can benefit from these lessons. Some may interpret the evidence to mean that if countries adopt a "good" deposit insurance system, they will be better insulated against crisis. The difficulty, however, is that the adoption of deposit insurance per se is a "stroke-of-the-pen reform," and the

—and keep schemes unfunded, or with much oversight, in a weak institutional environment

institutional building to ensure that the system is "good" takes considerable time. Without adequate institutional development, the risk that deposit insurance could lead to crises, less financial sector development, more poorly functioning financial markets, and ultimately slower growth and higher poverty levels is real. Thus, authorities considering deposit insurance should make an audit of their institutional framework the first step in the decisionmaking process. Countries that do decide to establish an explicit deposit insurance system should draw on these results of experience, which utilize known market forces to ensure prudence.

Conclusions

THE CONSISTENT MESSAGE OF THIS CHAPTER IS THUS THAT bank owners and other market participants should be viewed as necessary complements to official supervisors in monitoring banks. Whatever the prudential regulations that are put in place—and it may be that more is needed than simply focusing on capital adequacy (cf. Honohan and Stiglitz 2001)—ensuring compliance is the major stumbling block. Given information problems and the difficulty in understanding well how incentives are functioning, excessive weight on one group as the principle monitor is akin to excessive concentration in a bank's portfolio. It may appear to pay off nicely until failing miserably. The strategic approach for authorities is to use incentives wherever they can be applied to maximize the number of motivated, watchful eyes.

Easy access to an implicit or explicit safety net confers a subsidy on banks, which encourages excessively bank-dependent—and debt-intensive—economies. Putting in place the recommendations of this chapter and effectively eliminating or greatly reducing this subsidy will remove this distortion and encourage the nonbank financial sector to develop. To be sure, there are some risks here, to the extent that it is near-bank activity just outside the scope of the regulations that occurs, and regulatory design needs to be adaptive to avoid such arbitrage opportunities. To the extent, however, that it allows the emergence of nonbank types of finance, including market-traded equity and bonds, and the associated collective savings institutions and other financial services activities, this will help the allocation of risks and lower the cost of risk capital. Risk and fraud are present in nonbank finance, too, but the existence of risk is known to all participants and is rewarded by higher expected returns. Fraud needs to be dealt with through responsible disclosure standards and stiff penalties, as well as some consumer-oriented regulations. With a safer banking system in place, authorities will be better able to avoid going down the dangerous road of extending the safety net beyond banking.

There is no doubt that concentration of ownership and control, noted in chapter 1, can limit the efficacy of nonbank financial institutions and markets in providing independent sources of finance and independent checks on the powers of powerful interests. Along with increasing access to foreign financial services (chapter 4), however, broadening capital markets over time promises to provide greater diversity and stability to the financial sector. Improvements to basic financial infrastructure—enhancing disclosure and improving the protection of shareholders and creditors, as noted in chapter 1—will be instrumental in this task. To be sure, these recommendations may be difficult to implement, because politicians will need all their skills in combating powerful interests. Developing an awareness in society of the costs that many, including the poor, must pay for a weak incentive environment should help bolster support for improvements in the framework. The forces of globalization (chapter 4) may help in this effort.

Notes

1. Kahneman and Tversky's (1979) Prospect Theory holds that individuals' assessments of gains and losses can vary depending on their initial situation and specifically may be averse to losses or loss realization, such as not selling stock whose prices fall.

2. As Kindleberger (1996, p. 66) notes, "...the propensities to swindle and be swindled run parallel to the propensity to speculate during a boom...And the signal for panic is often the revelation of some swindle, theft, embezzlement, or fraud."

3. Bagehot (1873, p. 131) reminds that during the South Sea Bubble, one of the companies whose shares were quoted was a bit peculiar. "But the most strange of all, perhaps, was 'For an Undertaking which shall in due time be revealed.' Each subscriber was to pay down two guineas, and hereafter to receive a share of one hundred, with a disclosure of the object; and so tempting was the offer, that 1,000 of these subscriptions were paid the same morning, with which the projector went off in the afternoon."

4. As Levine (1997) notes, Hicks (1969) concluded that although the products in the early stages of the industrial revolution were invented several decades earlier, their large-scale manufacture had to await the financial revolution that permitted the financing of illiquid investments.

5. Bernanke (1983) documented the credit channel for the Great Depression of the 1930s. The role of a supply-driven "credit crunch" in exacerbating the East Asia crisis has been extensively debated (a representative collection of the research literature is in Domaç, Ferri, and Kawai forthcoming). To the extent that a summary conclusion can be drawn, it appears that, while an acute credit squeeze affected firms, especially SMEs in the early stage of the

crisis, the economic downturn soon meant that demand for credit also declined, and relaunching credit supply no longer seemed to be the most pressing issue—though scholars will remain divided on the degree to which it did remain a problem. For the future, the priority will be to ensure that both macropolicy stability and the regulatory environment will be sufficiently secure to make discussion of forbearance and subsidies unnecessary.

6. If three outliers are discarded, the correlation is 0.7 and a regression line implies an approximate one-to-one relationship between flow output costs and fiscal costs. This finding could be interpreted as suggesting that the different elements of cost are all correlated, and as supporting the use of fiscal cost as a general-purpose approximation to the unobserved total economic cost.

7. Other goals, such as antidiscrimination and promotion of home ownership and of exports, continue to be pursued through detailed measures of financial policy in some countries, but these will not be discussed here. There has been a decline in the perceived effectiveness of policy measures that seek to direct the flow of finance to specific economic goals (Caprio, Hanson, and Honohan 2001).

8. Official action to help prevent the outright failure of the highly leveraged hedge fund LTCM in 1998 was substantially driven by knowledge of the potential impact of such a failure on the stability of the banking system.

9. The ending of liquidity requirements in developing countries came about in emulation of the new, best practice in the OECD area, and lower liquidity requirements did alleviate somewhat the taxation of the financial sector. Although liquidity ratios—holdings of central bank reserves, cash, and government paper—were not needed for prudential purposes in high-income countries, developing countries have not been able to upgrade bank supervision and regulation sufficiently to offset the loss of this buffer, cf. Caprio and Honohan (2001).

10. Overly simple or inflexible rules can have unfortunate side effects. In a downturn, for instance, rigid bank capital requirements can accentuate the recession by constraining credit growth, especially if banks have to provision more against loan losses (Chiuri, Ferri, and Majnoni

2000). However, the theoretical solution of making the capital requirements explicitly cycle-dependent (Dewatripont and Tirole 1993) may, in practice be hard to implement credibly or without risking a degree of forbearance that could altogether undermine the incentive effect of having capital requirements.

11. It is not only emerging economies that underprovision. A recent Bank of Japan study (1998) found that 75.3 percent of loans classified in 1993–94 as doubtful at a sample of 18 banks became write-offs over the following three years—but required provisioning for such loans is only 52 percent; and that 16.7 percent of "category 2" loans, for which only a 2 percent provision is required, were written off.

12. The integration of financial sector supervision has received much attention, but is beyond the scope of this study. As integrated agencies are relatively recent, no formal quantitative research of their relative merits has been performed, and only anecdotal information (such as the continued difficulty in getting effective cooperation between separate departments in a single agency) is available. Still, as Goodhart (2000) argues, for emerging markets this issue is premature and likely of second order relative to fixing the overall incentive environment.

13. As Becker and Stigler (1974) note, "The appropriate pay structure has three components: an 'entrance fee,' equal to the temptation of malfeasance, a salary premium in each year of employment approximately equal to the income yielded by the 'entrance fee,' and a pension with a capital value approximately equal also to the temptation of malfeasance. As it were, enforcers post a bond equal to the temptation of malfeasance, receive the income on the bond as long as they are employed, and have the bond returned if they behave themselves until retirement. Put differently, they forfeit their bond if they are fired for malfeasance."

14. On the other hand, it is recently reported that senior executives of Daiwa Bank have been held personally liable for losses caused by an inadequately supervised trader (*Economist*, November 16, 2000).

15. In some transitional cases, authorities may have been partly motivated by the possibility of European

Union (EU) accession and the agreed model for deposit insurance there.

16. Of course, since "big money" also is "smart money," it may run first, and to the extent that authorities are concerned about a potential "systemic" crisis, they may elect to cover uninsured and large depositors, even including interbank claims, either through the deposit insurance fund or some other facility. Thus during the Continental Illinois difficulties in the United States, deposit insurance was extended to all creditors.

17. At times, governments have exceeded their own coverage limits, but the empirical findings recounted below show that having lower ceilings does seem to matter.

18. The requirement in EU law for member states to cover a common euro amount of deposits has placed upward pressure on coverage levels in countries aspiring to EU membership.

19. In the United States, as in some countries, there is a limit on the total amount of funds in the deposit insurance fund. Once that limit is reached, banks are no longer assessed until funds drop below the ceiling. In this situation, banks face a zero premium, and clearly no risk differentiation.

20. Demirgüc-Kunt and Detragiache (1999) found—although in a small sample of 24 countries—that the cost of crises also was higher with deposit insurance and weak institutional environments.

21. Similar arguments have been made in regard to foreign exchange reserves.

22. Any message that the coverage will be limited seems to be discounted in such institutional settings.

23. The latter can be significant in emerging markets, where it has taken from months to as long as eight years for depositors to be paid in accordance with deposit insurance statutes.

24. Neither private nor public systems, however, were designed for systemic crises, but rather to prevent episodes of individual bank failure from mushrooming into a systemic problem.

25. According to the La Porta and others (1997) database, Germany ranks among the highest in the protection of creditors' rights. Also, as Beck (2000) reports, although only fraudulent bankruptcy is subject to prosecution, in Germany fraud can include violating "orderly business practice," which can be broadly interpreted. Hans Gerling, a principal of Herstatt Bank, contributed about 150 million DM to creditors to avoid legal entanglements after that bank failed. Moreover, the German Banking Act prohibits any manager involved in fraudulent bankruptcy from ever holding a managerial post in banking—as determined by regulatory officials rather than criminal prosecution.

CHAPTER THREE

Government Failure in Finance

SINCE THE ADVENT OF BANKING, BOTH IN NORMAL TIMES and in times of crises, governments have taken ownership positions in banking either deliberately or indirectly as a result of a banking crisis. Instances of failed state owner-ship of banks, privatization followed by crises, and at best limited success in bank restructuring have occurred with sufficient frequency that a reconsideration of government's role in these related areas is overdue. Although many governments have retreated somewhat in their ownership stake in the banking sector in recent decades, government bureaucrats remain active in banking, and in the wake of crises regularly increase their involvement significantly, often for lengthy periods. Yet new research shows that, whatever its original objectives, state ownership tends to stunt financial sector development, thereby contributing to slower growth.

The stable and efficient provision of financial services—regardless of who owns the financial firms providing them—is a realistic goal for all countries, the achievement of which necessitates that governments focus on what they do best. The previous two chapters set out an ambitious agenda for government's role in laying the foundation and creating the regulatory superstructure for sound finance for development. This agenda will be difficult to achieve if the authorities' attention is absorbed by tasks in which they do not have an advantage, notably permanent or temporary ownership of banks, especially when the latter role conflicts with their position as regulator.

Whereas the previous chapter treated how governments should respond to handle *market* failures, this chapter reviews the evidence and makes recommendations on *government's* failures in owning and restructuring banks. Government failure as owner is attributed to the incentives imposed on it by the political process. The few cases of more successful

Government ownership of banks tends to stunt financial sector development—

as the political process distorts incentives

state banks appears to be linked to a stronger institutional environment and dispersed political powers. Without these advantages, authorities in developing countries generally need to reduce their ownership role, consider creative ways to use the private sector during crises, and focus on their agenda as provider of infrastructure and as regulator. Paradoxically, just as it may take a crisis to induce governments that are already in the sector as owner to get out of it, so too can crisis bring in—as temporary owners—governments that previously retreated or were not active in banking. When large systemic crises do occur and the government acquires an ownership stake, or otherwise takes control, strategies to secure its prompt and early exit should be part of the initial intervention design.

This chapter first reviews the arguments and evidence on state ownership of banks, combining both cross-country evidence with that of some individual country cases. It then turns briefly to a discussion of and evidence on the sequencing of bank privatization. Privatization without the necessary institutional framework has led to crisis and fiscal costs and thus should be tailored to country circumstances. A *credible* policy of preparing some banks for sale, coupled with new entry, including by foreign private banks, while improving this framework, appears to be sensible in weak institutional settings.

This chapter then turns to governmental failures as temporary owner during restructuring. Not surprisingly, some of the same principles adduced to the state's behavior as a long-term owner of banks also are applicable to this issue. Indeed, in times of crisis, bank restructuring is an opportunity for significant injections of fiscal resources, and it is important not only to limit the cost to taxpayers and the economy from the injections themselves, but to avoid reliance on bureaucrats to identify 'winners and losers.' Working with the market again emerges as a key consideration for a strategic crafting of government's response.

Bureaucrats as Bankers?

DESPITE MUCH DISCUSSION AND SOME HIGHLY PUBLICIZED increases in private sector activity in most countries' banking systems, more than 40 percent of the world's population lives in countries in which the majority of bank assets are in majority-owned state banks (figure 3.1). A glance at the map suggests that government ownership tends to be greater in poorer countries, as confirmed in figure 5 of the Overview.

Figure 3.1   State ownership in banking, 1998–99

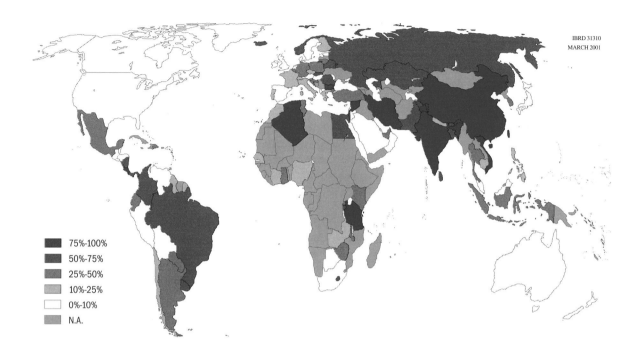

Note: The map shows the percentage of assets in state-owned banks; most of the observations are from 1998–99 (the World Bank Survey of Prudential Regulation and Supervision) and, where that data was not available, from La Porta, Lópes-de-Silanes, and Shleifer (2000). Thus, some very recent ownership changes, notably in Latin America, are not taken into account.

Source: World Bank survey on Prudential Regulation and Supervision, and other World Bank sources.

The incidence of state ownership has declined since 1970 (figure 3.2), but with the largest decreases in high-income countries. Over 30 developing countries, as of the late 1990s, continued to have over *half* their banking system assets in majority state-owned banks. Given that control is possible even with a lower share of ownership, these figures necessarily represent a lower bound on state control.

State ownership in banking continues to be popular in many countries for several reasons. First, proponents of state control argue that the government can better allocate capital to highly productive investments. Gerschenkron (1962) was among the first to make the case that in a weak institutional environment, private banks would not be able to overcome the deficiencies in information and contracting, or that it would take too long to do so. In the 1950s and 1960s, when many were looking for ways to have developing countries "take off" into self-sustaining

Figure 3.2 Government ownership of bank assets

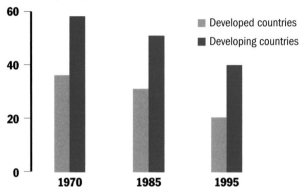

Share of the assets of the top 10 banks owned or
controlled by the government

**State ownership of banking still
is important in developing
countries.**

Source: La Porta, López-de-Silanes, and Shleifer (2000).

growth, state ownership of the banking sector appeared to be the way to
do it, a view that some may continue to hold. State ownership also makes
appropriation of the surplus from finance (financial sector taxation) and
directing credit much easier.

Second, there is the concern that, with private ownership, excessive
concentration in banking may lead to limited access to credit by many
parts of society. Indeed, one argument often heard in developing countries is that governments are reluctant to privatize because it would lead
to a concentration of credit at the expense of many groups in their country. Third, a related popular sentiment—reinforced by abuses at and
governance problems of private banks in many countries—is that private banking is more crisis prone. Rather than allocating resources wisely,
such failures as Barings Bank and Long-Term Capital Management
(LTCM—a hedge fund whose risky strategy was funded and mimicked
by banks) suggest to some that private banks will be more concerned
with gambling, a belief reinforced by postprivatization crises in countries such as Chile (in the early 1980s) and Mexico (in 1994).

A return to the focus of the previous chapter on incentives, however,
makes the first point debatable, because bureaucrats do not face incentives designed to reward efficient resource allocation. Elected officials
tend to be motivated by securing their political base and rewarding sup-
porters, a role that could conflict with that of resource allocation. And
all three arguments are very much empirical propositions.

Until recently, the primary evidence on this issue has been anecdotal. Although poorly regulated private banks have incurred large losses that are passed on to depositors or, more frequently, to taxpayers, some of the largest losses in history have been incurred by state banks. Two famous and long-established banks, Credit Lyonnais (nationalized by the French government in 1945 and privatized in 1999) and Banespa (purchased in 2000 by the Spanish bank BSCH, but previously owned by the State of São Paulo in Brazil), for example, each ran up losses estimated in the range of $22–28 billion under government ownership. It is now possible, however, to go beyond isolated case studies. Systematic analysis of available cross-country data indicates that state ownership, especially in low-income countries, is bad for financial sector development and stability, as well as for economic growth.

The key study, that of La Porta, López-de-Silanes, and Shleifer (2000), uses data from private industry sources covering the 10 largest commercial and development banks for each of 92 countries for 1970 and 1995, and finds that greater state ownership of banks in 1970 is associated with less financial sector development, lower growth, and lower productivity, and that these effects are larger at lower levels of income, with less financial sector development, and with weaker property rights protection.[1] Since they are using state ownership in 1970 to explain subsequent financial sector development and growth, there is no possibility that the latter is causing the former. Also, in explaining growth, they control for a wide array of institutional variables.[2] La Porta, López-de-Silanes, and Shleifer find that the channel from state ownership to lower growth is through the impact on productivity. State banks do not generally allocate capital to its highest use. Based on earlier research (chapter 1), through this channel, growth must be reduced as well, and they find no offsetting influence of state ownership on capital accumulation.

La Porta, López-de-Silanes, and Shleifer show that the effects of increasing private ownership are not only statistically significant, but economically meaningful as well. For example, the fitted regression line suggests that, had the share of government ownership in Bangladesh been at the sample mean (57 percent) throughout the period from 1970 instead of at 100 percent, annual average growth would have risen by about 1.4 percent, cumulating to a standard of living more than 50 percent higher than it is today. Although this projection holds other measured variables equal, applying the guidance of box 1.1, it needs to be noted that the implied privatization would also have had to be

The data are convincing: bureaucrats generally are bad bankers—

particularly in less developed economies

127

supported by the necessary institutional underpinnings emphasized below, a significant omitted variable in their approach.

State ownership tends to reduce competition—

Using a different data source, Barth, Caprio, and Levine (2001a,c) show that greater state ownership of banks tends to be associated with higher interest rate spreads, less private credit, less activity on the stock exchange, and less nonbank credit, even after taking account other factors that could influence financial development.[3] Thus greater state ownership tends to be anticompetitive, reducing competition both from other banks and from nonbanks. Barth, Caprio, and Levine also note that where state ownership is greater, the number of applications for bank licenses that are rejected tends to be higher and there are fewer foreign banks. With less competition, it would be surprising if greater state ownership led to a wider availability of credit, and La Porta, López-de-Silanes, and Shleifer instead find that the greater the state ownership, the larger is the share of credit going to the top 20 firms.[4]

limit access to credit—

and may heighten the risk of crisis

Last, state ownership appears to heighten the risk of crises. Admittedly, though Barth, Caprio, and Levine identified a positive impact of state ownership on the probability of a banking crisis, this impact was not statistically significant with their data.[5] But La Porta, López-de-Silanes, and Shleifer found that greater state ownership is correlated with various measures of financial instability. And, applying a logit model to the La Porta, López-de-Silanes, and Shleifer 64-country data set, Caprio and Martinez-Peria (2000) are able to show that greater state ownership at the start of the 1980–97 period was associated with a greater probability of a banking crises and (with far fewer observations) higher fiscal costs.

The above evidence is consistent with the theme of the last chapter on incentives. Rather than responding to principles of profit maximization, governments tend to be responsive to various interests, and especially to bolstering their support (box 3.1). Indeed, even within the gamut of state ownership, there is some evidence that form matters: Cull and Xu (2000) find that in the 1980s—when direct government financing was more available—Chinese state bank bureaucrats did a superior job allocating credit compared with government agency employees, that is, bank finance was allocated more in line with firm productivity than were direct transfers. One possible reason: these state bankers were paid bonuses related to the profitability of the bank. A contributing factor may have been the availability of direct budgetary funds to meet government agencies' needs, implying less pressure on state banks to engage in

Box 3.1   Political economy and financial policy

MOST PRESCRIPTIONS FOR FINANCIAL SECTOR policy implicitly envisage a government that seeks to achieve the common good, but this picture neglects both the incentives facing political actors and the political structures within which they operate. Even if they are not motivated by personal financial objectives, these actors are everywhere concerned with their political futures, and are therefore often beholden to sectoral interests. The extent to which sectoral interests hold sway over the decisions of political actors depends, in turn, on the political rules within which they operate, and perhaps also on social norms (cf. North 1999).

The nexus between the political arena and special interests in the financial sector can be especially close if only because (to quote Willie Sutton, that notorious bank robber of the 1940s) finance "is where the money is." All too often it has been the self-interest of government decisionmakers that has created and sustained the distorted incentives in the financial sector that have led to crisis, or even to the diversion of resources of state-controlled financial institutions to political or personal ends. What hope is there that good financial policy will be adopted if it is against the interest of the powers-that-be?

The persistence of a dysfunctional regulatory approach may thus be partly explained by politicians, as well as official regulators, having been "captured" by those they should be regulating. Regulatory policy is then more easily seen as operating in the private interest rather than that of the general public.[1]

Analyzing the role of political economy in influencing the worldwide shift toward financial liberalization, Kroszner (1998) has pointed out the way in which shifting technologies that alter the relative bargaining power of different interest groups, or the policy preferences of existing interest groups, can be influential in determining actual policy changes.[2]

Likewise, employing the same data on fiscal costs discussed in the text below, Keefer (2000) has recently explored the deeper political determinants, both of the fiscal costs of banking crises and of the propensity to exercise regulatory forbearance during crises. His hypothesis is that socially costly government forbearance action to shore up the financial system under its current management, or to allow the pursuit of risky behavior, may be adopted by politicians in order to ensure financial or political support from these interest groups, especially if political structures are weak. He provides evidence suggesting that, at least in less financially developed economies, checks and balances (as quantified in Beck and others 2000) do help to reduce both the fiscal costs of financial crisis and the probability that forbearance will be exercised.

Political economy analysis of such issues is clearly only beginning, but promises to be a fruitful area of research whose results will help ensure that government power is not misused in the regulation of finance.

1. Revealing the influence of contrasting political interests in different U.S. states, Kroszner and Strahan (1999) show that legislators from states with many small banks opposed the extension of interstate banking.

2. Romer and Weingast (1991) demonstrate similar patterns of influence in the run-up to the S&L crisis.

For instance, the first entry of foreign banks into several emerging markets has often been restricted to merger and acquisition, thereby securing the capital value of their remaining franchise—which might otherwise be competed away by the newcomers—for the existing owners. Likewise, when securities markets were being liberalized, partly to meet the government's need for additional loanable funds, most emerging markets opted for the sealed-bid, first-price auctions of government paper, generally thought to be more advantageous to primary dealers at the expense of the taxpayers interests.

inefficient directed lending. Indeed as direct government financing of state-owned enterprises (SOEs) declined in the early 1990s, the linkage between the credit decisions of state bankers and productivity faded.[6] In most settings, private banks are even more isolated from political pressures, which accounts in part for their superior performance. It is important, however, to note that in transition countries, abrupt privatization of banks is unlikely to work, as noted below, and some state ownership may be necessary as a buffer during the transition process.

State ownership can lead to a conflict of incentives

The first two chapters suggested that finance, including banking, will lead to faster growth and fewer crises where the information and contracting environment is stronger and where there are sufficient, well-motivated monitors to oversee intermediaries. With greater state banking, there tends to be less demand for better information and other parts of infrastructure, and weak monitoring. Barth, Caprio, and Levine find that monitoring by the market tends to be significantly weaker with higher state ownership. Governments are exposed to an incentive conflict when they have significant state ownership, as one part of government is then charged with monitoring another, so monitoring by official supervisors can be expected to be weaker as well.

State ownership need not always be bad for growth: La Porta, López-de-Silanes, and Shleifer find that at higher per capita income levels, the negative effect diminishes to become insignificant. Germany, with a longstanding tradition of high state ownership (as of 1998, 42 percent of commercial bank assets being in state-owned banks) is a clear outlier, but several other high-income countries, such as France and Italy, had periods in which state ownership was pronounced, though both have decreased this in recent years.

Governments with greater checks and balances and better institutional development might be expected to have more positive results from state ownership, both by providing better official and market oversight of government banks. Keefer (2000) finds that better checks and balances help to reduce both the fiscal costs of financial crises and the probability that forbearance will be exercised.[7] The quality of information, the vigor of contract enforcement, and even the personal stigma associated with nonrepayment of debt all can be expected to affect the costs of state banking. In developing countries, state-owned banks tended to allocate credit to state enterprise, which may explain the above-mentioned finding of weak productivity, as well as the outliers. Germany, for example, has had little state ownership of the enterprise sector (outside transport and finance), which has made it easier for bureaucrats to avoid the temptation of allocating credit to government firms. Moreover, the tough penalties in Germany for default and bankruptcy mentioned in chapter 2 help to make life easy for most banks, even those that are state run.

In sum, the data show poor performance of state banks in several dimensions. They tend to decrease financial sector development and economic growth, to concentrate credit, and to increase the likelihood and cost of banking crises. Although the findings do not demand elimination of all state ownership, the evidence is consistent with moving to sell government banks in a number of countries, especially where they dominate the sector. While it remains possible for developing countries to find ways to limit the damage done by state ownership, limiting such ownership itself will likely be easier to implement than the many institutional and political reforms needed to limit the abuses and inefficiencies of state banking.

Privatizing Banks

Evidence from countries that have made significant reductions in state ownership of the banking sector, though limited, confirms the above picture of the costs of state ownership, reveals the difficulty of bank privatization, and contains lessons for how it might be better conducted. The most detailed examination is for Argentina, which has seen a significant decline in the degree of state ownership—from about 50 percent of banking system assets in 1990 to half that level in 2000—and is consistent with the cross-country evidence. Clarke and Cull (1998) provide simulations of the present value of savings from privatizing Argentina's provincial banks and found impressive gains. Even if *nothing* were recovered from the residual entities that took over loss-making loans at the time of sale, and basing the simulations on the period 1991–96 (a time of general economic expansion when the banks should have been earning profits), the savings amounted to one-third of a typical province's public expenditure and could have financed its 1996 deficit for 12 years. Somewhat more realistic assumptions on recoveries put the savings at more than half government expenditure, and this with a high discount rate. Stated differently, the cost of retaining governmental ownership was large, and the cost of these injections, in combination with the discipline associated with the convertibility plan, led to privatization efforts.

The fiscal costs of state intervention add to the pressure to privatize

Figure 3.3 Nonperforming loans, Argentina, 1991

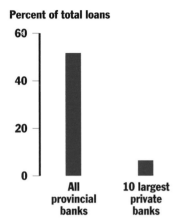

Percent of total loans

Source: Clarke and Cull (1999).

As seen in figure 3.3, prior to privatization, Argentine provincial banks were having serious difficulties: nonperforming loans (NPLs) were high and increased further after the preprivatization audits (mandated for banks accessing the Fondo Fiduciario, box 3.2). After the audits, and as a part of the actual sale, essentially all NPLs were removed from the balance sheet. Subsequently, the share of NPLs rose again, but only to levels comparable to the better private banks in Argentina. Since then, the privatized banks have remained more or less on par with other private banks on NPLs (although NPLs in 2000 went up at all private banks because of the general economic slowdown).

More generally, the newly privatized banks' balance sheets and income statements began to resemble more those of other private banks, especially in terms of their administrative costs relative to their revenues, and most importantly in terms of credit extended to public enterprises (figure 3.4, which shows the second cohort of banks that were

---

Box 3.2 Can bank privatization be sustained?

ALTHOUGH ECONOMISTS ALWAYS HOPE THAT THEIR research changes the minds of politicians, the lags between the establishment of new results and policy change can be long. Why else would politicians privatize banks? After all, state ownership frequently provides easy financing of government deficits and provides a source of political patronage in the form of jobs at the state banks and access to credit.

Argentina provides interesting insights. A decade ago, all 20 provinces owned at least one of the 27 provincial banks, which were found to have generally low portfolio quality, low efficiency, and low returns. Yet these banks remained state-owned until the Convertibility Plan ended their access to the discount window and also limited central bank funding of federal deficits. Thus provincial politicians no longer could hope for cheap financing and funding of provincial bank losses. With the Tequila Crisis in late 1994, the provincial banks were affected by a depositor run, forcing a reassessment of the state ownership decision. Given the (then) short maturity

of Argentina's capital markets, it would have been difficult to stretch out the financing of the bad assets in these banks, so the World Bank and the IDB helped create the Fondo Fiduciario, which extended loans to help provinces stretch out the costs of privatization, but only after newly established "good" banks—representing the good assets of the provincial banks—had been sold. As a result, about half the provincial banks were sold by late 1997, and by 2000 this ratio rose to two-thirds.

Still, politicians have a tendency to hang on. The weakest banks (highest NPLs) initially were the ones most likely to be privatized, and indeed postsale audits showed that their performance was worse than previously believed. On the other hand, large, overstaffed banks, which provide greater patronage, were less likely to be sold. This suggests that in countries with a few large state banks, either politicians—or their public— will have to be swayed by research results, or it will take a large crisis or significant tightening of their access to federal financing to get them to privatize.

Source: Clarke and Cull (1999).

Figure 3.4   Lending to state-owned enterprises in Argentina

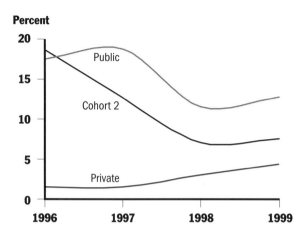

Note: The second cohort of 5 banks was the first group to be sold with assistance from Fondo Fiduciario (see box 3.2).
Source: Clarke and Cull (1999).

sold between September 1995 and March 1996). This dramatic change in lending supports the finding from the cross-country research that enhanced productivity follows privatization, in that SOE credit likely represented low-productivity loans. As part of the privatization process, the shedding of staff or their more efficient employment, though less significant for the overall economy, works in the same direction.

Notwithstanding this evidence, it is unclear to what extent bank privatization will continue, or how best to foster it. Argentine provinces only began privatization in earnest when their access to cheap refinancing and covering of losses was eliminated. Even then it took a crisis to accelerate the process (box 3.2). Other countries, such as Hungary, have first recapitalized banks before concluding that privatization was necessary to limit the cost to taxpayers.

Bank privatization is politically difficult, and if the same political forces continue in place, it is not likely that it will be successful. Argentine and Hungarian authorities clearly were motivated by the costs of maintaining state ownership. As seen in box 3.3, countries often turn to bank privatization only after long delays and sometimes failed restructuring.

Beyond waiting for crises, a possible way of fostering the sale of state banks is to encourage more rigorous enforcement of prudential regulation for all banks, so that the state banks' weaker position—and hence higher possible cost to taxpayers—will be evident, as it became in

Privatization can be politically difficult

133

Box 3.3 The rise, reprieve, and fall of state banks in Africa

EVEN AFTER LONG DELAYS, WHERE THE SAME strong interests that derailed earlier reforms still dominate a country's politics, outcomes from bank privatization will tend to be disappointing. This argues for most assistance to countries in which privatization is deemed to be politically desirable, feasible, and credible. Most African countries opted to create at least one large state bank after independence to support indigenous industries and state ventures, and to make banking services available for the broad population, including those in rural areas. In many countries these big state banks still dominate the banking sector and, after decades of politicized management and soft budget constraints, have been difficult to restructure or privatize. The disappointing results from restructuring and generally on privatization can be seen from three countries that attempted banking reform programs during the 1990s: Ghana, Tanzania, and Uganda.

Ghana

Ghana started economic reforms in the early 1980s after a politically unstable period of heavy state involvement in the economy. The state owned three commercial banks, three development banks, and the Cooperative Bank. There were also two foreign banks and a merchant bank.

All the state-owned banks were restructured and recapitalized under the financial reforms that started in 1987, with bad loans removed to an AMC. Management was improved through extensive technical assistance.

Both before and after restructuring, the primary function of the Ghanaian banks has been funding the deficit of central government and public enterprises (this averaged 73 percent of domestic credit in the 1990s). The very high T-Bill yields received by the banks helped offset the continued loan losses from other lending.

Bank privatization has been a stop-go process, being held up, for example, by disagreement be-

tween the privatization agency and external estimates of values on the price. With the program years behind schedule, the government decided to sell some shares in two state commercial banks domestically even before finding a strategic investor. This made it difficult subsequently to reduce the price to attract a strategic investor. Eventually, in late 1996 the government dropped its requirement that the strategic buyer should be a bank, and managed to sell the Social Security Bank to a consortium of foreign investment funds. By 1998, this newly privatized bank had about 13 percent of total banking system assets.

The largest bank, Ghana Commercial Bank (GCB), continued to have problems even after the restructuring of the late 1980s. With the failure of a planned sale in 1996 to a Malaysian manufacturing firm, it remains government-controlled, with just 41 percent held by Ghanaians after the initial public offering (IPO). In preparation for privatization in the mid-1990s it was found that there were serious reconciliation problems in the accounts and shortcomings in management, and some of the loss-making branches had never been closed. In 1997 the entire senior management of GCB had to be removed in the wake of a check fraud scandal.

Tanzania

Tanzania was starting to liberalize after two decades of African socialism. Twelve banks had been nationalized in 1967 and merged into a dominant commercial bank, National Bank of Commerce (NBC), which had a virtual monopoly for 25 years. The only other financial institutions were a small cooperative bank, which was also controlled by the state, and a few specialized state banks for housing.

By the mid-1980s, the NBC was insolvent, illiquid, and losing money at an alarming rate. Restructuring moved a significant portion of the NPLs out of the bank, closed some loss-making

(box continues on following page)

Box 3.3 *(continued)*

branches, and retrenched staff, but operating costs as a percentage of assets doubled and spreads became negative in 1992. The bank was recapitalized in 1992, but as the losses continued to mount, restructuring intensified with an "action plan" in 1994 that changed the board of directors, curtailed lending and laid off further staff. However, the salaries of the remaining staff were doubled by the new board of directors, thus offsetting the reductions in costs. The benefits from removing bad loans to the AMC were short-lived. By 1994, 77 percent of the remaining loans were nonperforming.

In 1995 another attempt to restructure failed. Finally, National Commercial Bank (NBC) was split in November 1997 into two banks and a holding company. The NBC holding company took the non-banking assets, for example, staff housing and the training center. The business bank, NBC-1997, took all lending and 45 percent of the deposits, and a service bank took the remainder of the deposits. The National Microfinance Bank was to provide basic depository services to the general population, and took the small deposits but no lending. The decision to set up a microfinance bank that would keep the rural branch network may have softened some of the political opposition to the privatization of the business bank. The separation proved difficult. Poor financial and operational controls led to the need for significant provisions on unreconciled balances, and there was a significant delay in producing financial statements after the split.

NBC-1997 was sold to the South African bank, Amalgamated Banks of South Africa Group (ABSA) in late 1999 with IFC participation. The microfinance bank remains unsold, but is now focusing on the provision of payments and savings services in its 95 branches.

Uganda

By the early 1990s, as Uganda was just starting to reemerge from the economic devastation of the tur-

bulent 1980s, the government had stakes in all nine commercial banks, and owned the largest two: Uganda Commercial Bank (UCB), with about 50 percent of the market, and the Cooperative Bank. As of late 1991, about one-third of the loans of UCB were nonperforming, and the negative net worth of the bank was estimated at $24 million.

Timid restructuring efforts started. Loss-making branches were converted into agencies rather than being closed. The AMC that was to take bad loans was not created until 1996 and, even then, there was a significant lag in transferring bad loans. There was a performance agreement in 1994 between the Ministry of Finance and the bank's board of directors, but the strategy pursued was to try to reduce the proportion of NPLs by growing the loan portfolio. Bank supervisors did not monitor compliance. Every improvement in profitability was temporary and losses continued to mount. By mid-1996 the financial position had deteriorated so that its negative net worth tripled from earlier estimates.

While the government's intention was that the restructuring would culminate in privatization, management of the UCB was actively opposed to sale. Eventually, after three years of unsuccessful attempts to restructure the bank, it was agreed that a reputable merchant bank be selected to implement the sale, giving the buyer greater freedom to define which assets and branches were to be purchased. Again there was a lag, and the merchant bank was finally hired in February 1996 and, at its request, top management was finally changed in July 1996. Losses were mounting throughout the delay, and UCB was losing market share. Audited financial statements for 1997 showed another fall in interest income, wiping out the core profits advertised to investors six months earlier. With few expressions of interest, a sale agreement was signed in late 1997 with a Malaysian industrial and real estate company. By December 1998, however, the deal had unraveled amid allegations of corruption.

Argentina during the crisis and then more clearly after the banks were sold. Notwithstanding the political forces that may favor limited information, the current international attention to international standards might encourage greater transparency and thus this result. Also, mandatory publication of the audits of state banks, preferably by international firms, will allow the owners—the country's citizens—to see what they own. Where privatization is limited by concerns about financing loan losses prior to sale, funding from multilateral development banks can help to stretch out the costs of privatization where longer-term markets are not sufficiently developed. As Clarke and Cull (1999) note, however, the fact that weaker banks are more likely to be sold suggests that preprivatization injection of funds should be avoided, as it may decrease the probability of sale and also can easily be squandered.

Privatization should be phased along with improvements to the infrastructure—

Since bank privatization can yield real benefits, and as there is considerable public ownership in many countries, moving to sell banks would appear to be an immediate imperative in many developing countries. When it occurs, though, privatization can also be badly designed and lead to crises. Stated differently, the above comparison on the gains from less state ownership were for "other things equal," such as the quality of financial sector infrastructure and the regulatory environment, and provided no sense as to the speed and sequencing of bank privatization.

Experience is both limited and ambiguous. Chile (with bank privatization in 1975 and a crisis in 1982) and Mexico (1992 and 1994, respectively) both appear to have been cases with an underdeveloped regulatory and supervisory framework, and both have made remarkable strides since their crises. The emphasis was on speed of sale, which was accomplished, but the costs of the subsequent banking crises (about 42 percent and 20 percent of GDP, respectively) were high.[8] Although both crises featured multiple causes, a weak regulatory environment appeared important and is widely acknowledged to lead to fraud, looting, and then crisis. While it is entirely possible that these problems then produce a lobby for better financial infrastructure and regulation and ultimately faster growth, as arguably occurred in Mexico and Chile, privatization in a weak framework, followed by crises, is just as likely to provoke opposition to market-based reforms. Thus, in order to avert postprivatization crises, authorities as soon as possible should strengthen these elements and exercise some caution—while still moving forward—in the privatization of the banking system. A *deliberate and credible* phasing out of state ownership over some period while the environment is being improved accordingly is suggested.

The Argentine case noted above supports this sequencing argument. On the eve of privatization they had a reasonably developed regulatory and infrastructure environment for finance, and indeed by 1997 had one of the toughest bank regulatory environments among emerging market countries (World Bank 1998). Minimum capital ratios were 11.5 percent, with risk weights varying as a function of credit and market risk. In addition, banks faced stiff disclosure requirements and were compelled to issue subordinated debt, and liquidity requirements were high (20 percent, with an extra 10 percent in the form of a puttable swap for dollar assets), among other factors. Moreover, the system as a whole was anchored by the top ten banks, nine of which by 1997 were majority foreign-owned, and the mix of public and private oversight, recommended in chapter 2, largely was in place. The decision to embark on a program of bank privatization in such a strong regulatory environment can be made with greater confidence.

—and the regulatory environment

When the environment is weak, however, the need for care in the privatization process has been dramatized by the experience in transition countries, where there is the risk of capture of the legal, regulatory, and supervisory apparatus by insiders, or oligarchs (Hellman, Jones, and Kaufmann 2000). Those who capture control of this apparatus and banks will soon become oligarchs. Whereas bureaucrats have been shown to be bad bankers, oligarchs may be even worse. More generally, when there is "regulatory capture," either through corruption or the control of banking and its regulation by the same interests, neither market nor official regulatory forces will work to support efficient and equitable development. The full story of the privatizations in Mexico in the early 1990s, with the purchase price sometimes allegedly paid from insider bank loans, and resulting in looting behavior that brought many banks down during the Tequila crisis, is only gradually coming to light (cf. the recent analysis by La Porta, López-de-Silanes, and Zamarripa (2000) mentioned in chapter 2 above). It too reinforces the need for an adequate regulatory environment for privatization.

Rapid privatization can come unraveled—

but excessive delays will have real costs

Still, the conundrum is that although premature privatization in weaker environments can lead to significant problems, lagging bank privatization can undermine real sector reforms. The costs of delay are amply demonstrated by the Czech Republic, which tried to move fast in the privatization of nonfinancial firms, but slowly in selling banks. Chapter 1 already touched on aspects of the acute problems of governance associated with the Czech experience when the assets of many privatized firms were looted during the 1993–96 period. Another aspect of this story was the way in which some of it was facilitated by continued lending from public sector banks (box 3.4).

Box 3.4 Looting in the Czech Republic

OBSERVERS CRITICIZE THE CZECH VOUCHER privatization as having led to tunneling, according to which dispersed ownership facilitated asset stripping from firms that had little effective corporate governance. Some go further and argue that tunneling occurs in legal systems that do not protect minority shareholders rights well (Johnson, McMillan, and Woodruff 2000). Cull, Matesova, and Shirley (2001), however, argue that tunneling cannot be the entire story, because once the most attractive assets were stripped, owners would have no more incentive to increase their equity position—precisely what occurred. They posit instead that there was looting—owners and managers of firms with low net worth borrowing and then defaulting on the debt—and control of firms a ticket into this game.

Although there should be limits to looting—banks might only be "stung" once—the dominance of the state as an important owner apparently allowed this activity to continue during the period 1993–96. According to La Porta, López-de-Silanes, and Shleifer's (2000) data, the government had a majority interest in just over half the banking system and a 20 percent stake—a level that has been found to be sufficient to give control—in 100 percent of the banking system. Cull, Matesova, and Shirley (2001) find that joint stock firms controlled by investment funds underperformed all others, and their ability to take on liabilities at a faster rate—borrow from the state banking system—contributed significantly to this performance.

The authors conclude that privatization design for the corporate sector is of second order importance compared with the need to create a competitively oriented banking system that will allocate credit in line with commercial, rather than political, practices.

Source: Cull, Matesova, and Shirley (2001).

Tunneling—the appropriation of the firm's assets by insiders—can occur even with private banks, but sustained looting—defined as borrowing with the expectation of not repaying—can only continue if the lending banks are not particularly concerned about their bottom line or can get compensated from government, both characteristics of public banks.

Privatize deliberately but carefully

Thus maintaining the status quo with a significant share of state-run banks can be dangerous for the economy. Moving slowly but deliberately with bank privatization, while preparing state banks for sale and addressing weaknesses in the overall incentive environment, would appear to be a preferred strategy. Preparation, in addition to improvements in infrastructure, could include some linkage of compensation for senior managers to the future postprivatization value of the bank, such as through stock options—an approach that appears to have helped in Poland. To be sure, this approach can only succeed if the process is credible, otherwise the deferred compensation will be too heavily discounted to have any value. Prolonged "contracting" of private managers likely will not work in banking, where it is too difficult to observe the outcomes of managers' decisions.[9] And, as mentioned, preprivatization recapitalization appears to be unwise, because it both risks dissuading officials of the need to sell the bank and can lead to a squandering of taxpayers' resources. Publication of as much information as possible on the privatization process and vigorous oversight by the media will help limit the ability of insiders to dominate, but this itself requires that the media be active and independent.

Countries that can attract foreign entry from good foreign names—an ability that likely will increase as e-finance drives down the cost of entry (chapter 4)—and from different countries are in a stronger position. Even though the regulatory environment may not be reliable, strong foreign banks both would bring good skills, products, and even a capacity to train local bankers, and would presumably be motivated to protect their reputations to behave in line with the highest fiduciary standards. Where powerful domestic interests or oligarchs are a barrier to sound banking, some reliance on foreign banking (see chapter 4 on its rise in some countries) may be the best alternative for development, even though it can be politically difficult to accept. Still, the possibility that foreign banks may be engaged in risky or criminal activities suggests that authorities cannot abdicate their own "due diligence." Regulators in home countries may be legally constrained by the information that they can share, but they should be as proactive as possible to alert developing and transition country authorities to concerns about their own banks—even if it is merely helping to translate—in language and in meaning—information that is available in their own, deeper markets.

Political factors undoubtedly will determine the speed of privatization. The experience of several countries, including Argentina and Hungary, suggests that where state banks are smaller, fiscal pressures greater, and political patronage lower or more dispersed, it will be easier to privatize (Clarke and Cull 2001).

Precisely how much needs to be done until a country can privatize its banks and how much of its banking system it can privatize in a given regulatory environment are decisions that necessarily have to be made on a case-by-case basis and undoubtedly involve art as much as science. What has been shown at this point is the direction of change that will help increase living standards in low-income countries. To be sure, the process of bank privatization is difficult, but the gains seem to be substantial.

Governments as Caretakers

Governments are often forced to take ownership positions during a crisis—

For more than a hundred years we have known what to do in a financial crisis: have some organization show up with a lot of money to restore confidence, have it lend freely to fundamentally sound organizations that need cash, and have it rapidly close down and liquidate businesses that aren't going to make it even if the crisis is successfully resolved. This is the way to restore confidence, and to keep the financial system doing its job of channeling money from savers and investors on the one hand to businesses that need capital on the other.

Bradford De Long (2000)

EVEN GOVERNMENTS NOT DISPOSED TO TAKE A LARGE(R) ownership position in the banking sector may find that bank owners have exercised the "put" option of handing over the bank's deposit liabilities with insufficient assets to repay them, especially in times of systemic crisis. Governments often then become involved in restructuring banks and even their assets—nonfinancial firms—in the process. In many cases, systemic crisis has led to significant increase in government ownership or "caretaking," even of some banks that have just recently been privatized (Mexico). This increase has tended to persist (figure 3.5). Yet the aforementioned evidence on governments' efficacy as "permanent" owners of banks implies that they will not excel at temporary ownership—restructuring failed or failing banks—either. In particular, if there is a tendency for political forces to dominate the economic judgments of bureaucrats in normal times, this tendency is even more marked during a systemic crisis, when the injection of substantial sums is in the offing, and the financial fate of powerful interests will be determined. This section considers what research can tell us about general principles—strategy, not tactics—for how governments should behave when crises raise the issue of injecting funds into the banking system.

but need to develop an exit strategy from the start

Systemic bank restructuring is a difficult and complex undertaking, and typically needs to be linked to wider corporate restructuring. The practitioners' literature calls for a comprehensive approach. Here we will not attempt to discuss the issues in any detail—not least because they have not yet been subject to systematic empirical investigation.[10] Some points, however, will be made on bank restructuring, in particular to highlight a simple though important message. Because government is not effective as a bank owner, it must devise its approach to bank restructuring to ensure that it gets out of a temporary caretaker position as

Figure 3.5   Government ownership of banks during the East Asia crisis

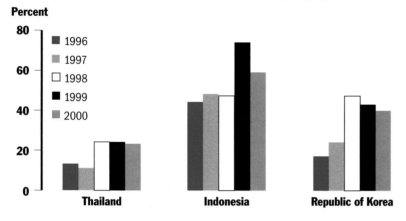

Assets in state banks, relative to total banking system assets

Note: Data is for year-end, except for the latest data, which is March 2000 for Thailand, and June 2000 for Indonesia and Republic of Korea.
Source: World Bank.

Government ownership of banks in time of crisis.

soon as possible. It must not use this position to pick the "winners and losers" itself, but rather should rely on the private sector for this key function. This message can be—and has been—carried over to the restructuring of corporates.

When a banking crisis occurs, authorities need to decide when and how to intervene. Much has been written on the former, starting with Bagehot (1873, to whom De Long refers above). When the problem is not systemic, bank creditors and supervisors should be left to proceed as usual. Indeed, well motivated subordinated debt holders and other creditors will have likely signaled the problem by not renewing credits and by pushing up the spreads at which problem banks borrow.

How should it be ascertained that a crisis is systemic, or when should the government intervene with other assistance? Although the application of mechanical trigger rules to this area is appealing—for example, all banks are on their own unless output has fallen by x percent or export or some other prices by y percent—most indicators either are available only with a lag (GDP), or are partial indicators of the severity of a problem (for example, the exchange rate). Moreover, the announcement of a rule based on specific commodity or stock prices or indices, interest rates, or exchange rates, can induce greater risk-taking once market participants are armed with the knowledge that some specific downside is covered. If a government states that it is willing to coinsure against a given decline in

Governments should only intervene when a crisis is systemic—

but defining a systemic crisis is not easy

141

an economic indicator, it may well be expected to intervene before that point is reached. For example, if authorities commit to intervene in crises if GDP falls by 5 percent—aside from the problem of estimating output—markets may expect support well short of that decline, to the point that intervention even in mild recessions might become the norm.

One possibility recently advocated (Mishkin 2000) is to announce a policy that, even in a systemic crisis, the first bank that fails will certainly not be bailed out, in the hope that each banker's uncertainty as to whether they will be first will motivate them to guard against excessive risk-taking. In this context, however, failure is usually a regulatory decision. Perhaps because of the difficulty of defining when a bank has become insolvent, this option has not yet been chosen in any country. Instead, many central bankers have decided on constructive ambiguity as the main solution.[11] Having chosen an approach based on discretion here, there are implications for the choice of how to intervene, noted below.

Given that the decision to intervene has been taken, that is, the problem is judged to have become "systemic," the government has several goals. First is to maintain or restore a functioning financial system. This goal is difficult to debate, though the best means of doing so are not always clear.[12] A second goal is to keep the lid on the budgetary cost of the crisis. Far from these costs being predetermined, research suggests that an easy or accommodating approach to intervention policy—before and after the crisis—can result in greatly magnified costs to the budget (and hence, as observed in chapter 2, in overall economic costs). The third goal, linked to the second, is for the government to ensure that their action helps decrease the likelihood of a subsequent crisis.

Fiscal Costs of Policy Choices

Does policy choice matter much in determining the fiscal cost of banking crises? Honohan and Klingebiel (2000) provide direct evidence as they examine the impact of different forms of intervention:

- Liquidity support of 12 months or longer in excess of total banking system capital.[13]
- The issuance of a blanket guarantee for depositors.
- Two measures of forbearance: (a) permitting insolvent banks to remain open, or (b) suspending or easing prudential regulations to redefine solvency.

- Repeated recapitalizations of banks.
- The formation of centralized asset management companies (AMCs, more on which below).
- An across-the-board public debt relief program.

Using regression analysis, they examine how much of the variation in the fiscal cost of 38 crises in industrial and developing economies (1980–97) can be explained using these indicators plus macro variables (the real interest rate and stock prices). They find that open-ended liquidity support, regulatory forbearance, and blanket deposit guarantees are significant contributors to fiscal cost, and tellingly the signs of all these variables are positive. Strict policy—less of each of the above variables—results in lower fiscal costs. To check for reverse causality—did big crises cause the easy policies—the authors try an instrumental variables, two-stage least squares approach, and find their original results confirmed.[14]

This lesson seems well illustrated by the experience of several African countries (box 3.3 above), whose insolvent and illiquid state-owned banks were given a reprieve in the mid-1990s as donor resources were mobilized to restructure them. The results of bank restructuring efforts there, drawn out as they were over a number of years, were disappointing. In some cases, banks were stabilized by extremely high interest rates offered on their holdings of government bills—in effect, an ongoing recapitalization.

As seen in table 3.1, the impact of these policies is large. Even relaxing one policy variable while maintaining strict values for the others still results

Easy policies can raise fiscal costs

Table 3.1 Estimated individual impact of an accommodating approach to resolution policies

Type of accommodating measure	Cases where it was used (percent)	Cost of adopting each accommodating measure (percent of GDP)
Forbearance (a)	24	6.7
Multiple recapitalization	24	6.3
Liquidity support	58	6.3
Forbearance (b)	84	4.1
Debt relief	21	3.1
Blanket guarantee	55	2.9

Note: The table shows how much each accommodating measure can add to fiscal costs. For example, permitting insolvent banks to stay open (forbearance a—see text) pushes up predicted fiscal costs by 6.7 percent of GDP, which is double the sample mean (each calculation uses the sample mean value of the other variables).

Source: Honohan and Klingebiel (2000).

in a substantial increment in costs—a plausible result, as any channel for government funding to banks in trouble can result in similar opportunities for rent seeking. Indeed, the much larger impact of, say, liquidity support compared with guarantees is likely a statistical artifact of the sample. Taken to extremes, as it often has been, open-ended liquidity support (through the lender-of-last-resort) is an alternative to announcing a blanket guarantee, and might only influence which government agency provides the funds. Many times the central bank ends up as the de facto owner of a bank to which it has provided what had been envisaged as merely temporary liquidity support. Of course, it would be disingenuous to interpret these results to mean that governments can switch from a previous policy of ease prior to a crisis—such as the Chilean forbearance of 1977 (box 3.5)—to a strict policy in the midst of a crisis and enjoy such large gains.

Still, the lesson that the consequences of easier intervention policies are significant for the fiscal position is important. Some point to the fact that industrial countries have engaged in forbearance, leaving insolvent banks open, as a justification for developing countries to do the same. To be sure, authorities have a choice to make, but industrial countries both generally have stronger regulatory and supervisory capacity, meaning that they are more likely to be able to control risk-taking—the clear threat when insolvent institutions continue in operation. Moreover, rich countries, with higher incomes and better-developed tax regimes, can better afford what appears to be second-best (or worse) policy. Thus, some argue that the cost of the U.S. savings and loan crisis would have been about one-fifth its final cost had it not been for forbearance—but still the total bill was under 3 percent of GDP.

Last, fiscal costs and cash costs are not the same. One common trap is for those designing restructuring plans to become preoccupied with minimizing the up-front cash costs of recapitalization at the expense of higher longer-term fiscal costs and neglect of the incentives that are created for the restructured banks (Honohan 2001c). Yet the former are small relative to the latter.

Sending the Right Signals

An intervention should be designed to reduce the likelihood of a subsequent crisis

The third goal noted above is the need to ensure that the manner in which authorities deal with the crisis provides signals and incentives that help decrease, rather than increase, the likelihood of a subsequent crisis. This may be the most difficult goal to weight appropriately in the midst

Box 3.5   Intervening sets the stage for the next crisis

FOLLOWING DECADES OF NEGATIVE REAL INTEREST rates and state ownership, Chilean authorities privatized banks in 1975 and in 1976–77 essentially allowed free entry into banking and finance. By late 1976 ten finance companies became insolvent, and then Banco Osorno. Initially the government announced that the central bank would "back" the bank, and then created an explicit deposit guarantee for banks, finance companies, and savings and loan associations, up to about $3,000—a limit it then breached for Banco Osorno depositors. Prior to this failure, the banks seemed to have been acting as if they did not expect government support, and the bankers' association even tried to organize a pool to cover failing banks, much like U.S. bank clearinghouses of the 19th century. Depositors also ran to the largest banks.

Banco Osorno clearly was gambling, but this does not presume that the owners thought that they would be able to put the losses to the government. Instead, they may well have been planning to pass the losses on to depositors, which is consistent with the prevalence of "self-lending," in their portfolio. One factor in the government's response was that the problems appear to have been a surprise, as they only had 10 bank inspectors for 14 banks and 26 finance companies, and these inspectors, because of the recent decontrol, could not have had significant experience with supervision.

Although the authorities allowed the finance companies to fail, and began to improve supervision, the failure of another bank (Banco Español) in early 1980, which was first sold to another business group (with no public or private capital injection) and then taken over by government in late 1981 with larger losses, signaled that government support was available. Although macroeconomic factors undoubtedly played a major role in the 1982 crisis, lax incentives stemming from earlier interventions appears likely. For example, by the end of 1981, real loans were six times the level of 1976, or an annual average growth rate of 43 percent. Banks were doubling their real portfolio every 18 months, not the usual behavior for bankers that are concerned about their own capital. As de la Cuadra and Valdes suggest, this appears to have been Ponzi finance on a large scale, and the lack of early rescue activity, when the problem did not appear to be systemic, shares part of the blame for the ensuing collapse, whose ultimate fiscal cost was more than 40 percent of GDP.

Source: De la Cuadra and Valdes (1992).

of a crisis, but perhaps is the most important. While governments should be prepared to change their role in a systemic crisis, such as by becoming a caretaker for banks, their approach and the actions they take need to be designed in such a way as to convince participants that this is a "one-time" event. One way is by making sure that the consequences of excessive risk-taking are borne by those who undertook them. Such a focus on incentives will also help restrain fiscal costs. As noted in box 3.5, the consequences of giving short shrift to this goal can be dramatic.

To see the importance of attention to incentives, consider what happens to firms outside the financial sector operating close to or actually in a state of insolvency. Those in control of these firms get the message

Reduce the conditions for moral hazard—

quickly that their poor performance is going to be costly to them. They generally find it difficult or impossible to raise new funds in any form. This precludes acting on profitable investment opportunities and may force the firm to sell important assets. All their creditors recognize that insolvency may also distort the incentives of management, making them more susceptible to fraud and moral hazard, and at the least reduces the incentives of owner and managers to exert effort.

Yet, in a private market economy, the economic functions of major nonfinancial firms need not cease when the firms themselves become insolvent. To the extent that they have a profitable core group of activities and new investment opportunities, the creditors' interests may be best served by continuing their operations. In addition, most firms have made large investments in fixed capital goods that are often difficult to resell. As long as the net present value of the firm's operating profits and tax losses carried forward exceeds its liquidation value, it makes sense to continue operations—albeit with minimal new investment, the divestiture of noncore activities, and the installation of new management. This is what a successful restructuring of a firm will achieve. What is relevant is that the imbalance between assets and liabilities is dealt with not by obtaining injections of new equity, but by marking down liabilities and equity to conform to the new, lower value of the assets and future cash flows. Equity holders generally see most of their claims wiped out while debt holders often have a portion of their claim converted to equity. New funding is provided *only* after this "marking to market" takes place. At the same time, old management is often replaced, a substantial portion of the firms' assets are sold, and workers are laid off. In other words, this is not a mere reworking of the firm's balance sheet, but rather very real changes are made in the way it does business, perhaps even in the business it does. For the economy, the happy result is that resources continue in their best use while all parties incur some costs for the firm's poor performance.[15]

In large part the restructuring of banks should follow the same general principles. Admittedly, banks differ from other firms in two senses: first, as noted in chapter 2, their particular fragility, and the possibility of contagion; and second, their centrality in the payments and credit mechanism. Banking in many economies may only count for a few percentage points of value added in the GDP statistics, but unlike any other sector of similar size or greater, has major macro implications when it is in distress. Although these differences justify a different approach in banking

—by imposing real costs on all involved parties—

and get resources back in productive use

compared with other financial and nonfinancial areas, they do not suggest that incentives matter any less. Indeed the evidence presented above on the links between bank ownership and financial sector development confirms that private incentives are every bit as important in this sector.

Unfortunately, as implemented in many countries, government-funded bank recapitalization programs—injecting capital usually in the form of bonds into banks—either mute or totally squelch the message that poor performance is costly, leaving out or minimizing the real restructuring. Recapitalization to support existing liabilities by itself leaves creditors completely protected, but forces no downsizing of the bank, no layoff of employees, no reallocation of peripheral assets to better uses; reduces the pressure to pursue delinquent borrowers; and even can reduce the accountability of regulators to the general public. Indeed, recapitalization without exacting some claim from the bank—and really exercising it—amounts to a transfer from taxpayers to shareholders, which is the group that keeps the residual value of the entity.[16] Yet, even in crises that owe their origins mainly to macro events, some banks virtually always are discovered to have been taking on substantial risk, so it is important that this message be sent, adjustments made, and consequences felt.

Many recapitalization programs avoid real restructuring

Restructuring is when the message is sent that this is the opportunity for making changes to ensure that banks are (back) on the track to providing needed financial services and allocating credit to its best uses. Note that many of the above messages that need to be sent are harsh ones, such as laying off staff or informing previously and possibly well-heeled and well-connected shareholders and senior managers that they are, in effect, wiped out. Clearly the losers from this process are much more narrowly concentrated than the larger society, which will reap the gains of greater efficiency and faster growth. Governments and the political process are not well suited to this task. As seen above, the government has no comparative advantage in banking itself, and even the basis for determining which banks get funds is not simple and straightforward—if it were clear, that is, if information problems were easy to solve, it would have been easy to prevent the losses in the first place. For the harsh messages that are sent as part of restructuring, not only is this not a clear area in which the public sector excels, but also one that is ripe for abuse. *The selection of individual winners and losers is what markets, not governments, do best.*

The market is better able to deliver the bad news

Nevertheless, some government involvement is required if taxpayer funds will be injected. Again, the debate can be framed in terms of the rules vs.

Government involvement should aim to protect the interests of the taxpayers—

discretion approach, though here the outcome is somewhat different. It is relatively easy to observe whether the government is providing support, and indeed most governments are eager to claim credit for such. Hence, leaving some discretion to officials as to *when* to intervene does not create significant opportunities for abuse. The size and targeting of support to individual banks, however, is more difficult to evaluate (does the choice make sense?) and monitor (is support being used well?), and creates a case for a greater reliance on a rule-based approach. Governments that inject equity will want to make sure that it is used wisely, that is to make sure that it goes to banks that are the least insolvent, regardless of the cause of the crisis, because there is a strong and necessary presumption that the most insolvent banks attained that status by dint of excessive risk-taking. If this presumption is not made, and the riskiest banks are not treated harshly, financial history teaches that banks will assuredly embark on an even riskier path. As agents of their country's taxpayers, authorities will also want to ensure that their funds are not looted. Yet they must recognize that they do not function well as bank owners and therefore can only take temporary equity positions in banks. One way to achieve both goals is for authorities to make some amount of funding available for recapitalization of banks, but only to those who do the following:

and to use the private sector to pick winners and losers

- Secure matching of private sector funds in some ratio.[17]
- Restrict dividends that can be paid or withdrawals by private partners and individual borrowers until the government is fully "bought out." Even the amounts and structure of compensation contracts for senior managers, such as by granting them deferred compensation in the form of stock options tied to the bank's equity value several years in the future, need to be controlled.
- Adhere to stringent transparency requirements.

As long as the amount of funding is such that some banks fail, this approach removes government from decisions as to which banks survive. The availability of (truly) private sector funding serves to identify the candidates, and the restrictions on different ways to take these funds out of the bank, combined with greater transparency, makes it more likely that the banks will not be looted and facilitates prompt exit by the government.

Consider the three banks shown in figure 3.6. All three are affected by a crisis, but Bank A's capital ratio—with sound accounting practices—is not expected to fall below the minimum 8 percent ratio assumed to hold in regulatory guidelines. Bank C, on the other hand, is assumed to

Figure 3.6   Stylized evolution of three banks through a crisis: sound, salvageable, and doomed

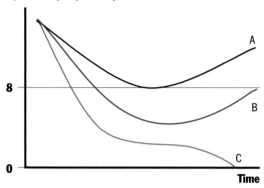

Source: Adapted from Ingves and Lind (1996).

continue to worsen, and it is important that it be closed, downsized, or split up, with the good bank surviving alone or merged. Banks like bank B appear to be salvageable, and this decision should depend on the time it would take for profits to be sufficient to rebuild capital and then earn returns for private owners. Private buyers are getting a claim on the franchise value of the bank—its future profits—and it is important that it be their expectations of profitability and their money that identifies the banks worth saving.[18] Government officials will need to be alert to other attempts to loot the surviving banks, and the failure of the banks engaging in the most excessive risk-taking will help convince market participants that the program is credible.

These are tough criteria, and only desperate banks will agree to such terms. That is the point: government assistance should only be injected into banks in dire straits, yet simultaneously to those with a real chance of survival. By openly stating the terms on which it will assist banks and their (new) shareholders, and ensuring that those terms provide good incentives for the restructured bank going forward, the government is making the best use of market forces while minimizing its direct ownership involvement.

This strategy is fine on paper, but will it work in practice? By and large, it already did, as many of these features characterized the U.S. Reconstruction Finance Corporation's (RFC's) program of taking temporary preferred equity positions in banks (box 3.6). Bank failure was clearly still

Box 3.6   Lessons from the Reconstruction Finance Corporation

THE RECONSTRUCTION FINANCE CORPORATION (RFC), which lasted from 1932 to 1957, loaned or invested more than $40 billion, mostly with funds borrowed from the U.S. Treasury or the public. As in many crises, initially it was thought that the banks were merely illiquid, but by 1933 officials realized that many banks had solvency problems and needed to be closed or needed additional capital, so a preferred stock program was established. At its peak, the RFC had capital positions in 5,685 banks, representing 40 percent of all insured banks in the United States. Officials' discretion was limited because "once the RFC received an application for assistance from a financial institution or commercial and industrial enterprise the agency only had the power to evaluate whether asset values were sufficient to secure assistance" (Mason 2000, p. 4). The combination of "sound asset values" with the restriction that the RFC could not hold more than a 49 percent stake in a bank (or firm) was intended to ensure that RFC funds did not go to deeply insolvent banks.

To be eligible for this program, however, banks had to agree to limit dividends and devote earnings to retiring the stock of the bank—essentially, buying out the government's position. Also, by law the identity of all recipients of any RFC assistance was made public, reducing the chance of political favoritism.

RFC staff had clear incentives. Hiring and promotions were outside the civil service framework, and much of the staff was located in decentralized field offices around the country that functioned relatively autonomously *provided* that they showed a profit. Intervention from Washington, including the possible replacement of field directors, occurred if the profitability guidelines were not met.

Individual deals had different features, not surprising in light of the RFC's decentralized structure. Some were contingent upon raising funds from the public, others upon capital infusions from management, and some of both that also relied upon the replacement of key officers and directors with those approved by the RFC. The consistent attention to safeguarding taxpayers' funds and the deliberate harnessing of the private sector stand out in this program.

It may be difficult to evaluate the success of efforts such as the RFC, but in this case, the intervention appears to have contributed to a recovery of confidence and output (until monetary tightening reversed both in 1937). The government recovered its initial capital and did not keep alive nonviable banks. In recent years, it is difficult to point to many similar records. Interestingly, the RFC took the same basic approach in its involvement with corporate restructuring, and saw similar success.

Source: Mason (2000 and correspondence with the author).

allowed: several thousand fewer banks opened their doors following the bank holiday of 1933, and failures continued for banks that did not meet the RFC's criteria. Selling this program to the banks was difficult—in a crisis, bankers can get into a game of "chicken" with authorities, as the next program may be more generous than the current offer. However, the requirement that when the U.S. deposit insurance system opened in 1934, only healthy banks would be allowed in, finally helped persuade banks in trouble to issue preferred stock to the RFC. Governments already offering explicit depositor protection can encourage participation by dropping coverage for weak banks that do not opt in to the program.

With the increase in the sophistication of financial engineering since the 1930s, it is not surprising to find a huge variety of innovative financial instruments being employed around the world in recent restructuring plans. They represent attempts—often ingenious, but not always successful—to tailor the government's commitments to the particular incentive issues involved. Careful, market-sensitive design of these instruments is essential if they are to be successful in achieving the desired effects at the least fiscal cost (cf. Honohan 2001c). Sometimes the terms have been too tough to attract new private capital. Sometimes the financial engineering has brought liabilities into the bank's balance sheet whose eligibility as capital could be disputed.

Once in the program, the issue for government is how to extricate itself as quickly as possible, and how it performs while being a temporary owner of banks and even of enterprises. Each of the banks that is saved then becomes a key player in the restructuring process for individual firms. Like the RFC, which took temporary equity positions under the same stringent terms in nonfinancial firms, restructuring agencies may also become involved at the firm level. But the essence of the approach is that it is decentralized, with firms' creditors, among which banks usually are key, taking the lead.

Instead, a centralized approach with banks' nonperforming loans being hived off into an AMC rapidly has become recommended practice in recent years, in part because of the apparent success of this approach in Spain in the early 1980s. Their success can be assessed in different dimensions. Klingebiel (2000) proposes the following:

- Did the AMC achieve their narrow objectives for which they were set up? (For those charged with rapid asset disposition, did they dispose of assets within a 5-year period? For restructuring agencies, did they sell off 50 percent or more of the assets under management within 5 years?)
- More broadly, did the banking system return to solvency, without problems reappearing, and was credit growth resumed? That is, did the banking system experience repeated financial distress, and did real credit to the private sector resume?

Unfortunately, it appears from Klingebiel's study that Spain was the sole clear case of success, in satisfying all these criteria, of seven countries

Shallow capital markets make restructuring harder in emerging markets

that included Finland, Ghana, Mexico, and the Philippines. The remaining cases, Sweden (1992) and the United States (1989), met the narrow criteria, but not the broader ones within a two-year window, although they did so quite well subsequently with clear recoveries, and should be classified as relative successes. Only Sweden's agency was charged with restructuring (box 3.7) and, like Spain and the United States, had the clear advantage that real estate and consumer loans dominated their portfolio, which can be bundled together and sold off in deep capital markets. In contrast, emerging markets have seen a greater prevalence of crises entailing significant effects on the corporate sector—with such loans being more difficult to restructure—and they lack the deep capital markets for asset sales.

Box 3.7   The Swedish experience: a Saab in every garage?

SWEDEN, WHICH EXPERIENCED A BANKING CRISIS in the early 1990s (and then a currency crisis with the realignment in Europe), often is held up as a model for developing countries to emulate in bank restructuring. With the onset of the crisis in late 1992—although problems were visible in the previous year—the government stepped in with a blanket guarantee covering all forms of bank debt. Securum, a "bad bank," was established to take over nonperforming loans, and later a Bank Support Agency was created. It gave out at least one guarantee—a promise to inject equity should a bank's net capital fall below 9 percent—which was not utilized. Securum moved quickly to dispose of assets, repackaging them and selling them relatively quickly—on the stock exchange and through other channels—and was completed by 1997. The net cost of the operation was estimated to be 2.1 percent of GDP, well below earlier fears.

Although these achievements were substantial relative to the potential size of the problem, Sweden enjoyed a number of advantages that many developing countries do not have. First, as noted in the text, many of the assets were real estate, which in contrast to

corporations are not that demanding in reorganization skills. Moreover, when developing countries find that many of their large enterprises are in need of restructuring, the political difficulty rises significantly. Second, a relatively homogeneous population and well-developed democratic institutions were an incomparable advantage in dealing with the disposition of assets. Thus, for example, the political opposition was represented on the Bank Support Agency, and there was a high degree of transparency for both agencies. Third, the legal framework was highly favorable to enforcement of bankruptcy. As Klingebiel notes, they score higher than the United States in enforcing creditors' rights, meaning that officials had a credible threat to speed up efforts. And funding and skills were not a constraint in the restructuring process.

Developing countries can aspire to these advantages, but they can also aspire to having a Saab in every garage. Without these advantages, it is not clear that the model as a whole is exportable. Some features, such as the lack of government interference with the private management of the banks, as in the RFC case (box 3.6) may be the most relevant parts of this lesson.

Sources: Englund (1999), Ingves and Lind (1996), and Klingebiel (2000).

Applying the same criteria to the Republic of Korea, Indonesia, and Thailand does not add to the clear success list, because there has been a marked tendency for the AMCs to hold on to assets. Because it has not yet been five years since they were established, Klingebiel's criteria could still be met. Still, the record with centralized AMCs in emerging markets is that they have a tendency to become long-term dumps, rather than active warehouses, for nonperforming loans. Although this result can be partly related to some characteristics of emerging markets—shallow capital markets and a dearth of restructuring skills—the record is also consistent with the failure to use the private sector in a transparent manner to identify those fit to survive. Interestingly, Mexico recently adopted a forced auctioning of assets if mediator-led reorganization efforts fail, which appears to be jump-starting a stalled process, and illustrates the promise of arm's-length rules and quick exit as a cornerstone for government's approach.

Greater concentration of firm ownership and wealth in recent crisis countries suggests a greater scope for abuses with the centralized AMC approach, and yet simultaneously greater difficulty in using the private sector. One remaining option is to use foreign entities, either to assist in managing the process or to buy and restructure problem assets, with the clear difficulty being that many societies are not prepared to have "national assets" pass from their hands. Otherwise, in line with the Becker-Stigler criteria, it will be important to ensure a great degree of transparency for the process, and high-efficiency wages to those involved in it (recalling the discussion of an appropriate balance of terror in chapter 2) can help reduce the likelihood of abuses. A serious threat that wrongdoing by public officials will at least result in their loss of a (sizable) pension may be the best tool to induce honest conduct. Successful resolution of banking crises will require a change of mindset and will win the confidence of domestic residents and foreigners alike. The outright failing of some banks at the start of the process, and convincing all that remaining banks are fit to survive, is the key to success, and using the private sector to identify the latter is the best practice available.

Conclusions

INCREASED POLITICIZATION OF BANKING DECISIONS WHEN THE government is involved means that the incentives for efficient and sound intermediation are impaired with state ownership, whether it is longstanding or temporary. Governments that attempt to be both owner and regulator likely will achieve success at neither. Cross-country and limited case study evidence shows that state ownership of banking leads to less development, less access to credit outside the largest firms, and a higher risk of crisis. Country authorities necessarily have to balance the hazards of privatization with the losses from state banking. A gradual program of credible privatization, preparing banks for sale and developing the regulatory infrastructure for participation by more private banks, appears to be a sensible path to navigate the dangers of action and inaction.

This evidence also suggests that authorities need to be planning for their own exit whenever they take a temporary stake in banking as part of systemic restructuring. As in earlier chapters, working with the market has been argued to be the preferred course for government, especially in letting market forces pick winners and losers. Foreign banks can play an important role in taking over from the state, all the more so if there is genuine concern about a few insiders dominating both banks and the bank regulatory apparatus.

Notes

1. The La Porta, López-de-Silanes, and Shleifer (2000) data could be limited by the focus on the top 10 banks, but as they note in virtually all countries this captures a large percentage of the banking system, which they have defined it to include development banks. However, the Barth, Caprio, and Levine (2001b) data, which are based on a survey of regulators, provides estimates of the percentage of assets in majority-owned state banks, and their data are highly correlated with that of La Porta, López-de-Silanes, and Shleifer for the 1990s.

2. In their growth regressions, these variables include: years of schooling, initial level of financial and economic development, inflation, the black market premium, an index of government intervention, tax and subsidy rates, and latitude.

3. Specifically, real GDP per capita, corruption, expropriation risk, bureaucratic efficiency, and the law and order tradition of the country. This study, as with most of the data underlying figure 3.1, is based on the World Bank Survey of Prudential Regulation and Supervision, and re-

fers to the percent of the entire commercial banking sector assets in majority-owned state banks, as of 1997–98.

4. Additionally, Cetorelli and Gambera (2001), who find some positive effects of greater bank concentration in promoting the growth of industrial sectors in need of external finance, report that this gain is negated by greater state ownership.

5. Although the original Barth, Caprio, and Levine (2001a) paper with about 60 countries found only an insignificant link between state ownership and crises, their forthcoming study, based on 105 countries, finds a significant link.

6. State bank lending to SOEs reportedly declined again in the late 1990s.

7. For countries with deep financial systems, the conclusion is reversed, which may also be rationalized by a political-economy argument, though less crisply. Proximity to the next election also appears to deter socially

costly policy reactions to crisis, reinforcing the message that political constraints are important. The variables employed by Keefer to indicate the level of public information available do not perform as strongly in the regressions, but are not inconsistent with the theory.

8. Postprivatization losses also can rightly be blamed, at least in part, on preexisting losses and weak initial conditions. Although many transitional economies experienced bank failures in the immediate years after transition started, often these problems occurred in state banks, represented the manifestation of losses in the prereform era, or were inevitable given the real sector turbulence, and virtually always were associated with a weak regulatory framework.

9. Governments could even consider retaining ownership and contracting out the management of banks to private parties, but perhaps fortunately have not done so, as management contracts have been found to work only in industries in which quality is easily verified and reputation is paramount (World Bank 1995). Thus hotels are an example satisfying both criteria for management contracts: output quality can be monitored by anyone (it is easy to see if the towels are clean) and quality matters (hotels with dirty towels lose business). However, it is difficult for depositors, creditors, supervisors, and even management to evaluate the health of bank portfolios, that is to tell if their portfolio is clean. And since the importance of reputation—once paramount in banking—in most countries is diminished by the presence of implicit or explicit deposit insurance, banking is not well suited to management contracts. Perhaps in recognition of this fact, there has been little experimentation with contracting out in banking.

10. A partial list would include Claessens, Djankov, and Klingebiel (1999), Dziobek (1998), Garcia (1999), and Lindgren and others (2000), and sources cited therein.

11. It may appear to be inconsistent for the authorities to maintain a constructive ambiguity about their policy stance, while insisting on transparency from others. There is clearly a tension between policy certainty and the strategic advantage to be gained from discretion. But, provided the government is seeking the common

good, there seems no reason to refrain from using strategic tools denied to private agents.

12. The common view, one that authorities have difficulty resisting, is that they must be proactive in rescuing depositors in a crisis, yet Baer and Klingebiel (1995) showed that in 5 crises in which depositors were allowed to take losses, there was a prompt recovery of output.

13. Many central banks limit liquidity support from the discount window to a short period, from 7 days to several months. Normally banks coming in for repeated liquidity support are subject to increased supervisory attention and indeed forced to seek other sources of funds, including where it exists the deposit insurance facility.

14. The instruments they employ—a measure of government corruption and the law and order tradition—rank high in terms of exogeneity. Also, they check a regression of the residuals on these instruments, and find no significance.

15. Actually, the same is true for banks: Bartholomew and Gup (1999) show that in non-U.S. G-10 countries, banks in most cases are rarely closed, and usually any liquidation involves a transfer of part of the bank's operations to other, presumably viable, banks.

16. State banks often are recapitalized—even though it is not clear how capital on their balance sheet differs from the contingent claims they hold on their governments—without sacking managers or other adverse consequences.

17. When banks are sold, the identity of the buyer matters—both Uganda and Ghana (box 3.1) had costly 'failed' privatizations to foreign manufacturing companies, which demonstrates the importance of finding 'fit and proper' buyers. Consistent with the message of this section, relatively clear definitions should be set out elaborating these criteria.

18. Since profits will depend on entry into the banking sector, authorities likely will have to agree to some limits on bank entry, otherwise prospective returns will be insufficient to attract responsible investors.

CHAPTER FOUR

Finance without Frontiers?

"Actually, every society that is based on an ancient structure and opens its doors to money sooner or later loses its acquired equilibria and liberates forces thenceforth inadequately controlled. The new form of interchange jumbles things up, favours a few rare individuals and rejects the others. Every society has to turn over a new leaf under the impact."
Fernand Braudel, *Capitalism and Material Life, 1400–1800*

I**N COMPARISON WITH THE SCALE OF GLOBAL FINANCE,** financial systems in individual developing countries are exceedingly small. China aside, only Brazil has a financial system as big as 1 percent of the world total. This chapter begins by explaining how small financial systems fall short of minimum efficient scale and that they have much to gain by sourcing some financial services from abroad.

Small systems increasingly interact with global finance

Along with the rapid—albeit uneven—expansion of international debt and equity flows, including foreign direct investment (FDI), there has also been a sharp recent increase in the provision of financial services in many developing countries by foreign-owned financial firms. In these three main dimensions, debt, equity, and services, financial globalization enlarges the scope for obtaining growth and other benefits from finance, but it also increases the risks. How far will this process go? In what respects should it be limited? In other words, what part of finance should remain domestic, and what should be provided from abroad?

This chapter continues by outlining the costs and benefits of capital account liberalization and proposing, as a basis for the remainder of the discussion, the premise that tight controls that result in a permanent wide gap between actual and market-clearing exchange rates and real wholesale interest rates are no longer a practical option.

Then the three main dimensions of financial internationalization are considered in turn:

- Internationalization of the provision of financial services, including entry of reputable foreign banks and other financial firms, can be a powerful generator of operational efficiency and competition, and should also prove ultimately to be a stabilizing force.
- Equity flows, including FDI, have tended to be larger than debt flows in recent years. We argue that the gains from admitting foreigners in terms of risk diversification likely outweigh any imported volatility in the price of listed equity.
- In regard to debt flows, the key variables are the interest rates and exchange rates at which the flows are contracted. Liberalization has resulted in domestic interest rates that are volatile and too high in many developing countries, reflecting exchange rate and other policy risks, and requiring careful risk management by financial intermediaries.

This chapter concludes with some remarks on the accelerating importance of technology and communications—a familiar feature of international finance, which has always been at the cutting edge, and is now reaching new heights with the advances of "e-finance."

Financial systems in developing economy are all small—
Against the backdrop of a vast global system, all but a handful of developing economies have financial systems that appear tiny. Taking the money supply (M2) as a rough but convenient overall measure, apart from China, only Brazil has more than 1 percent of the world total.[1] A mere 15 other developing countries even reach a threshold of 0.2 percent of world M2. Indeed, seven major countries account for fully three quarters of world M2, and, again leaving China aside, low- and middle-income countries account for only 9 percent (figure 4.1). The distribution of stock market capitalization is even more skewed. In effect, the market power of any developing country in global finance is altogether negligible. The financial systems of all developing countries are small and should be managed with that in mind.

Many systems are *extremely* small. Over 200 million people live in some 60 member countries of the World Bank whose tiny banking systems' assets fall short of $1 billion—the size of a single small bank in any of the advanced economies. Many of these countries also have small populations, but others are relatively large countries—nine of them with a population in excess of 10 million—whose financial systems are very poorly developed.

Figure 4.1 Share of developing economies in aggregate world money stock

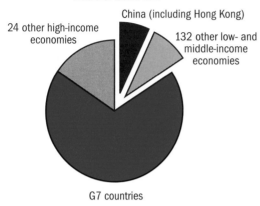

Share of world M2

China (including Hong Kong)

24 other high-income economies

132 other low- and middle-income economies

G7 countries

Source: International Financial Statistics.

Small financial systems underperform. They suffer from a concentration of risks. The smaller the financial system, the more vulnerable it is to external shocks and the less able its financial system is to insulate or hedge those shocks—unless the financial system is itself securely integrated in the world financial system through ownership and portfolio links. Small financial systems provide fewer services at higher unit costs, party because they cannot exploit economies of scale, and partly because of lack of competition. Regulation and supervision of small systems is disproportionately costly (Bossone, Honohan, and Long 2001).

For these countries, the policy imperatives of smallness are acute. They need to think in terms of outsourcing both financial services themselves (actively seeking to attract foreign-owned banks, insurance companies, credit registry firms, and so on) and some aspects of financial regulation.

They need to seek cooperative arrangements with neighboring countries in such dimensions as regional stock exchanges and international, regional cooperation in regulation of the securities, insurance, and banking industries. Examples of this sort of cooperation already exist, notably in West, Central, and Southern Africa, in the Eastern Caribbean, and in the Persian Gulf area (as well as in Europe). More will come.

Some services are more easily outsourced than others. For example, in considering the design of the arrangements for private provision of pensions, even in a small country the government may want to mandate contributions, create a collection system, and set minimum standards for pension contracts. As argued by Glaessner and Valdés-Prieto (1998),

—and smaller financial systems are more vulnerable to both domestic and external shocks

though, it could license international companies to offer those contracts to local contributors. In this case, the small country would be de facto importing supervision services, and avoiding much of the infrastructure needed for domestic securities markets.

There was a time when establishing a country's position in the world seemed to require a steel-making plant and a national airline. Economic realities mean that policymakers in those fields are now more concerned with the quality and cost of the steel that is available and the safety and reliability of air services, and with ensuring that airport infrastructure is adequately planned. In the same way, financial sector policymakers in small countries will increasingly think in terms of ensuring the quality and prices of needed financial services through regulatory and incentive design, regardless of whether those services are provided domestically or from abroad.

Capital Account Liberalization: Costs and Benefits

The move to capital flow liberalization has been fairly recent—

T HE GUSTING WINDS OF FOREIGN COMPETITION AND OF international capital flows have now been blowing through the financial systems of most developing countries for a decade or more. Yet it is not so long since most domestic financial intermediaries and markets operated behind substantial and effective regulatory barriers to international borrowing or lending, or more generally to international trade in financial instruments, and to cross-border ownership of financial firms.

It sometimes seems that a boom-and-bust roller coaster has been imported when the capital account has been liberalized. Undoubtedly, with the wrong incentives, this has been a threat, but there have also been tangible gains from external liberalization, and above all there is an inevitability about further opening-up to foreign capital markets and financial institutions.

After opening up to the rest of the world, individual countries are sometimes net importers of funds, sometimes net exporters. Sometimes an inflow or outflow of equity investments is balanced by an offsetting cross-border flow of debt finance. The maturity of inward and outward flows can also be different. Apart from the international flows that are involved, cross-border provision of financial services becomes important, and some of the financial firms operating locally may have foreign ownership.

Advocates of free capital movement point to several advantages, going beyond the static gains attributable to reallocation of loanable funds from capital-rich to capital-poor countries.[2] Because local equities can now be combined in a much wider portfolio, they become effectively less risky. That should increase their price, lowering the cost of capital for local companies. This in turn can make viable investment opportunities previously seen as too risky to finance, and in aggregate these can add substantially to growth. There is some evidence of an investment boom being associated with liberalization of equity markets. What is more important is that the quality or productivity of investment should also improve if the arrival of reputable foreign providers of financial services is associated, as it appears to be, with the kinds of improvements in the functioning of the financial system that come from financial development as discussed in chapter 1. (We review empirical evidence on some of these channels below.) Other dynamic advantages include the transfer of technology that can be embodied in or associated with capital inflows, and a possible disciplining effect on macroeconomic policy.

As international capital flows expanded, especially after 1973, concerns about their impact broadened from fear of speculative attack on an exchange rate peg, to a fear of macroeconomic destabilization triggered by overenthusiastic and reversible inflows. Numerous instances have been observed where capital flows, which had had the macroeconomic effect of bidding up local labor costs, have suddenly stopped (Calvo and Reinhart 2000), throwing the recipient economy into a recession. Nor are the victims of these sudden stops always countries where macroeconomic policy has been weak or the economy has been overheating.[3]

Despite a huge research literature, there is nothing near a professional consensus on whether the net impact of full capital account liberalization on growth, poverty, or volatility should be regarded as favorable or not. Growth regressions, which include various measures of international financial openness in growth regressions, tend to suggest either that there is no statistically significant relationship (Kraay 1998; Rodrik 1998c), or that any such relationship is limited to higher-income countries (Edwards 2000d).

—and there is no consensus on the net benefits

What is clear is that setting policy to cope with the stresses, as well as to take advantage of the benefits, of internationalization on the domestic financial system presents one of the greatest policy challenges today.[4] The impact and importance of international capital movements clearly extends beyond their impact on domestic financial intermediaries and markets. They are in the front line, however, and cannot remain unaffected because, regardless of what measures may be put in place to restrain capital movements, the actual openness to such movements is unlikely to diminish, given the rapid and continuing improvements in information technology and communications, allowing more and more of finance to be conducted across frontiers at essentially zero cost. While measures of control that have intermittent effect—that is, although constantly in place, they only bite in a crisis—could remain viable, the steady impact of other measures will be increasingly limited.

This, then, is a premise of the remainder of the chapter: that governments can no longer hope to maintain a permanent wide gap between actual and market-clearing exchange rates and real wholesale interest rates, without a panoply of administrative controls on international trade, as well as payments to an extent that is demonstrably damaging to growth and living standards. That premise, however, does not in itself rule out milder forms of control, including taxes and restrictions on international capital movements, on the purchase by foreigners of local equities and the admission of foreign-owned financial service companies, such as banks. These indeed are the three main areas where the actual empirical experience of, and impact on, small domestic financial systems needs to be understood, and we take them up in turn.

Financial Services: Allowing Foreign Provision

Emerging markets can benefit from importing financial services

THE FINANCIAL SERVICES INDUSTRY IN ANY COUNTRY STANDS to incur losses from the elimination of the protection that has allowed providers to operate at a high-cost, high-profit level over the years. Ease of communications and the removal of restrictions on borrowing and depositing abroad forces local banks to cut their costs, at least for large customers, and also forces them to improve the quality of their services, if they are to limit the loss of business. As we will see, most of the trading in local shares that is generated by depositary receipts (DRs—also see box 4.1) occurs offshore, and new initial public offerings from firms in developing countries are often now being made in mature markets, bypassing the local exchanges altogether.

Undoubtedly, the accelerating presence of the Internet will begin to make direct international financial transactions available even to small firms and individuals, although the speed of these developments and the extent to which they will displace the need for local presence of financial service companies remain unclear (Claessens, Glaessner, and Klingebiel 2000).

For the present, most financial service companies, whether they specialize in banking, insurance, fund management, or stock exchange services, still retain an important franchise based on local presence. Mostly these are locally owned firms, but increasingly foreign firms have also sought to enter. Privatization of banks, especially in transition economies,

---

Box 4.1   Depositary receipts and country funds

Depositary receipts

DEPOSITARY RECEIPTS (DRs) HAVE LONG BEEN USED to help U.S. investors to avoid transactions costs and some of the risks of holding or trading securities in an unfamiliar market, whether mature or emerging.[1] They can also be used to circumvent regulatory barriers facing U.S. investors, including institutional investors, to holding shares in non-U.S. firms. The first DR was established in the United States in 1927 for the British retail firm Selfridges. Now DRs are traded in other mature markets also. There are currently DR programs for about 2,000 firms, almost half of them from emerging markets. The wide range of companies whose shares are now indirectly traded in the United States now means (as shown by Errunza, Hogan, and Hung 1999) that U.S. investors can achieve essentially full diversification without moving outside the securities traded within the United States.

Issued typically by one of four large U.S. banks, a depositary receipt certifies that the depositary bank is holding shares in the non-U.S. firm as trustee for the holder of the certificate. Normally it is at the request of the non-U.S. firm that the depositary bank launches a DR program, with the objective of enabling the firm to reach a larger pool of worldwide investors. DRs can be offered for sale in the United States only in accordance with regulations established by the Securities and Exchange Commission (SEC), which ensures, inter alia, an adequate degree of disclosure of the foreign firm's accounts. The more disclosure, the more unrestricted the trading of the DR can be in U.S. markets. The high standards of

disclosure required for a DR program also benefit shareholders in the local market, and can indirectly generate pressure for increased disclosure, even for firms that do not have a DR program.

Country funds

The role of mutual funds, established in the U.S. (and European) markets, and specializing in the equities of specific emerging markets, or in regional groups of emerging markets, was important in the process of extending foreign ownership of emerging market equities, especially in the late 1980s and early 1990s. World funds hold diversified portfolios, including emerging market securities, and are increasingly important. There has also been a rapid growth in country funds marketed in the United States and specializing in specific industrial countries. Not only do these funds offer the usual risk-pooling and transactions cost benefits of collective savings media, but in some cases access to the markets was restricted to approved funds, which then represented the only way for foreign investors and local firms to gain access to each other. Nowadays, part of the emerging market security holdings of institutional investors in rich countries is directly held, but part is still in the form of country fund shares.

The first funds were closed-end, that is, their shares could not be redeemed—a suitable restriction when the funds were invested in illiquid markets. With increasing liquidity in the emerging markets, open-end funds have predominated. The price of the shares in closed-end country funds can deviate widely from the

(box continues on following page)

Box 4.1 *(continued)*

market value of the underlying shares. Such deviations are also found in mutual funds that invest in domestic securities and in country funds specializing in advanced markets. However, the deviations tend to be wider for emerging market country funds and to be highly variable. Even before the turbulence of 1997–98, the vari-

ance of country fund returns was found to be about three times as large as for the underlying assets (Hardouvelis and others 1994). Where the country fund is less restricted in its access to the emerging market than other foreign investors, it has tended to be at a premium to net asset value.[2]

1. Hence the usual designation American depositary receipts (ADRs). There is no difference between an ADR and a global depositary receipt (GDR), the latter term sometimes being preferred for marketing reasons. A Euro-denominated DR differs mainly in that dividends are paid to the holder in Euros, whereas dividends on ADRs and GDRs are paid in U.S. dollars at the current rate of exchange.

2. For further discussion, see Kaminsky, Lyons, and Schmukler (2001) and IMF (2000).

and fire sales of failed banks have provided great opportunities for banks from advanced countries to acquire a pre-existing branch network and thus to enter retail banking. Banks in several of the smaller Western European countries have been very active in Central and Eastern Europe, and the expansion of Spanish banks into Latin America has been dramatic—in some countries giving rise to policy concerns about increased concentration of ownership in the banking industry. Indeed, the share of banking assets controlled by foreign banks has soared in several countries in recent years (cf. IMF 2000; figure 4.2).

Despite worries that foreign firms could destabilize domestic finance—

Some countries, however, have remained slow to admit foreign-owned financial firms to the local market, fearing that they will destabilize the local financial system and put local financial firms out of business, with the ultimate result that particular sectors and particular national needs will be poorly served.[5] This section considers whether these fears are justified, and concludes that they are not.

There are certainly some potential drawbacks to excessive reliance on just a few foreign financial institutions, especially if they come from just one country. It can introduce a new source of contagion, as when domestic conditions induced credit contraction by Japanese banks in other East Asian countries (and in California), with significant consequences for the host country. Furthermore, it is conceivable that a government could find itself in a weak position to counter abuse of power by a cartel of dominant foreign-owned entities. And, while the prosperity of a bank tends to be correlated with that of the countries in which it operates, it is

Figure 4.2   Increase in the market share of majority foreign-owned banks, selected countries, 1994 and 1999

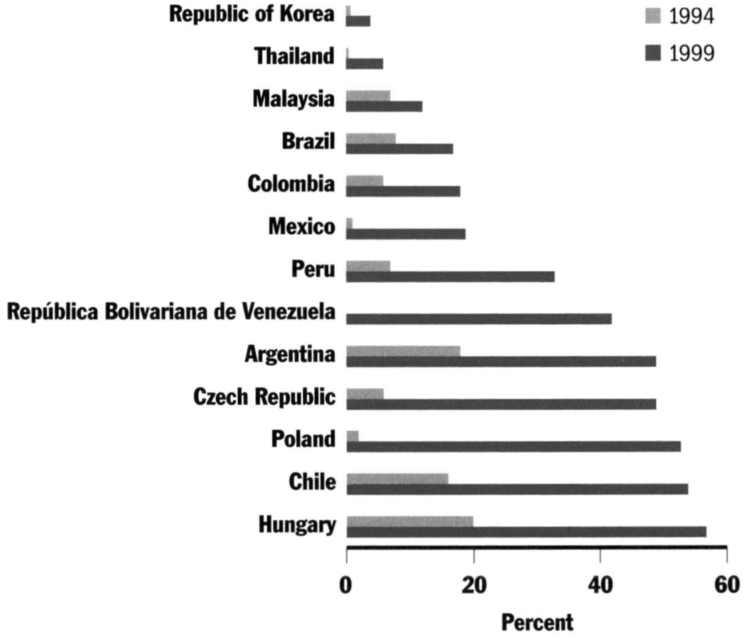

Source: Bankscope; IMF (2000).

plausible that foreign-owned banks would have a lower long-term commitment to the host countries.

Nevertheless, despite the growing presence of foreign-owned financial intermediaries, it is difficult to find any hard evidence for the proposition that admitting foreign firms has adverse consequences for the economy as a whole. Indeed, the indications are that, by improving overall operating efficiency, and by leveraging improvements in both official and private elements of the financial infrastructure, foreign entry helps create the conditions for improved financial intermediation and long-term growth (Levine 2000).

It is banking that has generated the greatest concern among those who oppose foreign entry. Now much evidence exists on how foreign banks behave and how they contribute to financial sector development and national economic growth.

In high-income and upper-middle-income countries, although they represent on average more than one in five of the banks, foreign-owned

—there is little evidence to support such fears

165

Foreign banks will become more than niche players

institutions still usually account for much less than 10 percent of local banking assets. They generally are niche players, often catering to foreign companies and concentrating on international trade business. In these environments, they tend to operate with lower unit costs and lower unit profitability than the domestic banks. In several of the more prosperous countries of Latin America and Central Europe, though (as well as in some advanced economies, such as in New Zealand), foreign-owned banks begin to play a larger role (cf. figure 4.2).[6]

Even before the recent expansion, foreign banks tended to have a larger share of the market in poorer countries. In 16 of these, the foreign banks account for more than a third of the system. Here the foreign-owned banks are more profitable on average than local banks, despite incurring higher operating expenses, which likely reflects their investment in higher-quality services. They also have higher interest margins and higher tax payments. The smaller the country, the more likely it is to rely on foreign-owned banks, but some larger countries, such as India, Indonesia, and Pakistan, also have a sizable share of foreign-owned banks.

Anecdotes to the contrary notwithstanding, there is no evidence that the local presence of foreign banks has destabilized the flow of credit. Instead, the entry of these banks has been associated with significant changes in the competitive environment and in the quality of regulation and disclosure.

Numerous case studies of bank entry into countries as different as Argentina, Australia, and Hungary document the dynamic impact of foreign entry on the efficiency and competitiveness of the local banking systems (see Levine 1996 and Claessens and Jansen 2000 for reviews). The very threat of entry has often been enough to galvanize the domestic banks into overhauling their cost structure and the range and quality of their services, with the result that foreign entry has often proved not to be as profitable for the entrants as they may have anticipated.

Statistical analysis of data on the accounts of individual banks confirms the impression that entry of foreign banks can make national banking markets more competitive. Thus, the higher the share of foreign-owned banks, the lower is the profitability and the higher are the loan-loss provisions (albeit compensated by a higher net interest margin) of domestically owned banks (figure 4.3).[7] The administrative efficiency of the incumbents may also improve. Although the raw change in overhead expenses is not statistically significant, this likely results from the

Figure 4.3   Estimated impact of foreign bank entry on domestic bank performance

Percent of total assets

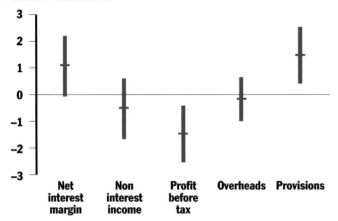

The entry of foreign-owned banks increases competition—pushing down the profit margins of domestically-owned banks, and inducing them to lend to sectors requiring higher gross margins to offset higher loan-loss provisions.

Note: The chart shows the impact of a 50 percent increase in the market share of foreign banks on the profitability of local banks. The vertical line shows the 95 percent confidence interval and the horizontal bar shows the point estimate; e.g., the net interest margin increases by 105 basis points +/– 110 basis points.

Source: Based on pooled national time-series cross-section regressions in Claessens, Demirgüç-Kunt, and Huizinga (2000).

apparent shift in the portfolio to riskier loans, which also entail higher administrative expenses.

Though not a magic bullet in this regard, this does suggest that opening up banking to foreign entry can help to extend the price and efficiency benefits of financial globalization to the smaller customer who still cannot easily access foreign-based financial services.

The fear that a local presence of foreign-owned banks might destabilize capital flows by exporting their resources at times of host country pressure does not appear to have been substantiated at the time of recent major crises. On the contrary, foreign-owned banks in Argentina drew on their external credit lines to meet at least part of the unprecedented deposit outflow in the Tequila crisis. To some extent, depositors have run to local branches of reputable foreign-owned banks in a crisis when they could have shifted their funds abroad (Claessens and Glaessner 1998). More generally foreign banks in Argentina and Mexico have proved, if anything, a stabilizing force in terms of overall credit flows (Cull and others 2000, Goldberg, Dages, and Kinney 2000).

Increased competition reduces domestic profit margins

The pressure on domestic banks from foreign competition could present prudential risks, if it erodes franchise value of high-cost operators to the point where they begin to gamble for resurrection, though in practice intensified domestic competition in a liberalized environment seems to have been a bigger source of problems in this regard, and the presence of foreign banks appears to reduce the risk of crisis (cf. Demirgüç-Kunt, Levine, and Min 1998). Also, there is the risk that some less reputable foreign bank entrants might prove to be unsound—the case of BCCI, which established itself widely in developing countries, as well as in the industrial world, must remain a cautionary tale. Evidently these considerations should be yet another reason for strengthening prudential regulation. Actually, the arrival of reputable foreign banks is usually associated with an upgrading of transparency, especially if the banks bring improved accounting practices with them. And if local banks want to establish a reciprocal presence in advanced centers in order to be able to match the range of international services offered by the foreign-owned banks to local clients, they will need to obtain a license there. To satisfy the host regulator that local regulation is adequate, such banks will, instead of preferring lax regulation, begin to pressure local regulators to upgrade, as in Mexico in the context of the North American Free Trade Agreement (NAFTA).

There is no evidence that systems relying on foreign banks disadvantage smaller customers

As to the concern that foreign banks neglect small customers, it is evident that a distinction must be made between the conduct of foreign-owned banks relative to domestic banks and the relative performance of systems in which foreign-owned banks have a large share. It is true that foreign-owned banks tend to specialize in other niches, leaving the small business segment to the local branches. There appears to be no statistical evidence, however, that systems with more foreign-owned banks neglect small customers. Indirectly some indication may be obtained from the experience of banking consolidation in the United States. When small banks, which have always tended to specialize in small firm finance, have been absorbed into a larger entity—while there has been some initial reduction of credit to that segment—the effect has been a transitory one; soon small business is as well served as it had been. The Argentine experience may point in the same direction. Banks acquired by foreign parents did not at first emphasize consumer or mortgage and property lending, and were disproportionately represented in the capital city, Buenos Aires. However, they soon entered the mortgage business aggressively, driving down profit margins on this business in the local banks (Clarke and others 2000).

Of the three dimensions of financial globalization reviewed here, entry by foreign-owned institutions thus appears to be the least problematic from a national point of view. Service quality and prices improve, and the risks are modest and containable. Producer interests in the financial sector may be damaged, in that market power of existing financial firms is reduced, but in the long run local firms that can match the efficiency of the entrants stand to prosper in a more dynamic environment.

Many countries do not have the luxury of choosing whether or not to admit the top tier of international banks. Indeed, there may be few or even no suitable applicants (see box 3.3 on the African experience). While entry by relatively inexperienced banks headquartered in neighboring countries can help achieve economies of scale, the benefits in terms of leveraging operational and infrastructural efficiency may be more limited. Such entrants certainly need to be closely scrutinized to make sure that their governance is adequate. If the business environment is poor, or if the market is small, set-up costs may be too high to justify entry and the authorities may have difficulty in securing suitable owners even when the largest bank in the country is for sale.

Overall, though, an open-door policy to the admission of qualified and reputable foreign financial firms seems overwhelmingly to be the best policy, and one that could have a strongly favorable impact on growth.

Opening the Equity Market

THE MOST DRAMATIC STRUCTURAL DEVELOPMENT IN international finance for developing countries over the past decade or so has been the growth in cross-border equity investment, whether in the form of FDI (where the investor takes a controlling stake) or in the form of portfolio investment in listed or unlisted equities.

By 1997 the stock of inward FDI represented on average 20 percent of GDP in developing countries, with a further 1.3 percent of inward equity portfolio investment (figure 4.4).[8] Although FDI was thus the dominant form of cross-border equity investment, the smaller quantity of portfolio investment is, perhaps, of greater direct relevance in considering financial sector policy.

For a country that has an active equity market, opening that market to foreign investors is a decisive step that can be expected to influence the level and dynamics of asset pricing. More than 30 sizable stock exchanges

Figure 4.4   Stock of foreign holdings of (gross) debt and equity, 1997

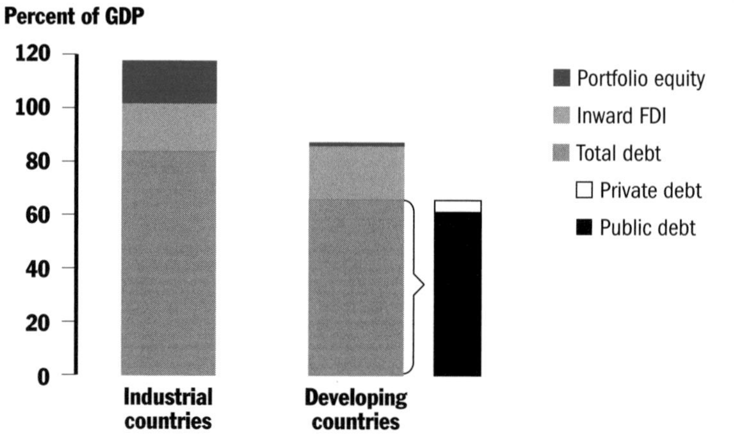

Source: Lane and Milesi-Ferretti (1999).

On balance, opening up equity markets has reduced the cost of capital—

in emerging market economies undertook significant liberalization mostly concentrated in a 10-year period from the mid-1980s to the mid-1990s. So it is natural to ask: Did the expected effects occur in practice? Were stock prices higher on average than they would otherwise have been? Was there an increase or a fall in the volatility of stock prices? In practice, these questions are tougher to answer than might appear at first sight. Overall, though (as elaborated below), it appears from research findings that prices have increased, thereby lowering the cost of capital, without an undue increase in volatility. Opening up has also accelerated improvements in disclosure and efficiency of the local stock markets, even though these have lost some of their share of the increased business in listing and trading of local equities.

but recent crises renewed fears about volatility

The dramatic stock market collapses in East Asia during 1997 and 1998—with equity indexes during 1998 in Indonesia, Malaysia, and Thailand *averaging* only between 20 and 30 percent of their end-1996 U.S. dollar values (and about 40 percent for Korea and the Philippines)—took much of the shine off what had seemed an almost trouble-free liberalization. However, by mid-2000, equity prices in Asia on average had recovered almost to their end-1996 level. Furthermore, much of the fall was a direct translation of the currency collapses in the region, and as such not necessarily attributable to the opening-up of equity markets to foreign investors. Nevertheless, the event clearly raises questions about the consequences, benefits, and costs, of equity market liberalization.

Nowhere has opening the equity market been a clear-cut leap from complete prohibition of foreign ownership of listed securities to a fully free market with all listed shares accessible to foreigners. Important intermediate steps have included the following:

- Phased increases in the ceiling on the proportion of the equity of each listed firm that foreigners can purchase.
- The establishment (in a mature market) of dedicated mutual "country" funds, with foreign shareholders, but which can invest in the local market.
- The launch of a depositary receipt (DR) program in the United States or other mature markets (box 4.1).

Beyond the headlines about the transmission of stock price volatility among open markets, there is a debate about the impact of equity market liberalization in part due to the difficulty in deciding when the liberalization occurred. Getting this right is crucial: if one assumes a liberalization date that is too late, some price movements will be misattributed to the period of closure, thereby dampening the estimate of any change. If one brings the assumed date of liberalization too early, however, the true effects of the change will also be understated.

Three general approaches have been adopted by researchers to dating stock market liberalization:

- The regulatory announcement approach, where the date of opening is related to the operative date of some relevant measure adopted by the host country, such as a significant expansion in the proportion of shares that can be held be foreigners.
- The investor action approach, where the date of announcement in the U.S. market of a country fund, or a DR program, is the key input.
- The statistical approach looks at the evolution over time of data on stock prices and other market-sensitive variables and determines the date of change by reference to an observed break in the statistical properties of the time series.

The first two approaches give widely different dates. Indeed, a comparison of the earliest and latest dates arrived at for each of 10 different countries in just 4 recent studies shows an average gap of 44 months (figure 4.5). Even if there were agreement on the date on which entry was effectively opened, it is likely that, as soon as the liberalization could

Figure 4.5   Equity market liberalization dates

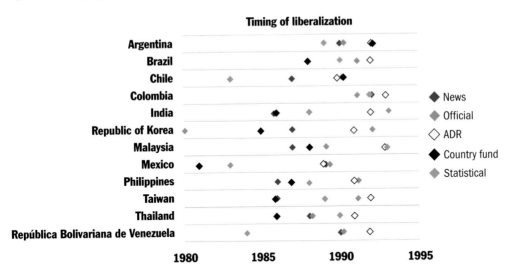

Note: The figure shows the estimated date of equity market liberalization for 12 countries based on five alternative approaches: (i) examination of news agency reports; (ii) official announcements; (iii) introduction of first ADR; (iv) introduction of the first country fund; and (v) shift in the statistical properties of asset prices and dividend yields.

Source: Bekaert et al. (2000); Henry (2000a); Levine and Zervos (1998b).

be foreseen, the market would anticipate the actual opening by bidding prices in advance to their expected new values. Here, then, is another complication in determining the relevant dates for analysis. The third (statistical) approach does prejudge the issue of whether there is a change in the dynamic properties of stock prices, but it does not predetermine the direction of this change as to average level of volatility.

With all the ambiguity concerning precise timing, it comes as no surprise to find that the measured impact of liberalization on equity prices, market capitalization, and trading volume is rather small. It is, however, statistically significant, even after controlling for other simultaneous but unrelated events that may also have affected the trend and volatility of stock prices, such as other policy reforms not directly related to the equity market, including tariff reductions and removal of other restrictions on foreign trade.

In their study of 20 liberalizing countries, for example, Bekaert, Harvey, and Lumsdaine (2000) identified 13 countries where the statistical break in series preceded a sustained reduction in dividend yield from about 5 percent to 3 percent per annum on average. Market capitalization jumped in these countries too: more than doubling on average in the first few years of liberalization, as more firms listed and others raised more capital. Although the turnover ratio of shares traded to capitalization did not show any clear-cut pattern, there was a sharp increase in liquidity as measured by the ratio of average value traded to GDP (as was first shown by Levine and Zervos 1998a). This latter liquidity variable is of key importance in that (as discussed earlier) it is the stock market indicator most reliably linked with economic growth.

Another study, focusing on the earliest regulatory announcement or investor action, reported cumulative excess returns of almost 40 percent around the time of liberalization, only a third of which could be associated with extraneous factors. This seems like a worthwhile, though not overwhelming, adjustment of local equity prices to their new prices reflecting the risk-pooling potential of the wider world market (Henry 2000a). In other words, the cost of capital is lower on average as a result of the equity market liberalization, but not dramatically so.

There is no clear theoretical presumption as to whether local stock prices will be more or less volatile after integration into the world market. Integration should insulate the prices from shocks that affect the nonmarket wealth or savings behavior of local investors, but could expose them more to fluctuations in world asset prices and to shifts in external investor preferences. The studies mentioned above do suggest a small average increase in the average comovement (*beta*) of liberalizing markets with the world market, but there is no evident pattern on asset price or rate of return volatility. Some countries saw an increase, others a decrease.[9]

An alternative approach sees asset price movements as characterized, not only by random shocks, but also by more gradual, cyclical fluctuations. When Kaminsky and Schmukler (2001) isolated such cycles from the stock price history of some 28 countries, they found that the amplitude of the cycles did increase in the immediate aftermath of liberalization, but that after about three years of functioning under the liberalized regime, the average amplitude of the cycle shrinks again. This suggests that liberalization heralds a transitional window of heightened vulnerability to a boom-and-bust cycle, but that as the market matures, the vulnerability diminishes (see figure 4.6).

Extracting the policy-relevant empirical signals from the very substantial noise that surrounds equity price movements is thus not an easy task. Overall, however, the fall in dividend yields, reflecting the increase in

Figure 4.6   Impact of liberalization on the amplitude of equity price cycles

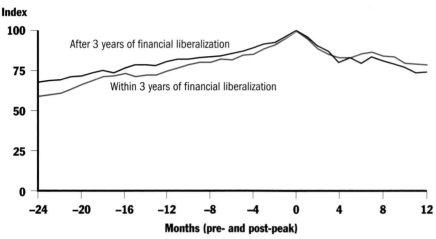

Industrialized countries

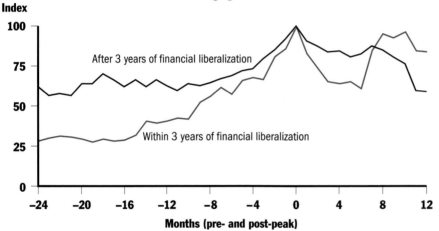

Emerging markets

After an initial period of increased volatility, liberalization is associated with reduced vulnerability.

Note: The figures are based on sorting stock market price peaks that occurred within 3 years after market liberalization from the remainder. The average price trend in the 24 months before and 12 months after a peak are plotted. For emerging markets there is a steep rise to the post liberalization peak and a sharp subsequent decline (though a bounceback after six months of decline is also evident).

Source: Based on Kaminsky and Schmukler (2001).

average equity prices, followed by new issues further increasing market capitalization, suggests that the opening-up of the equity market to foreign ownership tends per se to be relatively benign.

Liberalization of the capital account means not only access by foreigners to the domestic capital markets, but also access by domestic firms and households to the world market. Local investors also gain from the price increases but, in order to benefit fully from the risk diversification possibilities offered by the world financial market, it may be necessary for them to include foreign assets in their portfolio. This is a consideration that needs to be taken into account, for example, in designing the rules governing portfolio investment of pension funds and other collective investment vehicles. Liberalization of institutional outflows may seem more problematic, but allowing international portfolio diversification of institutional investments can, for example, help protect retirees from the risk of falling into poverty. The state-controlled national investment funds of Norway and Singapore are either wholly (Norway) or to a substantial extent (Singapore) held in foreign assets. Still, mutual funds, pension funds, and other institutional investors in many developing countries still face substantial regulatory barriers to investing abroad.

Diversification will reduce vulnerability

In addition to the East Asia case already mentioned, liberalized equity markets have also been hit by the other major international financial crises of the 1990s (Tequila in 1994–95; Russia-Brazil-LTCM in 1998), though again the origin of each of these crises was not the equity market. The behavior of particular groups of foreign investors in emerging equity markets during these crises has been studied in detail by several researchers. Their findings tend to confirm the plausible belief that swings in purchases and sales of emerging market equities have been important influences on price fluctuations, but also that the participation of foreign investors can help insulate markets from domestic shocks, while increasing their reaction to shocks elsewhere.

Foreign investors may dampen domestic volatility—

Tracking the net flows of a class of foreign investors and the corresponding price movements on a daily basis reveals a pattern of intertemporal interactions that deviates somewhat from the simple textbook model of prices adjusting instantaneously to new information.[10] Instead, the empirical evidence indicates that a price increase tends to generate a momentum in inflows over subsequent days, which in turn drives prices higher with the price movement also being drawn out over a period. It is as if the immediate impact of a piece of price-relevant news on the price is only a partial one. The foreign investors adjust their portfolios gradually, and this pushes prices up further, both because of the weight of money, and because of an expectation, generally realized, that the momentum of flows has further to go. This process can overshoot, and indeed it appears that at the time of crisis the fall in price does not reflect an outflow of funds by foreign investors as much as a failure of the expected inflow to continue.

—but also expose a country to contagion risks

The behavior of open-ended and closed-end mutual funds specializing in emerging markets throws further light on the behavior of foreign investors. More than 2,000 such funds are now in existence, and their holdings of equities in the top two dozen emerging markets reached about 5 percent of total market capitalization by the mid-1990s. For the open-ended funds, the relevant data is on their flows. They show that the ultimate investors, rather than the portfolio managers, are responsible for most of the sensitivity to price movements of their flows into or out of particular emerging markets. This applies both to own-price movements and to flows triggered by price movements in other markets, that is, what might be termed contagious flows. The evidence is that large withdrawals from mutual funds are mainly from countries where observable economic fundamentals are weak, inasmuch as indicators that prove in practice to be good predictors of future financial collapse have moved into the danger zone. Importantly, though, it is also found that the most liquid equity markets (such as Brazil in Latin America, and Hong Kong (China), Singapore, and Taiwan in Asia) suffer disproportionately from withdrawals, presumably reflecting attempts by the managers of mutual funds covering more than one country to minimize the average impact on the prices they receive when they have to shrink their portfolio in response to investor withdrawals (Kaminsky, Lyons, and Schmukler 2000a, 2001). Here is an unpleasant side effect of equity market development.

For closed-end country funds, further insight can be gained from movements in the gap, which (as with most closed-end funds in mature markets), tends to exist between the price of shares in these funds and the net asset value of the funds. Although there is not full agreement on the sources of such a gap, there are some interesting regularities. For example, where foreign access to the equity market is still quite limited, the country funds tend to trade at a premium. This likely reflects the pent-up demand by foreigners for the country's equities, which cannot be fully satisfied except through the country fund. As further liberalization occurs, the country fund price typically drifts to a discount on net asset value—often more than 5 percent, but quite volatile—thereby coming into line with a common, though not fully explained, feature of closed-end funds in most markets. At times of crisis, however, when the local market has collapsed, it is frequently observed that the price of country funds does not fall as much, with the result that they go to a premium on net asset value once more (figure 4.7). It seems that local investors react more strongly to local disturbances—perhaps because they hold a different view of the true significance of the local information

Figure 4.7 Mexico country fund discount, 1993–99

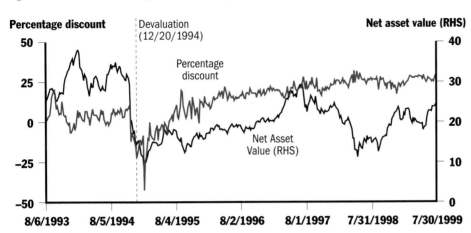

Note: While the fund traded generally at a discount to net asset value before the Tequila crisis, in the immediate aftermath of that crisis, with the local equity market sharply down, the fund price held up well, and moved to a premium on net asset value for several months. Local investors seemed to react more to the crisis than the foreign investors in the fund.

Source: Updated from Frankel and Schmukler (1996).

The figure shows the gap between the market price of the Mexico Fund, and that of its Mexican investments.

shock that has depressed the market, or perhaps because, being less well diversified than the foreigners, their wealth has been more affected by the shock. On this view, the country fund shareholders may expect the equity market to recover quickly enough for it not to be worth their while to attempt a costly arbitrage (Levy-Yeyati and Ubide 1998).

These glimpses into the mechanics of interaction between foreign investors and the local market show that foreign participation has consequences that go beyond an initial and permanent upward adjustment in the general level of local equity prices. Differences in information and in the reaction to information of the foreign investors, as well as differences in the time scale over which they adjust portfolios, has an impact on the dynamics of local equity prices. It may destabilize them, especially by transmitting world disturbances, as well as disturbances in countries with actual or perceived similarities through a form of contagion. They can also, however, have a countervailing effect to disturbances emanating from local conditions.[11]

It must be noted, however, that not all the increased trading activity in local equities takes place on the local exchange. For example, trading in closed-end country funds does not in itself trigger any trading on the local exchange, and the same is true of most trading in DRs, which simply change hands in the mature market. Perhaps 95 percent

A declining share of equity trading takes place on the local exchange

177

of trading in DRs does not involve the local exchange, though the remaining trades are mostly sufficient to avoid unexploited arbitrage opportunities between the two markets.

This can have an adverse impact on the importance of the local market to the extent that the major firms start to issue DRs. For these firms, activity and pricing can become dominated by the external mature market, so that the original issuing market becomes less and less important—eventually little more than a satellite to the DR market. In that respect, opening up can mean that much of the action moves abroad.

Internationalization has also resulted in some equities being delisted in emerging markets, often as a result of the takeover of listed firms by foreign entities. New issuers, especially in the technology sector, now sometimes choose to list only in a mature market.

On the other hand, the disclosure requirements of the DR program also tend to force improvements in disclosure in the local market even beyond what is formally required by the local regulations. Once a firm has satisfied the information requirements for a DR listing, neither they nor their competitors will find it easy to get away with lesser disclosure on home markets. In this way, the existence of DRs has been having an indirect effect on improving the quality of information disclosure even for firms that have not sought a DR listing, thereby enhancing the informational efficiency of the emerging markets. These positive effects of DRs surely outweigh the negative.

Access to financial services is more important than who provides them

The possible loss of business on local exchanges may concern the owners of the exchange, but should not be accorded much weight by the authorities—notwithstanding the possible costs of opening up for the employment and profitability of local brokers and others providing services associated with the local exchange. Thus, it is worth bearing in mind that generating more business for market professionals is not the primary policy goal of opening up the equity market. Instead the goal is to achieve the growth, macrostability, and antipoverty gains offered by overall financial development as discussed in chapter 1. If the migration of larger firms to foreign markets and the reduction in volume and liquidity on local markets had the effect of restricting access of small firms to equity finance as a result of consolidation and closure of some exchanges, that would be another matter, but some suggestions to that effect seem unduly alarmist. Harsh though the message may seem to financial sector producers, *it is access to financial services that matters, not who provides them.*

Debt Flows and Interest and Exchange Rates

BEFORE THE EXPLOSION IN INTERNATIONAL EQUITY investment, the classic form of international finance involved debt flows: international borrowing and lending. Analysis of these flows and the related policy issues forms one of the most active and long-established branches of economic and financial research. We confine ourselves here to a discussion of a handful of current policy issues with a special relevance to the functioning of domestic finance.[12]

Although most international lending and borrowing has long been expressed in terms of major international currencies (or originally in terms of gold-based currencies) openness to international flows has an indirect impact on domestic interest rates, and on the exchange rate. Here is where the risks arise, and where macroeconomic, fiscal, and monetary policy has long been directed to containing those risks. Specifically financial policy measures, too, can be contemplated, whether addressed to the flows themselves, to domestic interest rates, or to the exchange rate regime. This section briefly considers these three in turn. We note an emerging consensus that tax-like measures can be somewhat effective in damping short-term debt flows, but that piecemeal attempts to control the structure and pricing of domestic financial flows when the system is open to foreign flows are counterproductive and damaging. The liberalization both of domestic and international finance has resulted in a convergence of interest rate movements, although developing countries are now experiencing a structural risk premium. Some of this premium is attributable to exchange risk: adjustable pegs may accentuate this, especially in the presence of extensive but incomplete dollarization.

One clear lesson of the period of international financial liberalization of the past couple of decades is that the costs of domestic financial repression become quite unsustainable when the capital market is opened. Indeed, the heyday of financial repression was during the period between 1914 and 1973 when national financial systems operated largely in isolation from one another. This lengthy interruption of international finance markets was created by World War I and its inflationary aftermath, and continued with the protracted and doomed effort to restore the gold standard in major countries. It deepened with the attempts to protect national economies from the World Depression of the 1930s (a time when protectionism and a wider isolationism was on the rise and which prompted

Interest-sensitive flows force a review of financial policies

even Keynes to write "above all, let your finance be national"). It persisted through World War II. Thereafter, despite progressive trade liberalization, regulatory barriers to capital flows continued, chiefly because liberalization of capital outflows was seen as incompatible with pegged exchange rates and with policies of managed aggregate demand.

Behind the walls of exchange controls, managed finance emerged. With barriers against international movements of funds allowing considerable bite for domestic regulations, not only the currency, but also interest rates, banking (ownership and conduct), and stock exchanges were at first kept substantially under national control.

Although constrained from international business and with lending interest rates often pegged, banks benefited from ready access to cheap deposits as they were protected de facto from vigorous competition, whether domestic or foreign, and were often partially cartelized. In return, the banking system channeled sizable fractions of their loanable funds to government and its designated borrowers or sectors (Wyplosz 2001). Securities markets, where they were developed, also tolerated restrictive practices by insiders, and often rationed firms' access to the new issue market in the interest of maintaining orderly conditions.

The effectiveness of administrative controls on capital movements was limited, and it declined with improvements in transport and communication and with the increase in the volume of trade, associated with large payments flows whose timing and volume could be modified to conceal capital flows (Dooley 1996). Speculative pressure on exchange rate pegs—especially during the late 1960s—highlighted this declining effectiveness, although the volumes of speculative flows and the interest rate differentials they generated were modest when compared with later experience. When the system of fixed exchange rates was abandoned by the major industrial countries in the early 1970s, the perceived need to maintain capital controls also became less acute, and a process of dismantling them began.

Today, only three types of private market participant are likely to continue to be excludable de facto from the international capital markets, namely, low-income households, very small firms, and regulated financial firms. Even financial firms, however, that are excluded from direct participation in the global financial market are indirectly affected by it.

Domestic financial liberalization would be possible even without opening up the economy to international capital movements. With the opening-up, it becomes unavoidable. Open capital markets make attempts to fix interest rates and other domestic financial prices away from market-clearing prices altogether futile.[13] Large depositors have always responded to such attempts by placing their funds and making their investments abroad. Large firms make use of their access to foreign finance. Capital account liberalization thus weakens and distorts a repressed domestic financial sector, eventually forcing domestic liberalization. If the process is long drawn out, haphazard partial liberalization of external and domestic finance can result in a very risky and unsound situation emerging. This is well exemplified in the important and classic case of the Republic of Korea in the 1990s, where the sequencing of liberalization resulted in the large firms moving their borrowing abroad at inappropriately short maturities, and the domestic financial system turning to lower-grade domestic firms to which they in turn lent too much (box 4.2).

Box 4.2 Poor sequencing of the Republic of Korea's financial liberalization

DESPITE A RELATIVELY RAPID RATE OF RECOVERY, the collapse of the Korean economy in 1997 was a severe blow. Indeed, the Korean crisis had global implications, though in the event these were largely contained to a smaller scale than had at one time appeared likely. For some, the Republic of Korea's experience provided evidence that the financial liberalization on which the Republic of Korea had embarked only a few years before had been a mistake, and that a continuation of the previous practice of financial repression would have been a sounder policy. Others tell the story differently, asserting that the Republic of Korea's financial system had remained substantially repressed, and that a sham liberalization had not been to blame.

The full story is more subtle, although clear and strong lessons can be drawn. The Republic of Korea did liberalize its financial markets substantially, but it did so in the wrong order, encouraging the development of a highly fragile financial structure both in terms of the financial instruments employed (too much reliance on short-term bills), in terms of the financial intermediaries that were unwittingly encouraged (lightly regulated trust subsidiaries of the banks, and other newly established near-bank financial intermediaries), and in terms of market infrastructure development (failure to develop the institutions of the long-term capital market).

By liberalizing short-term (but not long-term) foreign borrowing, the Korean authorities made it virtually inevitable that the larger and better-known banks and *chaebols* would assume heavy indebtedness in short-term foreign currency debt. Restrictions on the use of derivatives limited the possibility of hedging. Meanwhile, the second tier of large *chaebols* greatly increased their short-term indebtedness in the domestic financial markets (funded indirectly through foreign borrowing of the banks). The funds borrowed were being invested in overexpansion of productive capacity.

The phasing of interest rate liberalization, too, was misconceived. Bank deposit interest rates were held

(box continues on following page)

Box 4.2 *(continued)*

well below competitive levels, thereby driving resources off bank balance sheet or away from the regulated banking sector altogether. Moral suasion meant that formal deregulation did not result in completely free market determination of many interest rates.

The reasons for this pattern of deregulation include a mechanical adherence to the importance of monetary aggregates (which induced the authorities to retain controls on these, while liberalizing near-substitutes), the preoccupation with maintaining an orderly long-term capital market (which distracted them from paying attention to the emergence of a new and much more disorderly short-term corporate paper market) and the persistence of directed policy lending (which meant that interest rate spreads needed to be wide enough to

allow for cross-subsidization, but at the cost of losing market share for the banks).

The quality of loan appraisal, bank regulation, and private credit rating was always in doubt. Over-optimism and complacency reigned.

In the end, it was not the bursting of a property bubble that ended the Korean expansion, but the refusal of foreign creditors to roll over their loans. A refusal prompted by their increasing unease at the loss of competitiveness and heavy indebtedness of Korean corporate borrowers. Even if the main sources of the Korean crisis lay elsewhere, the mistaken sequencing of financial liberalization contributed to the speed and severity of the crisis both by exposing the system to rollover risk and by encouraging excessive indebtedness of firms.

Source: Based on Cho (2001).

Higher interest rates in emerging markets reflect higher risks

With the progressive opening up of financial systems in developing countries, it was to be expected that market-clearing interest rates at home would increasingly become subject to international pressures. This has proved to be the case, as evidenced by the data. The rise in interest rates in developing countries from their repressed levels, however, has not stopped when they reached industrial country levels.

In both industrial and developing countries, treasury bill rates were unusually low in real terms in the later 1970s, reflecting the acceleration of inflation worldwide and, in developing countries, general continuation of financial repression. As real yields increased in industrial countries during the 1980s, developing countries lagged behind, but caught up as more and more developing countries liberalized their rates de facto, moving closer to market-clearing conditions. By the 1990s, median real rates in developing countries exceeded those in the industrial countries, presumably reflecting higher-risk premia (table 4.1, figure 4.8). The subsequent reduction in industrial country real rates from the mid-1990s, however, was not systematically followed in the developing world. Instead,

Table 4.1 Real interest rates

| Year | Real interest rates (percent, medians) | | | | | |
| | Money market | | Treasury bill | | Deposit | |
	Industrial	Developing	Industrial	Developing	Industrial	Developing
1975–79	−0.8	−1.3	−1.4	−4.8	−2.9	−4.7
1980–84	3.8	2.8	3.1	−0.7	0.9	−0.9
1985–89	5.1	4.1	4.9	1.0	2.5	1.3
1990–94	5.8	4.3	5.2	3.2	2.9	2.0
1995–99	2.7	6.4	3.3	5.0	1.7	3.4

Source: Honohan (2001a).

Figure 4.8   Real treasury bill yields for industrial and developing countries

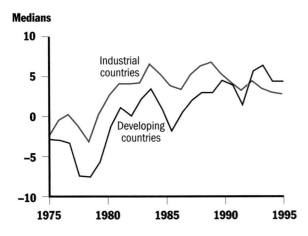

Medians

The figure shows how the median Treasury bill yield in developing countries, once well below, has caught up with and now exceeds that for industrial countries.

Source: Honohan (2001a).

wholesale interest rates in developing countries have moved to a premium over those of industrial countries on average. This predates the crises of 1997–98 and suggests a structural problem.

There are several likely sources of this premium: doubtless one factor relevant for many developing countries is their precarious fiscal position to which the fiscal costs of large banking crises and of state ownership will have contributed, which serves to underline the importance of the messages of the previous chapters. In many cases, however, they also likely reflect doubts not just about government policy credibility in general, but specifically exchange rate risk. To the extent that policy risk is the source, the premia are economically inefficient and costly: improved policy design might reduce them.

During episodes of financial crisis, whatever their origin, speculation about future exchange rate movements can become the dominant issue, destabilizing interest rates and threatening severe capital losses to some financial intermediaries and to some of their customers. It is an open question—widely discussed, but beyond the scope of the present study—as to whether choice of exchange rate regime can influence the level and volatility of interest rate premia. No matter what exchange rate regime one opts for, however, one must recognize that movements in world interest rates will tend to be transmitted to the domestic economy.

The well-known and plausible "uncovered interest parity" hypothesis—that domestic interest rates will equal those abroad plus the expected rate of currency depreciation plus a risk premium—works well on average over any period of several years (except under conditions of financial repression), and especially when there is a fairly steady rate of currency depreciation. It does less well in predicting short-term movements. When the interest differential is *unusually* high, that does not reliably predict a devaluation. In other words, there can be significant and unpredictable short-term fluctuations in risk premia, and higher interest differentials seem to be correlated with higher risk premia.[14]

Exchange rate risk weighs on financial intermediation

Exchange rate risk has become of central importance for the conduct of financial intermediation. If they are to tap external sources of funding, or meet the demands of their internationally trading customers, banks inevitably become exposed to the risk of sizable movements in foreign exchange rates.

Such risks may appear to be manageable with known techniques of risk measurement and hedging. Calculating and pricing the risk of an emerging market exchange rate is not straightforward, however. The risk is not likely to be stationary over time, and could be dependent on intrinsically unforecastable considerations, such as changes in the country's policy preference as between inflation and output stabilization. This is especially true of quasi-fixed exchange rate regimes, because of the large but rare devaluation events that they involve. Furthermore, attempts to hedge the risk, for example, by matching currency denomination of assets and liabilities, can often fall foul of counterparty credit risk. If the currency collapses, with widespread business dislocation, a bank's customers who borrowed in foreign currency may well be unable to service the debt. Yet many firms have been prepared to take on such risks, perhaps relying on an implicit safety net (see box 4.3). The assumption of sizable exchange risk by financial intermediaries or large corporate borrowers can impose a social cost if the bet

---

Box 4.3 Theory of twin crises—currency and banking

OPENING UP TO FOREIGN CAPITAL CAN FORM A lethal combination with implicit government guarantees provided to bank creditors. When added to exchange rate uncertainty and unhedged foreign exchange positions of banks and their borrowing clients, the mixture is explosive. The essential problem is that, by extending the implicit guarantee in a virtually unlimited way to foreign creditors—and in foreign exchange—the potential scale of moral hazard is enormously expanded.

Domestic banks are often keen to source funds abroad (and in foreign exchange) not only because of their ready availability, but because they typically have a lower interest cost, reflecting the lack of explicit exchange rate risk to the foreign depositor. They do, however, involve an exchange rate risk for the bank, even if it onlends these funds to local customers in foreign exchange, as exchange rate movements will affect the borrowers' ability to repay. The moral hazard is that, with a generous implicit safety net, banks and their depositors will proceed as if there were no risk. There are clear parallels with the discussion of chapter 2.

When the crisis occurs, this exchange rate element provides an extra twist not present in a domestic crisis. Domestic crises are characterized by a decline in the money price of most assets. After all, that's what makes it difficult for borrowers to repay money. For an open economy overborrowed in foreign exchange,

however, in addition to the fall in the money price of most domestic assets, the money price of a major liability—foreign exchange—actually increases, as the currency collapses.

The scale and timing of the currency collapse is linked to the market's expectations about the government's ability to meet the liability to bank creditors. If the banking system is insolvent at current exchange rates, and if the market expects the government to rely on the inflation tax to cover some of the bailout costs, a fixed exchange rate will be unsustainable. If so, the currency will collapse, *thereby worsening the insolvency of the banks*.

Even if the banking system is not insolvent at current exchange rates, a market belief that there will be a devaluation can be self-fulfilling, thereby "busting" the banks and triggering a bailout requirement that does end up being partly covered by the inflation tax.

This pattern has been well known to astute observers at least since the Chilean financial crisis of the early 1980s (Díaz-Alejandro 1985), but that did not prevent banks and their borrowers from going down the same route in East Asia, which helped to trigger not only the crisis of 1997–98, but also an explosion of theoretical analysis that has greatly deepened our understanding of the processes involved (cf., for example, McKinnon and Pill 1999; Burnside, Eichenbaum, and Rebelo 2000).

goes wrong. This has been argued as a justification for imposing regulations not only on banks, but also on nonfinancial firms, which restricts their foreign exchange exposure. The ease with which some Mexican banks evaded these controls in 1994, by use of special purpose derivatives, is a classic example of the practical difficulty of enforcing such controls (see box 4.4).

Box 4.4   Derivatives and capital control evasion

HISTORICALLY, CAPITAL CONTROLS HAVE BEEN evaded through a variety of techniques, such as under- or overinvoicing exports or imports, as well as by other practices, often illegal in nature. Wealthy individuals and large firms are able to evade controls rather easily, which is one reason why, when controls on capital outflows were removed in Italy, net inflows followed; not only were some more disposed to investing in Italy with the knowledge that they could get their money out easily, but also many wealthy Italians reportedly had Swiss bank accounts long before the controls were removed.

With the explosion of derivative products in recent years, however, evasion of capital controls or taxes is easier without breaking any laws, and it is also much more difficult to separate short- and long-term capital flows. Consider a few examples, from Folkerts-Landau and Garber (1997). Suppose first that there is a tax on gross inflows of capital, and foreigners want to make an equity investment. They can buy offshore an equity swap (a financial derivative that entitles them to receive the return on that investment position, presumably the reason they want the investment), and a domestic resident will be the counterparty, promising to pay the total return on that investment, and hedging this exposure by purchasing that investment (the equity)—without incurring any capital inflow tax. Other types of taxes—though not yet the specific one used in Chile—can be evaded with different derivative transactions.

Worse still, authorities cannot even tell short-term from long-term capital flows. These data are based entirely on "on-balance sheet" transactions, yet with derivatives this is only one part of the transaction. For example (again from Garber and Folkerts-Landau), suppose that a Mexican entity wants to buy a local stock on margin, which is forbidden. He can buy an equity swap from a firm in New York, promising to pay a floating rate return to the firm, and putting up some collateral. The New York firm is unhedged in this position, but can offset the risk by purchasing the stock on the Mexican market. That stock purchase, if sufficiently large, shows up as a long-term capital inflow into Mexico, but the offsetting transaction, the equity swap, is not recorded. Yet clearly the New York firm only purchased the stock to cover its position, and as soon as the swap expires— these are usually highly short-term transactions, which also contributes to the difficulty in tracking them— the equity position is extinguished. Derivatives thus have the ability to transform what appear to be the most stable form of capital inflow into one of the most volatile. Although it is difficult to quantify, it is likely that the large volume of supposedly long-term capital inflows lulled the Mexican authorities into thinking that their exposure to any reversal of flows was much less than it turned out to be.

Thus, even if capital controls are desired for the long term, such as because of the fear of multiple equilibria, they will be increasingly difficult to enforce in the future, as derivatives become more widely accessible. Authorities may be able to establish controls that cannot be evaded immediately, but the prospects for doing so permanently are low.

This risk of extreme currency movements resulting in losses to insufficiently hedged intermediaries (and businesses in general) is arguably the most acute problem generated by globalization for the functioning of the financial sector. A strongly capitalized financial sector with both the capacity and incentives for managing such risks is clearly needed. In addition, however, over and above the choice of exchange rate regime, a coherent, credible, and stable macroeconomic policy is needed to help reduce the risks.

Another effect of the increasing internationalization of trade, combined with currency uncertainty, has been a great expansion in the use of the dollar (or the DM/Euro) as a parallel currency in many countries, whether in the form of cash, in denominating bank accounts, or for pricing and contracting more generally. Often a surge of inflation and currency depreciation has triggered the first widespread dollarization in a country, and this process generally has not been reversed. Once asset holders are taxed through inflation or depreciation, they continue to hold a certain fraction of their wealth in dollars. A subsequent crisis often causes these holdings to ratchet upwards, despite a higher interest differential in favor of local currency assets (cf. Reding and Morales 1999).

When the economy becomes dollarized, currency speculation comes onshore, and is no longer just a question of international flows destabilizing exchange rates. Partially dollarized systems present special challenges to monetary management, and to the financial sector. For one thing, an economy in which prices are widely quoted in dollars is one in which a nominal exchange rate change tends to be quickly and fully passed through to local currency prices. Accordingly, a given change in the real exchange rate—such as may be required to adjust to a real external shock—tends to require a larger nominal exchange rate movement. Large nominal exchange rate movements can, however, as we have noted, have a considerable impact on the financial position of unhedged financial intermediaries and their customers. And in dollarized economies, the share of foreign currency assets and liabilities in financial intermediary balance sheets tends to be large. The tension between the need for a real exchange rate adjustment—to restore equilibrium in trade and current economic activity—and the costs, including bankruptcy costs, of the resulting nominal exchange rate movement has repeatedly presented policymakers with a difficult dilemma (box 4.5).

Their room for maneuver is also limited by the fact that the national monetary authority does not have an unlimited capacity to provide lender-of-last-resort facilities in respect of foreign currency deposits in the

Growing dollarization presents new challenges to the financial sector

Box 4.5   Dollarization—asset price and pass-through effects

DOLLARIZATION HAS TWO DIMENSIONS: THE currency denomination of assets and the use of foreign currency in pricing and internal payments. The impact on policy choices depends on how much of each type of dollarization has occurred. It is important to bear both dimensions in mind in considering what model of exchange rate policy applies in any given country.

Traditionally, thinking about the role of exchange rate changes related to a world in which both types of dollarization were unimportant (bottom left quadrant of the figure). In such conditions, exchange rate adjustment works mainly through its effect on the relative prices of current goods and services. This is the world of J-curves, elasticity pessimism or optimism and pass-through coefficients, familiar to international economics textbooks of the 1960s and 1970s.

Where it is finance that is highly dollarized, the role of the exchange rate as an asset price comes to the fore. This means that the authorities and market participants need to be acutely concerned with the capital gains and losses that will occur with changes in the exchange rate. Indonesia in 1997 provides a good example: wild fluctuations in the exchange rate had much

more impact on the solvency of unhedged firms than with the competitiveness of exports (upper left quadrant in the chart below; see also box 4.3).

The more it is that pricing of goods and services is in dollars, the faster and more complete the pass-through of exchange rate changes onto domestic prices will be. If there is little dollarization of financial assets, but pass-through is high, the economy is relatively insensitive to nominal exchange rate changes. Movements in the exchange rate are not effective in achieving real adjustment—they only change the price level. Something like the "classical dichotomy" between real and monetary sectors prevails (lower right quadrant).

Where both types of dollarization are high, the local currency loses its role as the main numeraire or measuring rod for economic transactions, as agents have switched to thinking in terms of dollars. Although government wages and payments are still made in the local currency, it is now seen as a risky asset. Holdings of cash are minimized, and the price of local currency-denominated securities builds in a substantial risk premium reflecting the unpredictability of the exchange rate—even if it has up to now been stable.

Influence of dollarization and pass-through on policy

Degree of dollarization of finance	Pass-through coefficient	
High	Exchange rate policy constrained by finance	Local currency riskier than dollar; little impact on current transactions
Low	Traditional position: nominal exchange rate is a real sector price	Classical dichotomy: nominal exchange rate does not matter
	Low	**High**

banking system. The rescue through liquidity support of even a solvent bank suffering a run from domestic depositors may thus be beyond the ability of a central bank in a dollarized economy. This is, of course, only an extreme example of the limitations placed on national policy instruments by global financial integration in its various forms.

Could the scale and volatility of speculative flows be reduced by the introduction of a tax on capital imports (or a tax-like control, such as a compulsory deposit) designed to penalize short-term movements, while leaving longer-term capital movements broadly unaffected? Adopted by a single country, such a tax cannot be a substitute for sound macroeconomic policy, for an appropriate exchange rate stance, and for adequate prudential regulation and risk management—but can it help?[15]

Using a mechanism of unremunerated reserves equivalent to a tax, Chile is one widely studied country that operated such a system through most of the 1990s. The effects of the Chilean system have been studied in some detail to assess whether it has had the hoped-for effects of lengthening the maturity of capital flows, and to what extent it has been vulnerable to evasion by the use of financial derivatives or otherwise.[16] The conclusions of this research are that, by progressively closing loopholes and extending the scope of the tax, the Chilean authorities were able to maintain its bite at a roughly constant share of the relevant capital flows. This process could not have been continued indefinitely. There was a clear impact on the maturity of flows, and probably a small impact on overall flows and on interest differentials. Complemented as it has been for much of the period by other restrictions on capital movements, both import and export controls the Chilean regime thus seems to have had a modest, but perhaps worthwhile role in protecting the Chilean economy from volatile speculative flows, and in allowing the authorities to raise interest rates to stabilize macroeconomic boom conditions; but there may also have been costs, for example in terms of reduced investment over the long run (Gallego, Hernández, and Schmidt-Hebbel 1999; Edwards 2000c).

The attractive feature of the Chilean design is the way in which it tilts incentives towards stability of capital flows rather than just prohibiting flows outright. The goal can be seen as working with the market to encourage a shift in the maturity of capital inflows without affecting net flows much over the longer term. It has relatively little impact except when it is needed, that is, when short-term inflows threaten to be large. Most observers agree that a standing regime of this type is likely to be

Chile offers a useful model of limited exchange controls

much more effective and have less adverse side effects than a hastily implemented attempt to ban outflows in a crisis. The ex post nature of the latter is likely to have a longer-term adverse effect on general confidence in the predictability and credibility of policy generally.[17] The recent experience of Malaysia offers an apparent exception to this statement, though this plausibly reflects the high initial credibility of the authorities with regard to the temporary nature of the restriction, as well as on their continued commitment to low inflation, both of which were facilitated by their long and favorable track record with inflation.

For all the dogmatic rhetoric that has surrounded the recent debate on the merits of capital controls, it would be difficult to justify an extreme position based on the evidence that has been advanced. Controls have their problems, but they can in some situations be effective.

Into the Future: Technology and Communications

Accelerating trends in technology and e-finance—

CONTINUING DEVELOPMENTS IN COMPUTING AND communications technology seem sure to reshape the way in which financial services are delivered worldwide. To some extent, the impact on developing economies will be an acceleration of the trends of recent years, but there will be qualitative changes, too. Economies of scale or scope for some financial services are declining and for others increasing, and the synergies between financial and other economic services are also changing and often increasing. This will alter the organization of the industry, with consolidation in some areas, and fragmentation in others.

The process has been under way for some time. Already by the 1980s, banks were being disintermediated by the growth of commercial paper and mutual funds on the one hand, while on the other, more and more banks were becoming involved in securities and insurance. Mergers and alliances seeking scale and scope have been occurring both within the banking, insurance, and securities market sectors, between firms in different sectors, and between financial and other information intensive services. These alliances are often designed to exploit cross-economies and to leverage brands. The tangled process of bundling and unbundling financial services and financial service firms seems likely to continue as market participants respond to the impact of technology.

The main driver is the pressure of much-altered cost structures, such as the oft-noted contrast between an average cost—in the United States —of over $1 for a physical transaction in a bank branch as against a couple of cents through the Internet.

Not only are new financial products and new market structures emerging, fundamentally new types of firms have arrived in the form of financial portals (which provide guidance on the availability of services and other topical information and, as such, are perhaps best described as an Internet counterpart to specialist magazines) and aggregators (providing an electronic analog to brokerage). None of these is unique to finance, but finance is uniquely well positioned to take advantage of electronic innovations, notably because physical delivery of financial products is typically of secondary importance. (One must not, however, ignore the continuing role of personal contact and trust in parts of finance.)

There has been an increase in the number and sophistication of electronic exchanges at which professionals trade financial instruments. Some of these operate as satellites of the traditional regulated exchanges, sometimes independently.

This whole process may present some opportunities for financial service providers in small developing countries. In particular, the trend toward unbundling of financial products may allow them to become involved in providing subproducts whose efficient production does not require large scale or sophistication.

The greater potential benefit in prospect for developing countries, however, will be for users of financial services. Technology should allow them to access these services on terms comparable to consumers in advanced countries, especially insofar as physical distance from the provider begins to lose much of its importance. Undoubtedly, the accelerating presence of the Internet will begin to make direct international financial transactions available even to small firms and individuals. Already, many banks in middle-income countries have begun to offer online banking, which is just the first step.

—which will primarily benefit the users of financial services

In the face of this pervasive technology, any attempts by governments to monitor or block e-finance transactions seem doomed to be either ineffective or prohibitively costly. International finance will surely be open to the middle classes, let alone the corporate sector.

Once the set-up costs have been incurred, access to Internet-based financial services can be provided remarkably cheaply. Of course, it is wise not to get carried away as to the immediate potential for reaching the poorest of the poor. Certain basic preconditions, such as literacy, electricity, and telephone service, must be achieved before anything else is done. Because of the lack of some or all of these, many of the smallholder coffee and cocoa growers in, say, West Africa, now at the mercy of middlemen exploiting local monopolies, will be able to make immediate use of, for example, the recently established Web-based business-to-business (B2B) futures exchange in coffee and other commodities.

Public policy, however, can help here. For example, broadband communications links now being put in place throughout India's postal system will potentially bring Internet-based financial services to some 150,000 access points. Speedy and cheap payments both by and to customers in relatively isolated locations, a simplification of procedures for insurance, current information concerning prices on agricultural commodity exchanges, as well as possible efficiencies in loan approval and other financial services, can all be envisaged. In addition, the same network could also be employed to effect speedy delivery of other public and private services at low cost. This will not solve all the barriers to access on the part of small firms and individuals, but it can do away with much of the heavy costs and lack of competition inherent in relying on local bank branches. Similar initiatives offer considerable potential to other countries, especially those with low population density where formal finance has hitherto not provided a comprehensive local physical presence.

To ensure that the potential benefits of electronic media are widely available to users of finance, including to users in developing countries, and that there are not new concentrations of market power, a number of wider policy issues will need to be considered by prudential and competition policy in the advanced countries where the major financial service providers will continue to be regulated. These include the following (Claessens and others 2000):

Policy issues

- Attention to a likely explosion in nonfinancial institutions bypassing the banking system to provide payment and deposit-type services.
- The complex issues of competition policy in an environment increasingly subject to network externalities.
- Securely identifying the relevant regulatory authority for financial firms whose chief geographical presence is in the Internet and whose range of activities corresponds to none of the traditional segments of the financial sector.

For policymakers in developing countries, the major questions emerging are likely to relate to the stability of domestic financial institutions in the face of the increased competition. Concerns about the consequences of the inevitable erosion of franchise value will be reinforced and will require proactive measures as discussed. The authorities will have to face up to the need to ensure that weakened firms exit the market and act preemptively to develop their exit policy.

Increased access to foreign financial services is likely to entail increased use of foreign currencies, which will accentuate the risks of exchange rate and interest rate volatility for countries that choose to retain their own currency. Once again, heightened prudential alertness will be needed.

The increased complexity of the financial instruments being offered by the financial system can mask the true risk of asset positions, and the speed with which their value can change. This can present problems, especially for small and less experienced users of financial services in developing countries, and there will be a need for education programs to heighten awareness both of these risks and of the dangers of fraudulent services being offered over the Internet.

The likely speed of these developments and the extent to which they will displace the need for a local presence of financial service companies remain unclear, but the question that will be increasingly asked is whether smaller developing countries need to have local securities and debt markets in the traditional sense, and even how much of banking needs to be domestic. The most fruitful way of thinking about this is to isolate the elements of domestic financial services that, given new technology, can be efficiently provided in small economies, and to plan institutional arrangements that allow these elements to be unbundled and provided locally while other services are efficiently imported.

The smaller the country, the more pressing are these considerations, but the general point here is not just one that applies to a minority of tiny countries. In an increasingly integrated and technology-driven global financial system, the relative costs of being small will likely increase, and the logic of planning policy on the basis of being small will apply with greater force to more countries. The global financial market has much to offer small financial systems. Working with this market, while respecting the risks it conveys, is the way forward. Risk management is crucial, but if it is mastered, the global market can help shift risk to those most ready to bear it and provide the instruments for doing so at the lowest cost. Better infrastructure and a more incentive-compatible regulatory framework will make it so.

Globalization and technology will accentuate the relative costs of small financial systems

193

Conclusions

THE OVERALL IMPACT OF FINANCIAL GLOBALIZATION ON THE domestic financial sector is thus profound. Liberalization of capital flows has effectively made domestic financial repression obsolete. The consequences have not been uniformly favorable. Following liberalization, domestic interest rates in developing countries have moved to a premium over industrial country rates, and can surge at times of currency speculation. Heightened interest rate and exchange rate volatility pose practical risk management difficulties for financial intermediaries, especially in partially dollarized economies, and reinforce the need for appropriate infrastructures and incentives for risk containment, as well as for good macropolicies.

On the other hand, the cost of equity capital has been reduced by allowing foreign investor access to local equity markets and allowing local firms to list abroad. Increased international flows through the equity markets have not been the major contributor to increased international sources of volatility.

In addition to opening access to foreign-sourced financial services, more and more countries have been admitting foreign-owned banks and other financial firms to operate locally. Although this can represent a threat to domestic owners of financial firms, the drawback is outweighed by improved service quality when reputable foreign firms leaven the domestic system with their better procedures and practices.

On all three fronts—debt, equity, and services—our assessment acknowledges the costs and risks of increased financial globalization, but there are strong benefits too. Graduated taxation of intermittent effect on inflows may in some cases cushion economies from the effects of volatile speculative capital flows, while maintaining the benefits of steady access to the global financial market. There can be little doubt, however, that aggressive attempts by individual governments to block financial flows are likely to backfire, and there is much to be gained from adopting instead a policy stance that supports deeper access of the local economy to top quality financial services in an internationally open context.

The financial systems of most developing countries are very small when compared with the global financial market. E-finance will make national frontiers even more porous than before. Foolish indeed is the government that does not make itself aware of these market realities and learn to work with them.

Notes

1. Contrast this even with the distribution of World GDP, where five other developing countries also reach 1 percent (ten, if measured at purchasing power parities (PPPs)).

2. The unsavory side of international finance cannot be ignored. Capital flight from poor countries, including the export of funds acquired through corruption, has long been a damaging aspect—and one rarely impeded by capital controls. There is increasing awareness, including among regulators in offshore financial centers, of the need to tighten measures against the use of international banking transactions to launder or conceal illicitly acquired funds.

3. The moral hazard resulting from implicit government guarantees, however, including for foreign creditors of the banking system, linked with unhedged exchange rate risk, has increasingly been implicated in the build-up before such sudden stops (see box 4.3).

4. The benefits include the wider potential that could be offered by international capital markets for national risk reduction (cf. de Ferranti and others 2000).

5. A somewhat xenophobic popular attitude to foreign banks is common, but not universal. When the share of foreign shareholders in Ireland's largest bank, AIB, exceeded 50 percent for the first time in 1999, with the effect that well over half of the Irish banking system is now majority foreign-owned, the event passed almost unnoticed and without any adverse public comment.

6. Analysis of an extensive firm-level database for Argentina confirms that it does tend to be the larger firms that are the foreign banks' borrowing customers. Interestingly, though, only where the foreign bank is headquartered elsewhere in Latin America does it tend to have a higher average loan quality (Berger, Klapper, and Udell 2001).

7. Cf. Claessens, Demirgüç-Kunt, and Huizinga (2000). They also note that the relative performance of foreign banks appears different and less positive in industrial countries.

8. Of course, these investment shares were not uniform across countries. In particular, as shown by Lane and Milesi-Ferretti (1999), Latin America and the transition economies have the largest share of portfolio equity.

9. In any event, it is worth bearing in mind that stock market price volatility is not robustly linked with growth (Levine and Zervos 1998a).

10. Here we draw on Froot, O'Connell, and Seasholes (2001). Their database represented the trades made by the customers of one large U.S. custodian bank.

11. It is important to stress that foreign investors are not always in the vanguard when there is selling pressure on local equities cf. Frankel and Schmukler (1996) for Mexico and Choe, Kho, and Stulz (1999); Kim and Wei (1999) for the Republic of Korea. In general, foreign investors seem to prefer to invest in large firms that export, and especially those with DR programs (cf. Kang and Stulz 1999).

12. Our discussion is complementary to that which can be found in the World Bank's annual *Global Development Finance* report.

13. Monetary policy can continue to influence the level of nominal interest rates, but in a generally market-clearing context.

14. For industrial countries, regressing quarterly exchange rate changes on the start-of-quarter interest differential results in a negative coefficient on the differential, instead of the predicted value of +1. For developing countries, though, the estimated coefficient on the differential of +0.59 is much closer to theoretical prediction (Honohan 2001a). Cochrane (1999) suggests that this interest parity puzzle, and several other well-known asset market anomalies, can be attributed to low asset prices (in this case, low foreign bond prices) being correlated with heightened risk.

15. Bouts of increased capital flow volatility also regularly unearth a proposal to implement such a tax on international capital movements not just in one country, but on a coordinated global basis, with the dual goal of damping speculative flows and generating a useful flow of international tax revenue. The practicalities of such a global scheme, however,—the so-called Tobin tax—have not yet been proved, and indeed widespread

skepticism as to how successfully it would function has left the proposal stillborn (cf. Haq, Kaul, and Grunberg 1996).

16. Though the tax rate is currently set at zero—reflecting the substantial capital outflows that have been associated with Chilean pension funds rebalancing their portfolios following a liberalization, which has permitted them to increase greatly their holdings of foreign assets—so that the system has no practical effect at present. As operated, the Chilean regime facilitates reserve accumulation by the central bank, a feature that highlights the potential role of reserves management as a tool of macroeconomic management in helping insulate countries from external capital account shocks.

17. Bartolini and Drazen (1997) provide a persuasive account of this mechanism.

References

World Bank Policy Research Working Papers can be obtained through the following Web site: http://econ.worldbank.org/.

Acemoglu, Daron, Simon Johnson, and James A. Robinson. 2000. "The Colonial Origins of Comparative Development: An Empirical Investigation." Cambridge, Mass.: MIT. http://web.mit.edu/daron/www/colonial8comp.pdf.

Adams, Dale, Douglas Graham, and J. D. von Pischke. 1984. *Undermining Rural Development with Cheap Credit.* Boulder, Colorado: Westview Press.

Agénor, Pierre-Richard, Joshua Aizenman, and Alex Hoffmaister. 1999. "Contagion, Bank Lending Spreads and Output Fluctuations." Policy Research Working Paper 2186. World Bank, Washington, D.C.

Allen, Franklin, and Douglas Gale. 2000. *Comparing Financial Systems.* Cambridge, Mass.: MIT Press.

Baer, Herbert, and Daniela Klingebiel. 1995. "Systemic Risk When Depositors Bear Losses: Five Case Studies." In George Kaufman, ed., *Banking, Financial Markets, and Systemic Risk, Research in Financial Services.* Greenwich, Conn.: JAI Press.

Bagehot, Walter. 1873. *Lombard Street: A Description of the Money Market.* London: John Murray.

Bandiera, Oriana, Gerard Caprio, Patrick Honohan, and Fabio Schiantarelli. 2000. "Does Financial Reform Raise or Reduce Saving?" *Review of Economics and Statistics* 82(2): 239–63.

Bank of Japan (Bank Supervision Department). 1998. "Utilization of Financial Institutions' Self-Assessment in Enhancing Credit Risk Management." *Quarterly Bulletin of the Bank of Japan* 6(1).

Barfield, Claude E. 1996. *International Financial Markets: Harmonization versus Competition.* Washington, DC: AEI Press.

Barron, John M., and Michael Staten. 2001. "The Value of Comprehensive Credit Reports: Lessons from the U.S. Experience." Forthcoming in Margaret J. Miller, ed., *Credit Reporting Systems and the International Economy.* Cambridge, Mass.: MIT Press.

Barth, James, Gerard Caprio, and Ross Levine. 2001a. "Banking Systems around the Globe:

Do Regulation and Ownership Affect Performance and Stability?" Forthcoming in Frederic Mishkin, ed., *Prudential Regulation and Supervision: Why It Is Important and What Are the Issues.* Cambridge, Mass.: National Bureau of Economic Research.

_____. 2001b. "Prudential Regulation and Supervision: What Works Best." Policy Research Working Paper (forthcoming). World Bank, Development Research Group, Washington, D.C.

_____. 2001c. "The Regulation and Supervision of Banks around the World: A New Database." Policy Research Working Paper (forthcoming). World Bank, Development Research Group, Washington, D.C.

Bartholomew, Philip, and Benton Gup. 1999. "A Survey of Bank Failures in non-U.S. G-10 Countries since 1980." In Irene Finel-Honigman, ed., *European Union Banking Issues: Historical and Contemporary Perspectives.* Greenwich, CT: JAI Press.

Bartolini, Leonardo, and Allan Drazen. 1997. "Capital Account Liberalization as a Signal." *American Economic Review* 87(1):138–54.

Baskin, Jonathan, and Paul J. Miranti, Jr. 1997. *A History of Corporate Finance.* New York: Cambridge University Press.

Beck, Thorsten. 2000. "Deposit Insurance as a Private Club: Is Germany a Model?" Policy Research Working Paper 2559. World Bank, Washington, D.C.

Beck, Thorsten, George Clarke, Alberto Groff, Philip Keefer, and Patrick Walsh. 2000. "New Tools and New Tests in Comparative Political Economy: The Database of Political Institutions." Policy Research Working Paper 2283. World Bank, .Washington, D.C. Forthcoming in World Bank *Economic Review.*

Beck, Thorsten, Aslı Demirgüç-Kunt, and Ross Levine. 2000. "A New Database on Financial Development and Structure." Policy Research Working Paper 2147. World Bank, Washington, D.C.

_____. 2001. "Law, Politics, and Finance." Forthcoming Policy Research Working Paper. World Bank, Development Research Group, Washington, D.C.

Beck, Thorsten, Ross Levine, and Norman Loayza. 2000. "Finance and the Sources of Growth." *Journal of Financial Economics* 58(1–2):261–300.

Beck, Thorsten, Mattias Lundberg, and Giovanni Majnoni. 2001. "Financial Development and Economic Volatility: Does Finance Dampen or Magnify Shocks?" Forthcoming Policy Research Working Paper. World Bank, Financial Sector Strategy and Policy Department, Washington, D.C.

Becker, Gary, and George Stigler. 1974. "Law Enforcement, Malfeasance, and Compensation of Enforcers." *Journal of Legal Studies* 3:1–18.

Bekaert, Geert, and Campbell R. Harvey. 2000. "Foreign Speculators and Emerging Equity Markets." *Journal of Finance* 55:565–613.

Bekaert, Geert, Campbell R. Harvey, and Robin L. Lumsdaine. 2000. "Dating the Integration of World Equity Markets." NBER Working Paper 6724. Cambridge, Mass.: National Bureau of Economic Research.

Berger, Allen, Robert DeYoung, Hesna Genay, and Gregory F. Udell. 2000. "Globalization of Financial Institutions: Evidence from Cross-Border Banking Performance." In Robert E. Litan and Anthony M. Santomero, eds., *Brookings-Wharton Papers on Financial Services* 3.

Berger, Allen, Leora Klapper, and Gregory F. Udell. 2001. "The Ability of Banks to Lend to Informationally Opaque Small Businesses." *Journal of Banking and Finance.* Forthcoming.

Berkowitz, David, Katharina Pistor, and Jean-Francois Richard. 2000. "Economic Development, Legality, and the Transplant Effect." Working Paper 39. Harvard University, Center for International Development (CID). http://www2.cid.harvard.edu/cidwp/039.pdf

Bernanke, Ben. 1983. "Nonmonetary Effects of the Financial Crisis in the Propagation of the Great Depression." *American Economic Review* 73(3):257–76.

Besley, Timothy. 1995. "Savings, Credit and Insurance." In Jehre Behrman and T. N. Srinivasan, eds. *Handbook of Development Economics, Vol. IIIA.* Amsterdam: North Holland.

Black, Bernard, and Reinier Kraakman. 1996. "A Self-Enforcing Model of Company Law." *Harvard Law Review* 109:1911ff.

Board of Governors of the Federal Reserve System. 1999. "Using Subordinated Debt as an Instrument of Market Discipline." Staff Study 172, Washington, D.C. December.

Booth, Laurence, Varouj Aivazian, Aslı Demirgüç-Kunt, and Vojislav Maksimovic. 2001. "Capital Structures in Developing Countries." *Journal of Finance* 56(1).

Bossone, Biagio, Patrick Honohan, and Millard Long. 2001. "Policy for Small Financial Systems." Financial Sector Discussion Paper 6. World Bank, Financial Sector Strategy and Policy Department, Washington, D.C.

Bossone, Biagio, and Larry Promisel. 2000. "Strengthening Financial Systems in Developing Countries: The Case for Incentives-Based Financial Sector Reforms." Paper prepared for the 1999 World Bank–IMF Annual Meetings, Washington, D.C.: World Bank.

Boyd, John, Ross Levine, and Bruce Smith. Forthcoming. "The Impact of Inflation on Financial Sector Performance." *Journal of Monetary Economics*, forthcoming.

Boyd, John, and Bruce Smith. 2000. "A User's Guide to Banking Crises." Paper prepared for the World Bank Conference, Deposit Insurance: Design and Implementation, June 2000. http://www.worldbank.org/research/interest/intrstweb.htm.

Braudel, Fernand. 1973. *Capitalism and Material Life, 1400–1800.* London: George Weidenfeld and Nicolson.

Brunetti, A., G. Kisunko, and B. Weder. 1997. "Institutional Obstacles to Doing Business." Policy Research Working Paper 1759. World Bank, Washington, D.C.

Burki, Shahid Javed, and Guillermo E. Perry. 1998. *Beyond the Washington Consensus: Institutions Matter.* Washington, D.C.: World Bank.

Burnside, Craig, Martin Eichenbaum, and Sergio Rebelo. 2000. "On the Fundamentals of Self-

Fulfilling Speculative Attacks." NBER Working Paper 7554. Cambridge, Mass.: National Bureau of Economic Research.

Calomiris, Charles W. 1992. "Getting the Incentives Right in the Current Deposit Insurance System: Successes from the Pre-FDIC Era." In James R. Barth and R. Dan Brumbaugh, eds., *The Reform of Federal Deposit Insurance: Disciplining the Government and Protecting Taxpayers.* New York: Harper Business.

_____. 1999. *The Postmodern Bank Safety Net: Lessons from Developed and Developing Economies.* Washington, D.C.: American Enterprise Institute.

Calomiris, Charles W., and Charles Kahn. 1991. "The Role of Demandable Debt in Structuring Optimal Banking Arrangements." *American Economic Review* 81(3):497–513.

Calomiris, Charles W., and Joseph Mason. 2000. "Causes of U.S. Bank Distress during the Depression." NBER Working Paper 7919. Cambridge, Mass.: National Bureau of Economic Research.

Calomiris, Charles W., and Andrew Powell. 2000. "Can Emerging Market Bank Regulators Establish Credible Discipline? The Case of Argentina." Washington, D.C.: World Bank. http://www.worldbank.org/research/interest/intrstweb.htm.

Calvo, Guillermo A., and Carmen M. Reinhart. 2000. "When Capital Flows Come to a Sudden Stop: Consequences and Policy Options." In Peter Kenen, Michael Mussa, and Alexander Swoboda, eds., *Key Issues in Reform of the International Monetary System.* Washington, D.C.: International Monetary Fund.

Caprio, Gerard. 1999. "Banking on Crises: Expensive Lessons of Financial Crises." In George Kaufman, ed., *Research in Financial Services, Volume 10.* Greenwich, Conn.: JAI Press.

Caprio, Gerard, Izak Atiyas and James A. Hanson, eds. 1994. *Financial Reform: Theory and Experience.* Cambridge, U.K.: Cambridge University Press.

Caprio, Gerard, James A. Hanson, and Patrick Honohan. 2001. "The Case for Liberalization and Some Drawbacks." In Caprio, Honohan, and Stiglitz, eds. *Financial Liberalization.*

Caprio, Gerard, and Patrick Honohan. 1999. "Restoring Banking Stability: Beyond Supervised Capital Requirements." *Journal of Economic Perspectives* 13(4):43–64.

_____. 2001. "Reducing the Cost of Bank Crises: Is Basel Enough?" In David Dickinson, ed., *Managing Money in the Economy.* London: Routledge. Forthcoming.

Caprio, Gerard, Patrick Honohan, and Joseph Stiglitz, eds. 2001. *Financial Liberalization: How Far, How Fast?* Cambridge, U.K.: Cambridge University Press.

Caprio, Gerard, and Daniela Klingebiel. 1999. "Episodes of Systemic and Borderline Financial Crises." World Bank, Financial Sector Strategy and Policy Department, Washington, D.C.

Caprio, Gerard, and Maria Soledad Martinez-Peria. 2000. "Avoiding Disaster: Policies to Reduce the Risk of Banking Crises." Discussion Paper. Egyptian Center for Economic Studies, Cairo, Egypt. http://www.eces.org.eg.

Catalan, Mario, Gregorio Impavido, and Alberto R. Musalem. 2000. "Contractual Savings or Stock Markets Development: Which Leads?" Policy Research Working Paper 2421. World Bank, Washington, D.C.

Cavallo, Michele, and Giovanni Majnoni. 2001. "Do Banks Provision for Bad Loans in Good Times? Evidence from G10 and non-G10 Countries." Forthcoming as Policy Research Working Paper. World Bank, Financial Sector Strategy and Policy Department, Washington, D.C.

Cetorelli, Nicola, and Michele Gambera. 2001. "Banking Market Structure, Financial Dependence and Growth: International Evidence from Industry Data." *Journal of Finance.* Forthcoming in April.

Chiuri, Maria Concetta, Giovanni Ferri, and Giovanni Majnoni. 2000. "The Macroeconomic Impact of Bank Capital Requirements in Emerging Economies: Past Evidence to Assess the Future." Forthcoming as Policy Research Working Paper. World Bank, Financial Sector Strategy and Policy Department, Washington, D.C.

Cho, Yoon Je. 2001. "Korea's Financial Crisis: A Consequence of Uneven Liberalization." In Caprio, Honohan, and Stiglitz, eds.

Choe, H., B. Kho, and R. Stulz. 1999. "Do Foreign Investors Destabilize Stock Markets? The Korean Experience in 1997." *Journal of Financial Economics* 54: 227–64.

Claessens, Stijn, Aslı Demirgüç-Kunt, and Harry Huizinga. 2000. "How Does Foreign Entry Affect the Domestic Banking Market?" In Claessens and Jansen, eds. (2000).

Claessens, Stijn, Simeon Djankov, Joseph Fan, and Larry Lang. 1999a. "Corporate Diversification in East Asia: The Role of Ultimate Ownership Structure Group Affiliation." Policy Research Working Paper 2089. World Bank, Washington, D.C.

_____. 1999b. "Expropriation of Minority Shareholders: Evidence from East Asia." Policy Research Working Paper 2088. World Bank, Washington, D.C.

Claessens, Stijn, Simeon Djankov, and Daniela Klingebiel. 1999. "Financial Restructuring in Asia: Halfway There?" Financial Sector Discussion Paper 3. World Bank, Financial Sector Strategy and Policy Department, Washington, D.C.

Claessens, Stijn, Simeon Djankov, and Larry Lang. 1999. "Who Controls East Asian Corporations?" Policy Research Working Paper 2054. World Bank, Washington, D.C.

_____. 2000. "The Separation of Ownership and Control in East Asian Economies." *Journal of Financial Economics* 58(1–2):81–112.

Claessens, Stijn, Simeon Djankov, and Lixin Colin Xu. 2000. "Corporate Performance in the East Asian Financial Crisis." *World Bank Research Observer* 15(1).

Claessens, Stijn, and Thomas Glaessner. 1998. "Internationalization of Financial Services in Asia." Policy Research Working Paper 1911. World Bank, Washington, D.C.

Claessens, Stijn, Thomas Glaessner, and Daniela Klingebiel. 2000. "Electronic Finance: Reshaping the Financial Landscape around the World." Financial Sector Discussion Paper 4.

World Bank, Financial Sector Strategy and Policy Department, Washington, D.C.

Claessens, Stijn, and Marion Jansen. 2000. *The Internationalization of Financial Services: Issues and Lessons for Developing Countries.* Dordrecht, Holland: Kluwer.

Clarke, George R. G., and Robert Cull. 1998. "Why Privatize: The Case of Argentina's Public Provincial Banks." Policy Research Working Paper 1972. World Bank, Washington, D.C.

_____. 1999. "Getting to Yes." World Bank, Development Research Group, Washington, D.C.

_____. 2001. "Political Determinants and Economic Effects of Bank Privatization in Argentina." Forthcoming in Frank Columbus, ed., *Political Science and Economics of Latin America.* Huntington, N.Y.: Nova Science.

Clarke, George R. G., Robert Cull, Laura D'Amato, and Andrea Molinari. 2000. "The Effect of Foreign Entry on Argentina's Domestic Banking Sector." In Claessens and Jansen, eds. (2000).

Cochrane, John H. 1999. "New Facts in Finance." NBER Working Paper 7169. Cambridge, Mass.: National Bureau of Economic Research.

Coffee, Jack C., Jr. 1999. "Privatization and Corporate Governance: The Lessons from Securities Market Failure." *Journal of Corporation Law* 25:1–39.

Cull, Robert, Jana Matesova, and Mary Shirley. 2001. "The Role of Looting in Czech Privatization." Forthcoming Policy Research Working Paper. World Bank, Development Research Group, Washington, D.C.

Cull, Robert, Lemma Senbet, and Marco Sorge. 2000. "Deposit Insurance and Financial Development." Policy Research Working Paper (forthcoming). World Bank, Development Research Group, Washington, D.C. http://www.worldbank.org/research/interest/intrstweb.htm.

Cull, Robert and L. Colin Xu. 2000. "Bureaucrats, State Banks, and the Efficiency of Credit Allocation: The Experience of Chinese State-Owned Enterprises." *Journal of Comparative Economics* 28:1–31.

de Ferranti, David, Guillermo E. Perry, Indermit S. Gill, and Luis Servén. 2000. *Securing Our Future in a Global Economy.* Washington, D.C.: World Bank.

de Gregorio, José, Sebastian Edwards, Rodrigo O. Valdés. 2000. "Controls on Capital Inflows: Do They Work?" *Journal of Development Economics* (63)1:59–83.

de la Cuadra, Sergio, and Salvador Valdes. 1992. "Myths and Facts about Financial Liberalization in Chile, 1974–83." In Philip Brock, ed., *If Texas Were Chile: A Primer on Banking Reform.* San Francisco: ICS Press.

De Long, J. Bradford. 2000. "Where Did All the Financial Crises Go?" *Fortune,* July 24. http://econ161.berkeley.edu/TotW/ea_20006.html.

Demirgüç-Kunt, Aslı, and Enrica Detragiache. 1999. "Financial Liberalization and Financial Fragility." In Boris Pleskovic and Joseph E. Stiglitz, eds. *Proceedings of the 1998 World Bank Conference on Development Economics.* Washington, D.C.: World Bank.

_____. 2000. "Does Deposit Insurance Increase Banking System Stability? An Empirical Investigation." Policy Research Working Paper 2247. World Bank, Washington, D.C.

Demirgüç-Kunt, Aslı, and Harry Huizinga. 2000a. "Financial Structure and Bank Profitability." Policy Research Working Paper 2430. World Bank, Washington, D.C.

_____. 2000b. "Market Discipline and Financial Safety Net Design." Policy Research Working Paper 2183. World Bank, Washington, D.C.

Demirgüç-Kunt, Aslı, and Ross Levine. 1996. "Stock Markets, Corporate Finance, and Economic Growth: An Overview." *The World Bank Economic Review* 10(2):223–40.

_____. 1999. "Bank-Based and Market-Based Financial Systems: Cross-Country Comparisons." Policy Research Working Paper 2143. World Bank, Washington, D.C.

Demirgüç-Kunt, Aslı, and Ross Levine, eds. 2001. *Financial Structure and Economic Growth.* Cambridge, Mass: MIT Press. Forthcoming.

Demirgüç-Kunt, Aslı, Ross Levine, and Hong-Ghi Min. 1998. "Opening to Foreign Banks: Issues of Stability, Efficiency and Growth." In Alan Meltzer, ed., *The Implications of Globalization of World Financial Markets.* Seoul: Bank of Korea.

Demirgüç-Kunt, Aslı, and Vojislav Maksimovic. 1998. "Law, Finance, and Firm Growth." *Journal of Finance* 53:2107–37.

_____. 1999. "Institutions, Financial markets, and Firm Debt Maturity." *Journal of Financial Economics* 54:295–336.

_____. 2000. "Funding Growth in Bank-Based and Market-Based Financial Systems: Evidence from Firm-Level Data." Policy Research Working Paper 2432. World Bank, Washington, D.C.

Dewatripont, Mathias, and Jean Tirole. 1993. *The Prudential Regulation of Banks*, Cambridge, Mass.: MIT Press.

DeYoung, Robert, Mark Flannery, Sorin Sorescu, and William Lan. 2001. "The Information Content of Bank Exam Ratings and Subordinated Debt Prices." *Journal of Money, Credit and Banking.* Forthcoming.

Diamond, Douglas W. 1984. "Financial Intermediation and Delegated Monitoring." *Review of Economic Studies* 51(3):393–414.

Diamond, Douglas, and Raghuram Rajan. 2000. "Banks, Short Term Debt and Financial Crises: Theory, Policy Implications and Applications." Chicago, Illinois: University of Chicago. http://gsbwww.uchicago.edu/fac/raghuram.rajan/research/croch.pdf.

Díaz-Alejandro, Carlos F. 1985. "Goodbye Financial Repression, Hello Financial Crash." *Journal of Development Economics* 19 (September/October):1–24.

Domac, Ilker, Giovanni Ferri, and Masahiro Kawai, eds. Forthcoming. *The Credit Crunch in East Asia.*

Dooley, Michael P. 1996. "A Survey of Literature on Controls over International Capital Transactions." *International Monetary Fund Staff Papers* 43:639–87.

Dziobek, Claudia. 1998. "Market-Based Policy Instruments for Systemic Bank Restructuring."

IMF Working Paper 98/113. International Monetary Fund, Washington, D.C. http://www.imf.org/external/pubs/ft/wp/wp98113.pdf.

Easterbrook, Frank H., and Daniel R. Fischel. 1991. *The Economic Structure of Corporate Law.* Cambridge, Mass.: Harvard University Press.

Easterly, William, Roumeen Islam, and Joseph E. Stiglitz. 2001. "Shaken and Stirred: Explaining Growth Volatility." In Bruno Pleskovic and Joseph Stiglitz, eds. *Annual Bank Conference on Development Economics, 2000.* Washington, D.C.: World Bank.

The Economist. 2000. "Japan's Corporate-Governance U-turn." November 16.

Edwards, Sebastian. 2000a. "Capital Flows and Economic Performance: Are Emerging Economies Different?" University of California at Los Angeles, Department of Economics, Los Angeles.

_____. 2000b. "Contagion." *World Economy* 23(7): 873–900.

_____. 2000c. "Exchange Rate Systems in Emerging Economies." April Prepared for the Meltzer Commission on the New Financial Architecture. University of California at Los Angeles, Department of Economics, Los Angeles.

_____. 2000d. "Interest Rate Volatility and Contagion in Emerging Markets." NBER Working Paper 7813. Cambridge, Mass.: National Bureau of Economic Research.

Eichengreen, Barry, and Carlos Arteta. 2000. "Banking Crises in Emerging Markets: Presump-tions and Evidence." University of California, Berkeley. http://elsa.berkeley.edu/users/eichengr/website.htm.

Englund, Peter. 1999. "The Swedish Banking Crisis: Roots and Consequences." *Oxford Review of Economic Policy* 15(3):80–97.

Errunza, Vihang, Ked Hogan, and Mao-Wei Hung. 1999. "Can the Gains from International Diversification Be Achieved without Trading Abroad?" *Journal of Finance* (December).

Evanoff, Douglas, and Larry Wall. 2000. "Subordinated Debt and Bank Capital Reform." Federal Reserve Bank of Chicago Working Paper WP 2000-07, August.

Fama, Eugene. 1965. "The Behavior of Stock Market Prices." *Journal of Business* 38:34–106.

Ferri, Giovanni, Li-Gang Liu, and Giovanni Majnoni. 2001. "The Role of Rating Agency Assessments in Less Developed Countries: Impact of the Proposed Basel Guidelines." *Journal of Banking and Finance* 25(1):115–148.

Folkerts-Landau, David, and Peter M. Garber. 1997. "Derivative Markets and Financial System Soundness." In Charles Enoch and John W. Greene, *Banking Soundness and Monetary Policy.* Washington, D.C.: International Monetary Fund.

Frankel, Jeffrey, and Sergio Schmukler. 1996. "Country Funds and Asymmetric Information." *Open Economies Review* 7 (fall):511–34.

_____. 1998. "Crisis, Contagion, and Country Funds." In R. Glick, ed., *Managing Capital Flows and Exchange Rates.* Cambridge, U.K.: Cambridge University Press.

Frankel, Jeffrey, Sergio Schmukler, and Luis Servén. 2000. "Global Transmission of Interest Rates: Monetary Independence and Currency Regime." Policy Research Working Paper 2424. World Bank, Washington, D.C.

Froot, Kenneth A., Paul G. J. O'Connell, and Mark S. Seasholes. 2001. "The Portfolio Flows of International Investors." *Journal of Financial Economics* 59(2):151–193.

Furman, Jason and Joseph E. Stiglitz. 1998. "Economic Crises: Evidence and Insights from East Asia." *Brookings Papers on Economic Activity* 2:1–135.

Gallego, Francisco, Leonardo Hernández, and Klaus Schmidt-Hebbel. 1999. "Capital Controls in Chile: Effective? Efficient?" Working Paper 59. Santiago: Central Bank of Chile. http://www.bcentral.cl/Estudios/DTBC/59/dtbc59.pdf.

Garcia, Gillian. 1999. *Deposit Insurance: Actual and Good Practices.* IMF Working Paper WP/99/54. International Monetary Fund, Washington, D.C. http://www.imf.org/external/pubs/ft/wp/1999/wp9954.pdf.

Gelb, Alan H. 1989. "Financial Policies, Growth, and Efficiency." Policy Research Working Paper 202. World Bank, Washington, D.C.

Gerschenkron, Alexander. 1962. *Economic Backwardness in Historical Perspective: A Book of Essays.* Cambridge, Mass.: Belknap Press of Harvard University Press.

Gertler, Mark, and Andrew Rose. 1994. "Finance, Public Policy and Growth." In Caprio, Atiyas, and Hanson, eds., pp. 13–45.

Glaessner, Thomas, and Salvador Valdés-Prieto. 1998. "Pension Reform in Small Developing Countries." Policy Research Working Paper 1983. World Bank, Washington, D.C.

Goldberg, Linda, B. Gerard Dages, and Daniel Kinney. 2000. "Foreign and Domestic Bank Participation in Emerging Markets: Lessons From Mexico and Argentina." Federal Reserve Bank of New York Economic Policy Review. vol. 6 no. 3

Goldsmith, Raymond W. 1969. *Financial Structure and Development.* New Haven, Conn.: Yale University Press.

Golembe, Carter H. 1960. "The Deposit Insurance Legislation of 1933: An Examination of Its Antecedents and Its Purposes." *Political Science Quarterly* 75(2, June):181–200.

Goodhart, Charles. 2000. "The Organizational Structure of Banking Supervision." LSE Financial Markets Group Special Paper 127 http://fmg.lse.ac.uk/publications/index.htm.

Greenspan, Alan. 1999. "Lessons from the Global Crises." Remarks before the World Bank-IMF, Program of Seminars, Washington, D.C., September 27, http://www.federalreserve.gov/boarddocs/speeches/1999/199909272.htm.

Grossman, Sanford, and Joseph Stiglitz. 1980. "On the Impossibility of Informationally Efficient Markets." *American Economic Review* 70:393–408.

Haq, Mahbub-ul, Inge Kaul, and Isabelle Grunberg. 1996. *The Tobin Tax.* New York: Oxford University Press.

Hardouvelis, Gikas, Rafael La Porta, and Thierry Wizman. 1994. "What Moves the Discount on Country Equity Funds?" In Jeffrey Frankel, ed., *The Internationalization of Equity Markets.* Chicago: University of Chicago Press.

Hellman, Joel, Geraint Jones, and Daniel Kaufmann. 2000. "Seize the State, Seize the Day: State Capture, Corruption, and Influence in Transition Economies." Policy Research Working Paper 2444. World Bank, Washington, D.C.

Henry, Peter Blair. 2000a. "Equity Prices, Stock Market Liberalization, and Investment." *Journal of Financial Economics* 58(1–2): 301–34.

_____. 2000b. "Stock Market Liberalization, Economic Reform, and Emerging Market Equity Prices." *Journal of Finance* 55:529–64.

Hicks, John R. 1969. *A Theory of Economic History.* Oxford, U.K.: Oxford University Press.

Honohan, Patrick. 2001a. "How Interest Rates Changed under Liberalization: A Statistical Review." In Caprio, Honohan, and Stiglitz, eds. *Financial Liberalization.*

_____. 2001b. "Perverse Effects of an External Ratings-Related Capital Adequacy System." *Economic Notes* 30(3). Forthcoming.

_____. 2001c. "Recapitalizing Banking Systems: Implications for Incentives, Fiscal and Monetary Policy." Policy Research Working Paper 2540. World Bank, Washington, D.C.

Honohan, Patrick, and Daniela Klingebiel. 2000. "Controlling the Fiscal Costs of Banking Crises." Policy Research Working Paper 2441. World Bank, Washington, D.C.

Honohan, Patrick, and Joseph E. Stiglitz. 2001. "Robust Financial Restraint." In Caprio, Honohan, and Stiglitz, eds., *Financial Liberalization.*

IFC (International Finance Corporation). 1998. *Financial Institutions: Lessons of Experience.* Washington, D.C.

IMF (International Monetary Fund). 2000. *International Capital Markets Developments, Prospects, and Key Policy Issues* (by a staff team led by Donald J. Mathieson and Garry J. Schinasi). International Monetary Fund: Washington, D.C.

Ingves, Stefan, and Goran Lind. 1996. "The Management of the Banking Crisis—in Retrospect." *Quarterly Review*, Sveriges Riksbank, No. 1: 5–18.

Islam, Roumeen. 1999. "Should Capital Flows Be Regulated? A Look at the Issues and Policies." Policy Research Working Paper 2293. World Bank, Washington, D.C.

James, Estelle, James Smalhout, and Dimitri Vittas. 1999. "Administrative Costs and the Organization of Individual Account Systems: A Comparative Perspective." Policy Research Working Paper 2099. World Bank, Washington, D.C.

James, Estelle, and Dimitri Vittas. 2000. "The Decumulation (Payout) Phase of Defined Contribution (DC) Pillars: Policy Issues in the Provision of Annuities and Other Benefits." Policy Research Working Paper 2461. World Bank, Washington, D.C.

Jappelli, Tullio, and Marco Pagano. 1999. "Information Sharing, Lending and Defaults:

Cross-Country Evidence." Working Paper 22, Centre for Studies in Economics and Finance, University of Salerno, May.

_____. 2000. "Public Credit Information: a European Perspective." Washington, D.C.: World Bank. Forthcoming in Margaret J. Miller, ed., *Credit Reporting Systems and the International Economy*. Cambridge, Mass.: MIT Press.

John, Kose, Anthony Saunders, and Lemma Senbet. 2000. "A Theory of Bank Regulation and Management Compensation." *Review of Financial Studies,* Vol. 13, no. 1, Spring, 95–125.

Johnson, Simon. 2000. "Private Contracts and Corporate Governance Reform: Germany's Neuer Markt." Cambridge, Mass.: MIT. http://web.mit.edu/sjohnson/www/research.htm/

Johnson, Simon, Rafael La Porta, Florencio López-de-Silanes, and Andrei Shleifer. 2000. "Tunneling." *The American Economic Review Papers and Proceedings* 90(2, May):22–7.

Johnson, Simon, John McMillan, and Christopher Woodruff. 1999. "Property Rights and Finance." Cambridge, Mass.: MIT. http://web.mit.edu/sjohnson/www/research.htm/

Jordan, John, Joe Peek, and Eric Rosengren. 1999. "The Market Reaction to the Disclosure of Supervisory Actions: Implications for Bank Transparency." *Journal of Financial Intermediation* 9(July): 298–319.

Kahneman, D., and Andrei Tversky. 1979. "Prospect Theory: An Analysis of Decision under Risk." *Econometrica* 47:263–91.

Kaminsky, Graciela, Richard Lyons, and Sergio Schmukler. 1999. "Managers, Investors, and Crises: Mutual Fund Strategies in Emerging Markets." Policy Research Working Paper 2399. World Bank, Washington, D.C.

_____. 2000. "Mutual Fund Investment in Emerging Markets: An Overview." Policy Research Working Paper 2529. World Bank, Washington, D.C.

_____. 2001. "Economic Fragility, Liquidity, and Risk: The Behavior of Mutual Funds during Crises." Forthcoming as Policy Research Working Paper. World Bank, Development Research Group, Washington, D.C.

Kaminsky, Graciela, and Sergio Schmukler. 2001. "On Financial Booms and Crashes: Regional Patterns, Time Patterns, and Financial Liberalization." Forthcoming as Policy Research Working Paper. World Bank, Development Research Group, Washington, D.C.

Kane, Edward. 2000. "Designing Financial Safety Nets to Fit Country Circumstances." Policy Research Working Paper 2453. World Bank, Washington, D.C.

Kang, Jun-Koo, and René M. Stulz. 1999. "Why Is There a Home Bias? An Analysis of Foreign Portfolio Equity Ownership in Japan." *Journal of Financial Economics* 46(1):3–28.

Kaplan, Idanna. 1999. "The Put Option Approach to Banking Crises in Emerging Markets: Valuing Implicit Deposit Insurance In Thailand." University of Washington, Department of Economics, Seattle.

Keefer, Philip. 2000. "When Do Special Interests Run Rampant? Disentangling the Role of

Elections, Incomplete Information and Checks and Balances in Banking Crises." Policy Research Working Paper 2543. World Bank, Washington, D.C.

Keeton, William R. 1992. "The Reconstruction Finance Corporation: Would it Work Today?" Federal Reserve Bank of Kansas City, *Economic Review*, no. 1.

Keynes, John Maynard. 1923. "A Tract on Monetary Reform." Reprinted in his *Collected Writings* (Donald Moggridge, ed.), Cambridge University Press, vol. IV.

Khanna, Tarun, and Krishna Palepu. 1999. "Emerging Market Business Groups, Foreign Investors and Corporate Governance." NBER Working Paper 6955. Cambridge, Mass.: National Bureau of Economic Research.

Kim, Woochan, and Shang-Jin Wei. 1999. "Foreign Portfolio Investors before and during a Crisis." NBER Working Paper 6968. Cambridge, Mass.: National Bureau of Economic Research.

Kindleberger, Charles, P. 1978, 1996. *Manias, Panics, and Crashes: A History of Financial Crises.* New York: John Wiley and Sons.

King, Robert G., and Ross Levine. 1993a. Finance and Growth: Schumpeter Might Be Right." *Quarterly Journal of Economics* 108(3):717–37.

_____. 1993b. "Finance, Entrepreneurship, and Growth." *Journal of Monetary Economics,* 32(3):513–42.

Klingebiel, Daniela. 2000. "The Use of Asset Management Companies in the Resolution of Banking Crises: Cross-Country Experiences." Policy Research Working Paper 2284. World Bank, Washington, D.C.

Klapper, Leora. 2001. "Bankruptcy around the World: Explanations of Its Relative Use." Forthcoming as Policy Research Working Paper. World Bank, Development Research Group, Washington, D.C.

Kraay, Aart. 1998. "In Search of the Macroeconomic Effects of Capital Account Liberalization." World Bank, Development Research Group, Washington, D.C.

Kroszner, Randall S. 1998. "On the Political Economy of Banking and Financial Regulatory Reform in Emerging Markets." *Research in Financial Services* 10:33–51.

Kroszner, Randall S., and Philip E. Strahan. 1999. "Obstacles to Optimal Policy: The Interplay of Politics and Economics in Shaping Banking Supervision and Regulation Reforms." University of Chicago, Graduate School of Business. http://gsbwww.uchicago.edu/fac/randall.kroszner/research/KrosStrahNBERfinal.pdf.

Laeven, Luc. 2000. "Banking Risks around the World: The Implicit Safety Net Subsidy Approach." Policy Research Working Paper 2473. World Bank, Washington, D.C.

Lane, Philip, and Gian Maria Milesi-Ferretti. 1999. "The External Wealth of Nations: Measures of Foreign Assets and Liabilities for Industrial and Developing Countries." IMF Working Paper 99/115. International Monetary Fund, Washington, D.C. http://www.imf.org/external/pubs/ft/wp/1999/wp99115.pdf.

_____. 2000. "External Capital Structure: Theory and Evidence." CEPR Discussion Paper 2853. London: Centre for Economic Policy Research.

La Porta, Rafael, Florencio López-de-Silanes, Andrei Shleifer. 1999a. "Corporate Ownership around the World." *Journal of Finance* 54:481ff.

_____. 1999b. "Investor Protection: Origins, Consequences, Reform." http://www1.worldbank.org/finance/html/investorprotection.html

_____. 2000. "Government Ownership of Banks." Harvard University, August. http://www.economics.harvard.edu/faculty/laporta/laporta.html

La Porta, Rafael, Florencio López-de-Silanes, Andrei Shleifer, and Robert W. Vishny. 1997. "Legal Determinants of External Finance." *The Journal of Finance* LII(3):1131–50.

_____. 1998. "Law and Finance." *Journal of Political Economy* 106 (6):1113–55.

La Porta, Rafael, Florencio López-de-Silanes, and Guillermo Zamarripa. 2000. "Soft Lending and Hard Landing: Related Lending in Mexico." Harvard University, Department of Economics, Cambridge, Mass.

Levine, Ross. 1996. "Foreign Banks, Financial Development and Economic Growth." In Barfield, ed.

_____. 1997. "Financial Development and Economic Growth: Views and Agenda." *Journal of Economic Literature* 35:688–726.

_____. 2001. "International Financial Liberalization and Economic Growth." *Review of International Economics*, forthcoming.

Levine, Ross, Norman Loayza, and Thorsten Beck. 2000. "Financial Intermediation and Growth: Causality and Causes." *Journal of Monetary Economics* 46(1):31–77.

Levine, Ross, and Sara Zervos. 1998a. "Capital Control Liberalization and Stock Market Development." *World Development* 26:1169–84.

_____. 1998b. "Stock Markets, Banks, and Economic Growth." *American Economic Review* 88(3):537–58.

Levy-Yeyati, Eduardo, and Angel Ubide. 1998. "Crises, Contagion and the Closed-End Country Fund Puzzle." IMF Working Paper 98/143. International Monetary Fund, Washington, D.C. http://www.imf.org/external/pubs/ft/wp/wp98143.pdf.

Li, Hongyi, Lyn Squire, and Heng-fu Zou. 1998. "Explaining International and Intertemporal Variations in Income Inequality." *Economic Journal* 108(1):26–43.

Lindgren, Carl-Johan, Tomás J. T. Baliño, Charles Enoch, Anne-Marie Gulde, Marc Quintyn, and Leslie Teo. 2000. *Financial Sector Crisis and Restructuring: Lessons from Asia.* IMF Occasional Paper 188. Washington, D.C.: International Monetary Fund.

Lustig, Nora. 1999. "Crises and the Poor: Socially Responsive Macroeconomics", Presidential Address at the Fourth Annual Meeting of the Latin American and Caribbean Economic Association, Santiago, Chile, October 22, 1999. http://www.lacea.org/Conferences_files/presidential.pdf.

Manove, Michael, A. Jorge Padilla, and Marco Pagano. 2000. "Collateral vs. Project Screening: A Model of Lazy Banks." Department of Economics, Boston University.

Martinez-Peria, Maria Soledad, and Sergio Schmukler. 2001. "Do Depositors Punish Banks for 'Bad' Behavior? Market Discipline, Deposit Insurance and Banking Crises." *Journal of Finance* 56(3).

Mason, Joseph R. 2000. "Reconstruction Finance Corporation Assistance to Financial Intermediaries and Commercial and Industrial Enterprise in the U.S., 1932–37." World Bank, Financial Sector Strategy and Policy Department, Washington, D.C. http://www.lebow.drexel.edu/mason/RFCWB.pdf.

McKinnon, Ronald I., and Huw Pill. 1999. "Exchange Rate Regimes for Emerging Markets: Moral Hazard and International Overborrowing." *Oxford Review of Economic Policy* 15(3):19–38.

Merton, Robert C., and Zvi Bodie. 2000. *Finance.* Upper Saddle River, N.J.: Prentice-Hall.

Miller, Margaret J., ed. Forthcoming. *Credit Reporting Systems and the International Economy.* Cambridge, Mass.: MIT Press.

Mishkin, Frederic S. 2000. "Moral Hazard and Reform of the Government Safety Net." In Joseph R. Bisignano, William C. Hunter, and George Kaufman, eds., *Global Financial Crisis: Lessons from Recent Events.* Boston: Kluwer Academic Press.

Modigliani, Franco, and Enrico Perotti. 1998. "Corporate Law Enforcement and the Development of Security Markets: Theory and Evidence." *Managerial and Decision Economics* 18:519–28.

Morduch, Jonathan. 1999. "The Microfinance Promise." *Journal of Economic Literature* 37(4):1569–1614.

Narayan, R.K. 1999 (originally published in 1952). *The Financial Expert.* Chicago: University of Chicago Press.

Neusser, Klaus, and Maurice Kugler. 1998. "Manufacturing Growth and Financial Development: Evidence from OECD Countries." *Review of Economics and Statistics* 80:636–46.

North, Douglass C. 1999. "Understanding the Process of Economic Change." London: Institute of Economic Affairs, Occasional Paper 106.

Obstfeld, Maurice. 1998. "The Global Capital Market: Benefactor of Menace?" *Journal of Economic Perspectives* 12(4):9–30.

Paulsen, Jo Ann. 2000. "The Rise, Reprieve, and Fall of State Banks in Africa." mimeo. Financial Sector Policy and Strategy Department. World Bank, Washington, D.C.

Phillips, Ronnie J. 1995. "Credit Markets and Narrow Banking." Jerome Levy Economics Institute Working Paper 77. Blithewood, N.Y.

Rajan, Raghuram G., and Luigi Zingales. 1998. "Financial Dependence and Growth." *American Economic Review* 88(3):559–586.

Reding, Paul, and Juan Antonio Morales. 1999. "Currency Substitution and Network Externalities." University of Namur, FUNDP, Namur, Belgium.

Rocha, Roberto, Richard Hinz, and Joaquin Gutierrez. 1999. "Improving the Regulation and Supervision of Pension Funds: Are There Lessons from the Banking Sector?" Washington, D.C.: World Bank Social Protection Discussion Paper 99/29.

Rodrik, Dani. 1998a. "Globalization, Social Conflict, and Economic Growth." Prebisch Lecture, *The World Economy* 21(2), March.

_____. 1998b. "Symposium on Globalization in Perspective: An Introduction." *Journal of Economic Perspectives* 12(4):3–8.

_____. 1998c. "Who Needs Capital-Account Convertibility?" In Stanley Fischer and others, *Should the IMF Pursue Capital-Account Convertibility?* Essays in International Finance No. 207. International Finance Section, Department of Economics, Princeton University, May 1998.

Romer, Thomas, and Barry Weingast. 1991. "The Political Foundations of the Thrift Debacle." In Alberto Alesina and Geoffrey Carliner, eds., *Politics and Economics in the Eighties.* Chicago: University of Chicago Press.

Rousseau, Peter L., and Paul Wachtel. 1998. "Financial Intermediation and Economic Performance: Historical Evidence from Five Industrial Countries." *Journal of Money, Credit, and Banking* 30:657–78.

Sebsted, Jennifer, and Monique Cohen. 2000. Microfinance, Risk Management and Poverty." Background paper for *World Development Report 2000–2001.*

Shleifer, Andrei, and Lawrence Summers. 1990. "The Noise Trader Approach to Finance." *Journal of Economic Perspectives* 4(2, spring).

_____. 2000. *Inefficient Markets: An Introduction to Behavioral Finance.* New York: Oxford University Press.

Squire, Lyn. 1989. "Project Evaluation in Theory and Practice." In Hollis Chenery and T. N. Srinivasan, eds. *Handbook of Development Economics, Vol. II.* Amsterdam: North Holland.

Srinivas, P. S., Edward Whitehouse, and Juan Yermo. 2000. "Regulating Private Pension Funds' Structure, Performance and Investments: Cross-Country Evidence." Washington, D.C.: World Bank Social Protection Discussion Paper 00/7.

Stiglitz, Joseph E. 1994. "The Role of the State in Financial Markets." *Proceedings of the World Bank Annual Conference on Development Economics 1993.* Washington, D.C., pp. 19–52.

_____. 2000. "Capital Market Liberalization, Economic Growth, and Instability." *World Development* 28(6):1075–86.

Stiglitz, Joseph E., and Andrew Weiss. 1981. "Credit Rationing in Markets with Imperfect Information." *American Economic Review* 71:393–410.

Sylla, Richard. 1997. "The Rise of Securities Markets: What Can Government Do?" In Gerard Caprio and Dimitri Vittas, *Reforming Financial Systems: Historical Implications for Policy.* New York: Cambridge University Press.

Udry, Christopher. 1994. "Risk and Insurance in a Rural Credit Market: An Empirical Investigation in North Nigeria." *Review of Economic Studies* 61:495–526.

Vittas, Dimitri. 1998. "Regulatory Controversies of Private Pension Funds." Policy Research Working Paper 1998. World Bank, Washington, D.C.

_____. 2000. "Pension Reform and Capital Market Development: 'Feasibility' and 'Impact' Preconditions." Policy Research Working Paper 2414. World Bank, Washington, D.C.

White, Eugene. 1997. "Deposit Insurance." In Gerard Caprio and Dimitri Vittas, *Reforming Financial Systems: Historical Implications for Policy.* New York: Cambridge University Press.

World Bank. 1995. *Bureaucrats in Business: The Economics and Politics of Government Ownership.* New York: Oxford University Press.

_____. 1998. *Argentina Financial Sector Review.* Washington, D.C.: World Bank. http://www-wds.worldbank.org/pdf_content/000178830981117035548333/multi_page.pdf.

Wurgler, Jeffrey. 2000. "Financial Markets and the Allocation of Capital." *Journal of Financial Economics* 58(1–2):187–214.

Wyplosz, Charles. 2001. "Financial Restraints and Liberalization in Post-War Europe." In Caprio, Honohan, and Stiglitz, eds., *Financial Liberalization.*